e-Government in Asia: Origins, Politics, Impacts, Geographies

ELSEVIER
ASIAN STUDIES SERIES

Series Editor: Professor Chris Rowley,
Cass Business School, City University, London, UK;
Institute of Hallyu Convergence Research, Korea University, Korea
Griffith Business School, Griffith University, Australia
(email: c.rowley@city.ac.uk)

Elsevier is pleased to publish this major Series of books entitled Asian Studies: Contemporary Issues and Trends. The Series Editor is Professor Chris Rowley of Cass Business School, City University, London, UK and Department of International Business and Asian Studies, Griffith University, Australia.

Asia has clearly undergone some major transformations in recent years and books in the Series examine this transformation from a number of perspectives: economic, management, social, political and cultural. We seek authors from a broad range of areas and disciplinary interests covering, for example, business/management, political science, social science, history, sociology, gender studies, ethnography, economics and international relations, etc.

Importantly, the Series examines both current developments and possible future trends. The Series is aimed at an international market of academics and professionals working in the area. The books have been specially commissioned from leading authors. The objective is to provide the reader with an authoritative view of current thinking.

New authors: we would be delighted to hear from you if you have an idea for a book. We are interested in both shorter, practically orientated publications (45,000+ words) and longer, theoretical monographs (75,000–100,000 words). Our books can be single, joint or multi-author volumes. If you have an idea for a book, please contact the publishers or Professor Chris Rowley, the Series Editor.

Dr Glyn Jones
Email: g.jones.2@elsevier.com

Professor Chris Rowley
Email: c.rowley@city.ac.uk

e-Government in Asia: Origins, Politics, Impacts, Geographies

Barney Warf
Department of Geography
University of Kansas
Lawrence
United States of America

AMSTERDAM • BOSTON • HEIDELBERG • LONDON
NEW YORK • OXFORD • PARIS • SAN DIEGO
SAN FRANCISCO • SINGAPORE • SYDNEY • TOKYO
Chandos Publishing is an imprint of Elsevier

Chandos Publishing is an imprint of Elsevier
50 Hampshire Street, 5th Floor, Cambridge, MA 02139, United States
The Boulevard, Langford Lane, Kidlington, OX5 1GB, United Kingdom

Library of Congress Cataloging-in-Publication Data
A catalog record for this book is available from the Library of Congress

British Library Cataloguing-in-Publication Data
A catalogue record for this book is available from the British Library

ISBN: 978-0-08-100873-7 (print)
ISBN: 978-0-08-100899-7 (online)

For information on all Chandos Publishing publications
visit our website at https://www.elsevier.com/

 **Working together
to grow libraries in
developing countries**

www.elsevier.com • www.bookaid.org

Publisher: Glyn Jones
Acquisition Editor: George Knott
Editorial Project Manager: Tessa De Roo
Production Project Manager: Priya Kumaraguruparan
Designer: Matthew Limbert

Typeset by TNQ Books and Journals

I dedicate this book to the brave cyberdissidents in China, Vietnam, and other totalitarian countries who have given so much, including their lives, to promote freedom of speech and expression.

Contents

Acknowledgment

This book grew out of an earlier article (Warf, 2014) on the geography of e-government in Asia. It seeks to build upon and elaborate that analysis both conceptually and empirically. I thank the staff and editors at Elsevier for their help and support. A special shout-out to my son Derek as well as Curren and Susan, Sandy, and Abe, my colleagues at the University of Kansas, and the folks at Drinking Liberally. Thanks also to Bob Antonio, Phil, and Serina.

List of figures

List of tables

Introduction

Today, more people are more connected technologically to one another than at any other time in human existence. For the bulk of the world's people, the Internet, mobile phones, text messaging, and various other forms of digital social media such as Facebook have become thoroughly woven into the routines and rhythms of daily life (Kellerman, 2002; Zook, 2005). The extremely rapid growth of the Internet—now used by 49% of the world's population—has unleashed enormous changes in how the planet's netizens (Internet users) communicate, are entertained, shop, obtain information, and interact. For many users these uses extend well beyond e-mail to include bill payments, stock trading, "e-tail" shopping, digital gambling, video games, telephony (e.g., Voice over Internet Protocol), hotel and airline reservations, chat rooms, downloading television programs, digital music, and pornography, as well as popular sites and services such as YouTube, Facebook, and Google. In all these ways, and more, cyberspace offers profound real and potential effects on social relations, everyday life, culture, politics, and other social activities. Indeed, for rapidly rising numbers of people around the world, the "real" and the virtual have become so deeply shot through with one another that simple dichotomies like online/offline fail to do justice to the degree to which these worlds are interpenetrated. In this light, access to cyberspace is no longer a luxury, but a necessity. As its applications have multiplied, the Internet is having enormous impacts across the globe, including interpersonal interactions and everyday life, identity formation, retail trade and commerce, and the structure and form of cities, in the process generating round upon round of non-Euclidean geometries in the context of a massive global wave of time–space compression.

The Internet has also changed how governments interact with their citizens. Indeed, it would be astonishing if, given how widespread the Internet has become, states did *not* utilize it in some form or another. Electronic government, or e-government, may be defined simply as the use of web-based applications, to enhance access government services and deliver them more efficiently. Definitions of e-government vary (Yildiz, 2007), but all involve the use of the Internet to deliver government information and services, change administrative procedures, and improve citizen input and participation. Web 2.0, which allows users to interact with government bureaucracies rather than just passively receive information, has expedited this process considerably. Burn and Robins (2003, p. 26) argue "eGovernment is not just about putting forms and services online. It provides the opportunity to rethink how the government provides services and how it links them in a way that is tailored to the users' needs." Good e-government is citizen-centric and enhances transparency and accountability, although not all e-government is good. The topic has been extensively scrutinized by scholars (for a review, see Rocheleau, 2007). However, the bulk of such work concentrates on e-government in economically developed countries, while developing ones have been largely overlooked (Basu, 2004). This silence is important, as e-government has

e-Government in Asia: Origins, Politics, Impacts, Geographies. http://dx.doi.org/10.1016/B978-0-08-100873-7.00001-5

become increasingly widespread not only in the economically developed world but also in developing countries as well.

This book examines e-government in Asia (here defined to exclude the Middle East), including its Central, South, East, and Southeast components. It has two primary goals: first, it seeks to illustrate that e-government has made steady gains throughout the region and is reshaping societies and everyday lives. Second, it demonstrates that social and spatial contexts matter: e-government preparedness, implementation, policies, and effects are highly uneven among (and often within) Asian countries. In short, e-government cannot be understood without geography. The volume seeks to achieve these goals through a series of reasonably detailed case studies of every country on the Asian continent, examining the origins of e-government (often legislative in nature), the telecommunications infrastructure involved (notably Internet penetration and broadband), and the major e-government programs initiated and their effects. It also examines the digital divide in each nation and steps taken to rectify it. Finally, it also summarizes Internet censorship in each state, for that too is part of how governments and their citizens interact.

1.1   E-government forms and consequences: an overview

E-government reshapes both how state agencies interact with one another and how they interact with the public at large, and is thus common to many "reinventing government" discourses. There are many types and levels of e-government, ranging from simple one-way delivery of information, in which citizens are passive consumers, to integration that allows user input and citizen feedback. Typically, e-government is divided into three forms: government-to-business (G2B), government-to-government (G2G), and government-to-citizens (G2C) (Fountain, 2001a,b). G2B e-government includes digital calls for contract proposals; submissions of bids, bills, and payments; and Internet management of supply chains. Among other things, G2G e-government enhances interactions among different government offices and agencies such as through paperless flows of information. These changes are frequently alleged to increase citizen accessibility, improve efficiency, create synergies, and generate economies of scale in the delivery of government services. E-government may also encourage a democratization of public bureaucracies by moving them from classic hierarchical forms of control to more horizontal, collaborative models (Ho, 2002; Ndou, 2004). The most common type is G2C e-government, which is used, inter alia, for the digital collection of taxes; electronic voting; payment of utility bills, fines, and dues; applications for public assistance, permits, and licenses; online registration of companies and automobiles; and access to census and other public data; it may include e-voting. Online access facilitates acquisition of information, reduces uncertainty, and reduces trips to and waiting times in government offices. In very remote rural areas, e-government such as distance education or telemedicine offers advantages to people who may not receive these services at all. Local governments often use the Internet to entice tourists and foreign investors; interactive municipal sites give residents access to information about schools, libraries, bus schedules, and hospitals.

By making public records more open, e-government improves transparency and helps to galvanize objections to arbitrary state actions.

There are many alleged benefits of e-government. If it improves the delivery of public services, it may raise satisfaction with existing administrations; conversely, in countries plagued by chronic corruption, the increased efficiency resulting from e-government may minimize the growth of public employment and increase trust in government. Electronic payment of dues and fines limits the opportunities for graft, while digital hotlines allow citizens a voice in the circles of governance. Concerns over e-government include the potential invasions of privacy that it invites, local and national security (i.e., hacking of government files), and the inequality of access generated by digital divides (about which we see later) (Belanger and Carter, 2008).

A common view of e-governance, typically rooted in a technologically determinist perspective, naively implies that its impacts are so similar among countries that there is a generic, universal model of e-government that can be applied everywhere identically (e.g., Grant and Chau, 2005). Such a view divorces the Internet and its consequences from local political, cultural, and economic contexts. More sophisticated understandings focus on the different institutional and political environments in which e-government is adopted, thus acknowledging that there are bound to be significant differences in impacts. As noted, one goal of this project is to emphasize that even in the ostensibly placeless world of the Internet, place still matters; i.e., that profound geographical variations exist in the levels of adoption of e-government among (and within) countries and their consequences.

E-government consists of a series of diverse practices that vary over time and space in response to varying political climates and institutional contexts. Chadwick and May (2003) describe three models of e-government—managerial, consultative, and participatory—drawn from the experiences of the US and the European Union. Managerial e-government maximizes the speed and efficiency of delivery of government services to citizens. The consultative model incorporates citizen input in various ways, so that information technologies are seen as inherently democratizing (e.g., Internet voting, polling, referenda, and electronic conferences with officials). Finally, the participatory model includes input from nonstate actors, including corporations and nongovernmental organizations. These views constitute a continuum of social access in which the consultative and participatory models are the most socially inclusive forms.

In similar fashion, Layne and Lee (2001) offered a well-received conception of developmental stages of e-government, ranging from simple online presence (i.e., a webpage); interfaces that allow citizen access to data and services; vertical integration in which citizens can actively participate (e.g., for license applications); and horizontal integration, in which one or a few centralized websites offer a broad range of government functions. Empirical assessments of e-government initiatives typically focus on the quality of websites, including criteria such as user-friendliness, missing links, readability, the publications and data displayed, contact information for public officials, number of languages in which content is provided, sound and video clips, ability to use credit cards and digital signatures, security and privacy policies, and opportunities for citizen feedback.

Important components to the successful implementation of e-government include decisive leadership, cooperation by bureaucrats, sufficient funding of e-government initiatives, clear lines of responsibility and accountability, explicit metrics of success or failure, and effective mechanisms for feedback (Rose and Grant, 2010). Some authors conceptualize this in terms of multiple stakeholders and their interests. Thus, e-government is as much an administrative process as a technological one. These comments serve to illustrate that the adoption of e-government is highly contingent and path-dependent, and is shaped by a variety of cultural, legal, and political forces. The highly political nature of e-government implementation and its effects imply that its usage changes over time and space, and that its consequences are inevitably geographically differentiated.

1.1.1 Theorizing e-government

Understanding e-government conceptually involves a journey into the immense thicket of literature concerning the changing nature of the state in late capitalism. An enormous body of work has traced the rise of neoliberalism, mounting global competitiveness, the emasculation of the welfare state, and their linkages to contemporary globalization and international trade, and needs not be recapitulated here. The influential perspective of Castells (1996, 1997) distinguished earlier *information* societies, in which productivity was derived from access to energy and the manipulation of materials, from later *informational* societies that emerged in the late 20th century, in which productivity is derived primarily from knowledge and information. In his reading, the time–space compression of postmodernism was manifested in the global "space of flows," including the three "layers" of transportation and communication infrastructure, the cities or nodes that occupy strategic locations within these, and the social spaces occupied by the global managerial class. Suffice it to say that it is no accident or coincidence that e-government arose on the heels of the microelectronics revolution of the late 20th century, and that it represents part of a broader process by which capitalism has brought the state to heel, including enormous pressures to deregulate, downsize, reduce employment, and improve efficiency.

In the developing world, international donors and actors such as the World Bank, IMF, and USAID have increasingly turned to e-government as a means to promote "good governance." Combatting corruption is high on the list of expectations for its adoption and implementation. Jane Fountain's (2001a) *Building the Virtual State: Information Technology and Institutional Change* has been widely acclaimed for its neoinstitutional analysis of the use of information technology, including virtual agencies and single portals through which citizens can access numerous public services. This last model has been widely adopted in Asia, as shall soon be seen.

The literature on e-government comes primarily from those working within public administration and political science. Many theorizations emphasize various "stages" models ranging from the primitive to sophisticated, or more condescendingly, from the immature to the mature (e.g., Fath-Allah et al., 2014). For example, Holliday and Kwok (2004) differentiate between emerging, enhanced, interactive, and seamless forms of e-government along a continuum. Layne and Lee (2001) offer a four-stage model. Davison et al. (2005) similarly identify a series of steps in the transition from government to e-government, including three models of "maturity" ranging from simple digital presence to full-scale, interactive service delivery. Often metaphors of life stages, evolution, contagion, or learning curves are deployed. Stages, steps, levels, and continuums can be important descriptors of the degree of sophistication of e-government systems, but one must avoid the implication that there is some teleological inevitability behind them, i.e., all countries must march mechanically through a predefined set of stages. Variations and jumping stages are possible and common. Again, there is no single trajectory: national context matters, and it is impossible to understand e-government within its spatiotemporal coordinates.

Perhaps the most common theorization of e-government is the technology acceptance model (TAM), introduced by Davis (1989, 1993). Drawing on a tradition of technological and innovation diffusion, the TAM approach emphasizes how users accept and utilize specific technologies, particularly computer-related ones. It operates at the interface of social and personal psychological variables. Experience, education, cultural norms, and gender roles are part and parcel of this phenomenon, as are personal considerations such as self-assurance. Potential users judge an innovation based on its perceived usefulness and ease of use, including convenience and heightened job performance, all of which may be shrouded in uncertainty. Significant factors that enter into the adoption of a technology include its potential savings in terms of time and cost. Such decisions are also made in light of social pressures from peers and supervisors, and are embedded within the wider context of policies, regulations, and the legal environment. Some assert that the TAM model considers citizens to be little more than consumers, while others stress that the differences are considerable. The TAM approach has often been applied to e-government to understand its variable adoption among countries and groups (e.g., Carter and Belanger, 2005; Hung et al., 2006). This view is not so much wrong as it is self-evident and pays little attention to the roles of power, conflict, class, and inequality in shaping access to all technologies, including the Internet.

E-government is sometimes held to inevitably promote democracy by making governance more transparent (Netchaeva, 2002; Rose, 2004; Prasad, 2012), a claim that mirrors Utopian expectations of the Internet in general. Johnson and Kolko (2010, p. 17) note that "Many current models of e-Government have an unstated assumption that a desire to fulfil democratic functions motivates the creation of e-Government initiatives and that the ultimate goal of e-Government initiatives is increased transparency and accountability." Certainly there is some merit to this line of thought. The best and most effective forms of e-government have generally been found in democratic societies, which tend to be wealthier ones. E-government may improve trust and accountability, and minimize corruption, and in some cases allow for citizen input and feedback. More efficient e-government raises citizen satisfaction. Yet the extent to which e-government enables democracy, or vice versa, is almost impossible to determine empirically. The relation may be simultaneously determinant, i.e., a two-way street. Moreover, authoritarian governments also use e-government (e.g., China), often to legitimate themselves in the eyes of the populace, without democratic inklings. There is, therefore, more than one trajectory involved here.

1.2   E-government and digital divides

Internet usage is characterized by significant social and spatial digital divides, that is, discrepancies in terms of ease and cost of access at several spatial scales (Crang et al., 2006; Goldfarb and Prince, 2008; Korupp and Szydlik, 2005; Stevens, 2006). For many economically and politically marginalized populations—the familiar litany of the poor, elderly, undereducated, and ethnic minorities—cyberspace is simply inaccessible. Globally, Internet access closely reflects the geographies of uneven development and the associated variations in wealth and power. Internet penetration rates vary greatly across the world: in economically developed countries the vast majority of people have access, particularly in places such as Scandinavia, where Internet usage is essentially universal. In contrast, in the developing world, Internet penetration rates are considerably lower, but rising rapidly. Digital divides also exist *within* countries, meaning that the poor, elderly, ethnic minorities, and rural areas exhibit lower rates of usage (Chakraborty and Bosman, 2005; Mills and Whitacre, 2003). However, the rapid rise in Internet users—approximately 15% annually— indicates that digital divides are rapidly changing. Finally, the growth of broadband services, including mobile ones, is increasing Internet access significantly (Arminen, 2007; Kellerman, 2010).

The digital divide is a major obstacle to the successful adoption and implementation of e-government (Yigitcanlar and Baum, 2006). E-government is useless to those without access to the Internet; thus e-government and the digital divide are deeply intertwined phenomena (Helbig et al., 2009). Fountain (2001a, p. 48) notes, "An increasingly digital government favors those with access to a computer and the Internet and the skills to use these sophisticated tools competently." People who lack the requisite technical skills, the income to acquire a personal computer at home, schools or jobs that provide Internet access, or the ability to utilize public Internet points such as libraries or cybercafes are excluded from the benefits of e-government. Sadly, and ironically—because those who need the information that the Internet offers typically benefit the most, and those with abundant sources of input need it less—the digital divide may enhance, not simply reflect, the inequalities surrounding e-government. Those most in need of government services have the least opportunity to access them in digital form. Dugdale et al. (2005) found that those who use government services the most are least likely to use the Internet. Therefore, Becker et al. (2008) conclude that due to the digital divide, the adoption of e-government is primarily a demand side rather than supply-side problem. Thus, as Hossain (2005) posits, e-government may exacerbate, not reduce, social inequalities.

Finally, given that e-government relies on Web 2.0 technology and the potential collection of vast quantities of data about individuals, issues of privacy are of paramount importance. As Goranson et al. (2013, p. 338) argue, volunteered information "provides a mechanism for collecting increasingly accurate spatial and temporal data about an individual, privacy must be protected above all." Many Asian governments have long autocratic antidemocratic traditions, and many do not have clearly stated and well-enforced regulations concerning privacy protection, so as e-government unfolds across the region, the potential for abuses must be kept in mind.

1.3 Obstacles to implementing e-government

If e-government were easy to implement, every country would have it. Despite its manifest benefits, however, there are substantial obstacles that inhibit its introduction. Foremost among these are poverty, illiteracy, and low-Internet penetration rates, including the digital divide. For those concerned with just getting by, the Internet is some alien, remote phenomenon at great distance from their daily lives. For many people living in rural areas, computers are a distant dream. Owning a personal computer is impossible, and even cybercafes are not affordable. Not knowing how to read and write certainly prevents people from taking advantage of it. Lack of computer literacy, including basic technical skills, and a phobia of things digital also play a role. Frequently, in rural areas in developing countries, electricity is often in short supply, irregular, and unreliable.

Restrictive gender roles are also important. In the developed world, the gendered digital divide has all but disappeared. But in many developing countries, where women enjoy significantly fewer advantages than do men (including literacy), access to technologies is especially difficult. Women's incomes and literacy rates are often lower than those of men. Many women are overwhelmed by the demands of childcare and domestic chores. Strategies to enhance access thus must specifically target women.

Finally, fluency in a tongue that is not widespread restricts access to Internet content. Most material that governments place on the Web is either in English or a dominant native tongue. For Indians who do not speak Hindi, Filipinos who do not speak Tagalog, minorities in Myanmar who do not speak Burmese, or Tamils in Sri Lanka who do not speak Sinhalese, language is an obstacle to e-government access.

Governments too have their own problems implementing e-government. Leadership may be poorly coordinated, haphazard, and lack clear priorities. Perhaps the most serious matter is resentment by public officials and employees. For those who may have acquired their jobs through patronage, be suspicious of limitations on bribe-taking and graft, or simply operate in a very conservative culture that regards changes as unnecessary, e-government is an unwelcome intrusion. Many workers lack the necessary information technology skills, and vendors may be unreliable. Bloated offices may dislike the idea of streamlining and downsizing. Thus, because e-government is, at its heart, a political (and not simply technical) process, it is often resisted by entrenched bureaucracies, which rightly view it as a "disruptive technology," Hanna (2008, p. 128) notes

> *IT units and their managers often stand as barriers to change. They have a vested interest in stand-alone systems; coordinated services and shared infrastructure or the more recent web-based technologies may erode their monopoly on information and technology–oriented services.*

Reducing corruption is one of the most touted benefits of e-government (Andersen, 2009; Bertot et al., 2010; Kim et al., 2009; Neupane et al., 2014) and a principal incentive behind many countries' implementation of it, such as China. However, while Internet-based governance may reduce corruption, the reverse is also true: corrupt government hierarchies can thwart e-government. For example, corruption has been tied to the failure of some telecenter projects in India, and e-government programs have lagged behind in Indonesia, Pakistan, and Bangladesh due to it.

In addition, insufficient funding may lead to shortages of equipment, which may quickly become outdated. Funds intended for this purpose may be siphoned off by corrupt managers. Turf battles among different government agencies may interfere with long-term e-government plans. Finally, there may be vulnerabilities in terms of cybersecurity, including susceptibility to hacking, viruses, worms, and malware.

These limitations are sometimes insurmountable, and e-government initiatives can collapse without accomplishing their goals or even being implemented altogether. Indeed, there is a long, sad history of failed e-government projects (Dada, 2006). This line of thought serves as a healthy reminder of the contingent nature of e-government and undermines teleological interpretations that view it as unstoppable or inevitable. Because e-government is deeply political, it is always open to different pathways, some of which succeed while others do not.

1.4   E-government and Internet censorship

Censorship might seem to be an odd topic for a book on e-government. Yet to the extent that governments limit access to the Web, and its contents, it shapes the number of people who have access to e-government services. Of all of the innumerable myths that swarm around cyberspace, one of the most insidious is that the Internet is an inherently emancipatory tool, a device that necessarily promotes democracy by giving voice to those who lack political power, and in so doing undermines authoritarian and repressive governments. For example, the chair of Citicorp, Walter Wriston (1997, p. 174) argued that "the virus of freedom… is spread by electronic networks to the four corners of the earth." Such visions appeal widely to Western policy makers, who tend to exaggerate the extent and power of ostensibly freedom-loving cyber-dissidents. Closely associated with this idea is that the global community of netizens is a self-governing one in which the state has become largely irrelevant (Goldsmith and Wu, 2006). The reality, unfortunately, is more complex and depressing, and the necessary corrective calls for a state-centered approach. As Lake (2009) notes, "the Web is not nearly the implacable force for freedom that some of its champions have portrayed. The world's authoritarians have shown just as much aptitude for technology as their discontented citizens." Many governments across the planet aggressively limit access to the Internet, and as Kalathil and Boas (2003) demonstrate, Internet opposition to censorship and political activism is typically confined to small groups of educated individuals, often diasporas, and has relatively little impact among the masses of their respective states.

Internet accessibility reflects, inter alia, the willingness of governments to allow or encourage their populations to log-in to cyberspace. Repressive governments often fear the emancipatory potential of the Internet, which allows individuals to circumvent tightly controlled media channels. Theorizations of Internet censorship can draw fruitfully on contemporary geographic discussions of the state, power, and discourse; Foucauldian perspectives loom large in this regard. Critical analyses of cyberspace, for example, point to geosurveillance, invasions of privacy, and the formation of digital panopticons (Crampton, 2007; Dobson and Fisher, 2007). Such work has demonstrated that clearly the Internet can be made to work against people as well as for them. Far from being innately emancipatory in nature, cyberspace can be used to reinforce hegemonic powers, spy on citizens, cultivate a climate of fear, and prevent or minimize dissent.

There are multiple motivations for Internet censorship, and thus several forms and types, including political repression of dissidents, human rights activists, or comments insulting to the state (e.g., in China, Iran, Myanmar); religious controls to inhibit the dissemination of ideas deemed heretical or sacrilegious (as found in many Muslim states); protections of intellectual property, including restrictions on illegally downloaded movies and music; or cultural restrictions that exist as part of the oppression of ethnic minorities (e.g., refusal to allow government websites in certain languages) or sexual minorities (i.e., gays and lesbians). Typically, governments that seek to impose censorship do so using the excuse of protecting public morality from ostensible sins such as pornography or gambling, although more recently combating terrorism has emerged as a favorite rationale. Deliberately vague notions of national security and social stability are typically invoked as well.

Governments face a choice in the degree of censorship, including its *scope* (or range of topics) and *depth* (or degree of intervention), which ranges from allowing completely unfettered flows of information (e.g., Denmark) to essentially prohibiting access to the Internet altogether (e.g., North Korea); most opt for a position between these two poles. Most frequently, interventions to limit access or shape the contents of cyberspace reflect highly centralized power structures, notably authoritarian one-party states concerned with an erosion of legitimacy. As Villeneuve (2006) points out, states seeking sovereignty over their cyberterritories often generate unintended consequences to censorship (e.g., diminished innovation, negative publicity that may lead to pariah status, reduced tourism, or offended corporations), results that policy makers rarely anticipate or acknowledge when putting such systems into place.

Essentially, censorship involves control over Internet access, functionality, and contents (Eriksson and Giacomello, 2009). Precise filtering is almost impossible, but there is a wide variety of methods used to control the flow of digital information, including requiring discriminatory ISP (Internet service provider) licenses, content filtering based on keywords, redirection of users to proxy servers, rerouting packets destined for a specific IP address to a blacklist, website blocking of a list of IP addresses, tapping and surveillance, chat room monitoring, discriminatory or prohibitive pricing policies, hardware and software manipulation, hacking into opposition websites and spreading viruses, denial-of-service attacks that overload servers or network connections using "bot herders," temporary just-in-time blocking at moments when political information is critical, such as elections, and harassment of bloggers (e.g., via libel laws or invoking national security). Content filtering often relies on keyword matching algorithms that evolve as the Internet's lingo changes, and filtering may occur at the levels of the ISP, the domain name, a particular IP address, or a specific URL. Most forms of filtering are difficult to detect technically: the user may not even know that censorship is at work. Most ISPs lack the ability to block transmission to an individual IP address or URL, so governments undertaking this task in volume frequently purchase foreign (usually American) software for this purpose.

Filtering mechanisms suffer the risk of overblocking, or "false positives," i.e., blocking access to sites that were not intended to be censored, and underblocking, or "false negatives," i.e., allowing access to sites that were intended to be prohibited (Murdoch and Anderson, 2008). Most common and particularly important is self-censorship, as the bulk of Internet users well understand the boundaries of politically acceptable use within their respective states. Often cultivating a persuasive, hegemonic view of dominant powers is more efficient than outright force. Typically both persuasion and coercion are combined as local contexts demand. Once formal censorship is initiated, no matter how benign or transparent, the temptation to enlarge its scope, or what Villeneuve (2006) calls "mission creep," is always there.

Generally, authoritarian governments in countries with low Internet penetration rates resort to relatively crude measures, such as restricting public access through licenses and monitoring of cybercafes. A national, sanitized intranet may be offered as a substitute for the global Internet. Cuba, Vietnam, and Burma/Myanmar exemplify this approach. As more people move online, including rising home personal computer ownership rates, a more complex, expensive, and cumbersome set of censorship mechanisms is called for, including firewalls and blocking or filtering website access. Arrests and imprisonment of cyberdissidents may be common. China, Kazakhstan, and Saudi Arabia are prime exemplars of these tactics. A third stage involves widespread Internet access, in which "soft" censorship tactics are the norm, particularly self-censorship and encouraging ISPs to police their users. Singapore and Russia illustrate this type and degree of government intervention. Finally, at least in the hopes of many optimistic observers, widespread Internet usage can overwhelm the state's capacity to control dissent, as is increasingly the case in China today.

The institutions used to enforce such policies, which are typically outgrowths of older media regulatory regimes concerned with newspapers, radio, and television, are usually government ministries of information and communication. The degree of centrality in the management of Internet censorship varies considerably. Because the state is not a monolithic entity but composed of diverse agencies, sometimes working at cross-purposes, rather than view censorship as the simple repression of oppositional discourses it is more instructive to think of it in terms of multiple, sometimes contradictory authorities that invoke diverse strategies of suppression of various groups and individuals for a broad array of reasons and motivations. Adding to this complexity is the rapidity with which the Internet has grown and changed technologically; often government censors have difficulty keeping up-to-date with changing technologies (e.g., text messaging) or slang terms used to communicate hidden meanings.

However, Internet censorship should be seen as part of a more complex array of contested relations in cyberspace: the Web is not simply a tool of government control but an arena of conflict. Thus, the Internet also serves various counterhegemonic purposes, including human rights groups and ethnic or political movements in opposition to governments. Attempts at censorship are often resisted, sometimes successfully, by local cyberactivists, such as through the use of anonymizing proxy servers in other countries that encrypt users' data and cloak their identities. Today, numerous groups in civil society use the medium to connect isolated once-invisible populations (e.g., gays and lesbians), unite and empower women's movements, give voice to human rights activists, and allow political minorities to promote their own agendas. Thus, Internet usage both reflects and in turn shapes prevailing political orders. In authoritarian regimes with relatively weak civil societies, opposition to state control is often weak and ineffectual; in more democratic states, opposition can be organized, vociferous, and effectual. When seen as a contested terrain of political struggle, the interactions between government Internet censors and the various groups that resist such impositions resemble a cat-and-mouse game that continually evolves over time. As the context of Internet censorship changes, including rising penetration rates, deregulation of telecommunications providers, and new geopolitical circumstances (e.g., openness to foreign investment), both government authorities and their opponents resort to changing tactics. Overt control over cybercafés, for example, may give way to government blockages of dissident websites, while opposition groups may utilize foreign proxy servers, anonymizing software, or texting by cell phones to circumvent such obstacles. The outcome of such contestations is inevitably path dependent, contingent, and unpredictable.

1.5   Asian e-government in context

Asia is so large and so diverse that it defies easy generalizations. With roughly four billion people—home to more than half of the world's population—it exhibits an enormous diversity in terms of levels of economic development, standards of living, political systems, languages, religions, and cultures. Several of the world's most populous states (China, India, Indonesia) are found there. Buddhism has long been central to the cultures of East Asia and the Indochinese peninsula, whereas Hinduism prevails in India, and Islam is dominant in Central Asia, Pakistan, Bangladesh, Malaysia, and Indonesia. Only the Philippines is a primarily Christian country. Asian countries have long, rich histories that include enormous tragedies (e.g., famines, plagues, genocides) and wars (World War II, the Korean and Vietnam conflicts, India and Pakistan, and secessionist uprisings and civil rebellions in numerous states).

Long impoverished through centuries of colonialism and more recently neocolonialism, much of Asia has enjoyed rapid economic growth, particularly along the Pacific Rim. Capitalism has relentlessly inscribed itself across the continent, pulling billions along with it. Globalization has been unkind to the middle classes of Europe and the United States, but it has pulled billions of Asian people out of poverty. A large middle class with disposable incomes, urban shopping malls, and cities crowded with cars testify to this newfound wealth. Annual GDP growth rates of 6–10% annually have not been uncommon. Japan, of course, pioneered Asian industrialization, followed by the second generation of "tigers" in the 1970s and 1980s (Hong Kong, South Korea, Taiwan, and Singapore), the third generation in Southeast Asia in the 1990s (e.g., Thailand, Malaysia, and Indonesia), and, of course, looming over all, China, now the world's second largest economy. More recently India, too, has enjoyed substantial rates of growth. A tidal wave of foreign investment fueled much of this prosperity as many shifted to export-led industrialization strategies, turning Asian countries into major producers of textiles and garments, steel, ships, automobiles, electronics, toys, and, increasingly, producer services such as telecommunications, finance, and engineering. Many Asian countries have substantial trade surpluses, often with the United States, and some have become large creditors as a result. Typically, the more globalized the economies of Asian countries, the better off they are: contrast, say, Singapore, Taiwan, China, and South Korea with Nepal, Myanmar, Bhutan, or North Korea.

For better or worse—or more likely, both—the traditional, agrarian, impoverished Asia is dying or dead. The ancient land of peasants stooped over rice paddies has given way to a new, modern, wealthy, globalized, and digitized set of societies. Pockets of the past remain, of course, primarily in the countryside, but even there longstanding ways of living are being reshaped by urbanization, television, and cell phones. Death rates are down and life expectancies are up. Massive rural-to-urban migration has swollen the cities: today most countries in Asia, including China, are primarily urban. Numerous megacities—Shanghai, Bangkok, Kolkata, Surabaya, Karachi, Dhaka, Tianjin, Manila—testify to this new landscape. Services have replaced agriculture in many countries as the largest form of employment.

The political geography of Asia has been remade time and again. Communism established a foothold over China, North Korea, Vietnam, Laos, and, courtesy of the Soviet Union, in Central Asia and Mongolia. During the decades of the Cold War, the economic, political, and cultural influence of the United States was dominant in many other states, notably Japan, South Korea, Taiwan, and much of Southeast Asia. Communism collapsed, however, and remains in name only in hypercapitalist kleptocracies such as China. Only in the Democratic People's Republic of Korea—a misnomer if there ever was one—and Vietnam does it exert much influence. Today Asian countries exhibit different political regimes ranging from well-functioning democracies to tyrannical dictatorships. The Korean peninsula has both. The late 20th century witnessed different military regimes give way to democratic forms of government, such as in South Korea, Thailand, Taiwan, the Philippines, and Indonesia. North Korea remains an iconoclastic hermit kingdom largely removed from the world system and impoverished as a result. China, Vietnam, and Myanmar, as well as almost all of Central Asia, remain ruled by authoritarian governments with abysmal records of censorship and human rights abuses. Conversely, India is the world's largest democracy, which has made inroads in several other states as well.

It is against this background of enormous size, cultural diversity, and rapid growth and change, with highly uneven patterns of economic and political development, that e-government began in Asia in the 1990s. Its uptake has been uneven over space and time: richer countries invariably have better and more sophisticated systems than do poor ones. The literature on Asian e-government includes many national and local case studies, but remarkably few overviews. Holliday (2002), Wescott (2011), and Warf (2014) offer brief summaries of the nature and implications of e-government in the region, while Hachigian (2002) wrote an insightful paper on the Internet in single-party Asian states. The collection edited by Sodhi (2015) contains a series of detailed case studies.

E-government in Asia arrived in the 1990s amidst a period of intense restructuring of the region's governments, including neoliberal reforms initiated at the behest of the

World Bank, USAID, and the International Monetary Fund. Asian governments have a long tradition of government-led development, so it is not surprising that many are effective in adapting the Internet for governance purposes, both at the national and local levels. This process included insistent calls for modernization of the region's governments and administrative practices, streamlining of bureaucracies, liberalization, privatization and deregulation, and reduction of systemic corruption. Many governments initiated e-government programs in response to demands from donors for greater transparency and accountability.

The most common measure of e-government success (or lack thereof) is the United Nation's e-government readiness score, which combines assessments of countries' digital infrastructure, Internet affordability, human capital resources, public webpage designs, and the scope and effectiveness of government services delivered online. This index varies widely across the region (Fig. 1.1): the highest ranked countries include South Korea (a perfect 1.00), which has the world's most developed e-government; Singapore (0.847); and Japan (0.802), while conversely Southeast and most Central Asian countries tend to lag behind, including Laos and Cambodia (0.290), Myanmar (0.270), Nepal (0.2664), East Timor (0.236), and Afghanistan (0.17).

A second measure of e-government is the United Nations' e-participation score, a measure of the degree to which policies are citizen-centric, including the proportion of populations that participate in e-government programs, the interactive properties of government webpages (i.e., user-friendliness), and the prevalence of programs to enhance access in low-income and rural communities, that is, to mitigate the digital

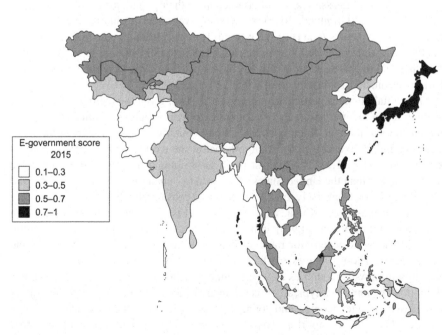

Figure 1.1 e-Government scores, 2015.

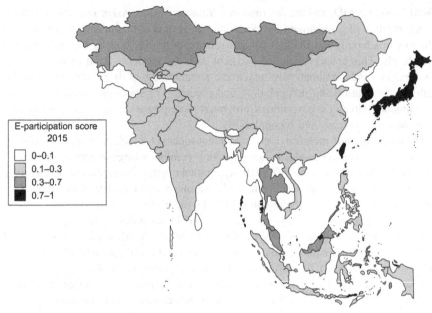

Figure 1.2 e-Participation scores, 2015.

divide. Obviously, e-government is closely tied to Internet penetration rates, but it also reflects the diffusion of technical skills, literacy, and the willingness or ability of states to use the Internet to assist (as opposed to control) their populations. The index is not without its faults (Grönlund, 2011). As with e-government readiness, e-participation varies unevenly across Asia (Fig. 1.2): South Korea scores a perfect 1.0, followed by wealthy and well-connected Singapore and Kazakhstan (0.947) and Japan (0.736); at the other end of this scale lie North Korea, Laos, Cambodia, Myanmar, East Timor, Turkmenistan, and Tajikistan, all of which score near 0.

The digital divide is particularly important in Asia, given the region's pronounced inequalities in income and rates of economic growth, which are replicated in social and spatial variations in Internet access among countries. Internet penetration in the region in mid-2016 averaged 44% (slightly below the world average of 59%) but varied markedly (Fig. 1.3). The highest penetration rates were found in South Korea (92.5%, higher than the United States), followed by Japan (91%), Taiwan (84%), and Singapore (81%). Conversely, Internet access was considerably lower in impoverished countries such as North Korea, where the Internet is essentially illegal, Afghanistan (12%) and Turkmenistan (14.9%). In between these extremes are middle-income countries with moderate penetration rates, such as Malaysia (68%), Kazakhstan (54%), and China (52%). These averages mask social and spatial variations: digital divides are present within Asian countries as well as among them, although much less is known about this phenomenon: typically it is urban areas, the relatively well educated, those with above-average incomes, and younger people, who enjoy the most access.

One of the most important issues concerning Internet access, and therefore e-government, is the use of mobile or cellular phones. Over the last 20 years, the mobile

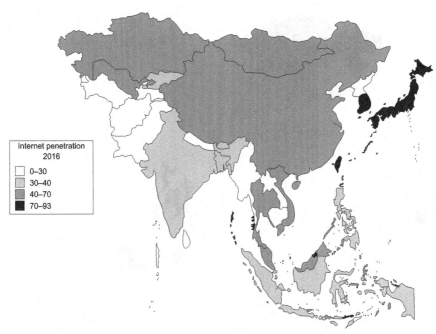

Figure 1.3 Internet penetration rates, Mid-2016.

or cellular telephone has become the most widely used form of telecommunications in the world, surpassing even the Internet in numbers of users (Campbell and Park, 2008; Comer and Wikle, 2008; Ling and Donner, 2009). Rapid decreases in the cost of mobile phones, and the minimal infrastructure necessary for their operation (i.e., cell towers), have made them affordable for vast numbers of people, including in the developing world. Today there are more than 10 times as many mobile phones as landlines. For many people who cannot afford a personal computer, or even a cyber-cafe, mobile phones are the major means of connecting to the Internet. Accordingly, mobile e-government, or m-government, has become increasingly important (Trimi and Sheng, 2008; Loo and Ngan, 2012; Hung et al., 2013). The growth of cellular or mobile phones and social media outlets such as Facebook and Twitter likewise has paved the way for mobile governance, or what Linders (2012) calls the shift from e-government to "we-government." Asia is very well endowed with mobile phones: most countries have more cell phones than people (Fig. 1.4). Surprisingly, while penetration rates are universal in wealthy countries such as South Korea and Japan, the highest rates are found in poorer ones such as Kazakhstan, Vietnam, and Thailand.

Finally, several Asian governments have taken steps toward reducing the digital divide, with varying degrees of success. For example, China has sought to increase Internet access in remote rural areas (Harwit, 2004; Chen and Lai, 2010) and has promoted the mobile Internet there (Loo and Ngan, 2012). Similar programs exist in South Korea (Moon et al., 2012), Thailand (Srinuan et al., 2012), and Malaysia (Nair et al., 2010). The Indian government initiated several commissions to bridge the country's digital divide, with limited success, such as Gyandoot, a series of digital information kiosks

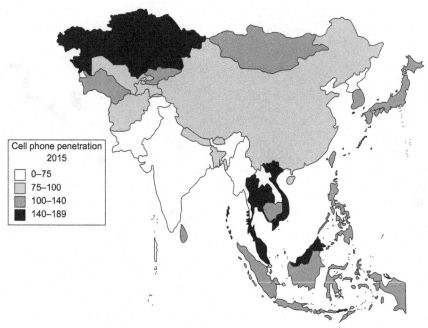

Figure 1.4 Mobile phone penetration rates, 2015.

in Madhya Pradesh launched in 2000 (Rao, 2005; Monga, 2008). In Sri Lanka, the government established 600 Nenasala centers in rural areas to provide access to government information and services (Karunasena and Deng, 2012). In Central Asia, progress toward reducing the digital divide has occurred much more slowly than in most of the world and is often handicapped by governments fearful of losing control over a vital means of information control. Using funds from the Agency for International Development, the Kyrgyz government has created a small network of subsidized telecenters (Best et al., 2009). Some governments cling to the older model of state-owned telecommunications, such as Uzbekistan, in which UzbekTelecom retains a legal monopoly status even as it is being privatized. In such cases, service tends to be poor and prices for dial-up and ISPs are relatively high and certainly out of reach of low-income residents. However, as the Internet has become increasingly graphical in nature, reliable access to government services requires broadband communications, a domain in which many Asian countries still have far to go. Broadband is generally widely available in rich countries, whereas in poorer ones it may be confined to cities.

1.6   Summary of chapters

Following this introductory chapter, the subsequent ones examine each of the major regions of Asia: Japan and Korea, the greater Chinese realm (including Taiwan), Southeast Asia, South Asia, and Central Asia.

Chapter 2 examines two countries with some of the best developed e-government systems in the world, South Korea and Japan, as well as one of its worst, North Korea. South Korea is widely acknowledged to have the most sophisticated e-government program on the planet, and Seoul is perhaps the world's most hardwired city. South Korea has exported its e-government programs to several other countries. Japan, too, has an excellent system, when it is not stymied by overly conservative bureaucrats. The tyrannical dictatorship in North Korea, in marked contrast, reserves the Internet for a tiny elite and uses it largely to wage cyberwar against its neighbors and enemies.

In Chapter 3, the focus is on China, notably the People's Republic. Here e-government assumes a strictly top-down form, through a series of "Golden" initiatives and China Online. Beyond the usual hyperbole about improving efficiency and transparency, many observers suspect the real motivation is to enhance the prestige of the Communist Power and its dictatorial rule. If China's e-government is reasonably good, those in Hong Kong and Taiwan are excellent, and, unlike the mainland, geared to serving the needs of their residents.

Southeast Asia, the subject of Chapter 4, contains a wide variety of cultures, economies, standards of living, and political systems. It would be noteworthy if the region's e-governments did not reflect that diversity. In Vietnam, it is strictly Leninist and similar to China's. In Laos, Cambodia, and Myanmar, e-government is in its infancy and barely developed. Thailand's system is good and making progress, and Malaysia's even better, the best in the Muslim world. Tiny Singapore is one of the world's leaders in e-government, a model for others to follow. Enormous Indonesia is making progress but hampered by lack of funding and corruption. In the Philippines, e-government takes the form of SMS messages in the texting capital of the world.

Chapter 5 concerns South Asia. India reveals a startling array of e-government programs, and has arguably done more than any other developing country to combat the digital divide through multiple telecenters programs, many of which allow farmers to register land and check on crop prices. Corruption has declined as a result. Pakistan and Bangladesh have systems not as well developed, although they too have addressed corruption through e-procurement; both have public systems that allow users to check on *hajj* pilgrims to Mecca. The chapter concludes by turning to the two island states of Sri Lanka and the Maldives.

Central Asia's e-government is, on the whole, the least well developed on the Asian continent, as detailed in Chapter 6. Hampered by poverty, poor leadership, corruption, and lack of funding, most governments there confine their Internet interactions with citizens to one way flows of information such as downloadable forms. Surprisingly, even war-torn Afghanistan has some semblance of e-government. Mongolia, the most democratic state of the group, has taken significant steps, including bringing the Internet to nomads in yurts.

Finally, the conclusion, Chapter 7, wraps up this multitude of case studies by pointing to broad themes that run throughout the course. It reiterates that there is no standard "one-size-fits-all" model of e-government, noting that it must be understood within varying cultural and geographical contexts. It summarizes the major factors that both enable and inhibit e-government in Asia. It dwells on the impacts of e-government programs, such as the reductions in corruption and waiting times, telehealth and distance education programs, and how they have improved transportation and public safety. It also reviews initiatives to curb the digital divide. Finally, it summarizes the sad story of continued Internet censorship in the region.

1.7   A note on strategy

The implementation of e-government is often quite similar in many countries. Grand plans are announced with the vision of transforming the country into an e-society, often surrounded by clouds of hyperbole about international competitiveness, gains in productivity and transparency, and lifting the poor. These are sometimes followed by a series of legislative actions that pave the way, such as protecting intellectual property and electronic signatures. Typically the rhetoric amounts to much more than the less impressive reality. For this reason, the focus in this book is not so much on what governments *say* but what they *do*, which are often quite different things. Moreover, rather than obsess with the similarities, attention is devoted here to the differences among countries with the aim of illustrating that e-government means quite different things in different contexts.

Many countries follow similar routes to establishing e-government. Thus, there is a certain similarity in the summaries that follow. They open with a brief account of the telecommunications infrastructure, followed by notes concerning the legal and legislative history that enabled electronic governance. The case studies then proceed to summarize major national e-government programs, followed by provincial and municipal examples, as well as obstacles to e-government implementation. Next attention often turns to the digital divide and attempts to rectify it. Finally, as appropriate, governments' propensity to censor the Internet is analyzed.

Japan and Korea

2

On the easternmost edge of Asia, three countries display markedly different approaches to e-government. Two—Japan and South Korea—are world leaders in this regard, whereas North Korea, a tyrannical, despotic state, uses the Internet primarily as a means of social control and to wage cyberattacks against other nations. Thus, Japan and South Korea illustrate e-government at its best while North Korea reveals it at is very worst.

2.1 Japan: e-government in the Land of the Rising Sun

Japan occupies a unique niche in Asian, and global, history, the first non-Western country to challenge the West in its own terms. With roughly 125 million people, it is a wealthy and formidable economic powerhouse. The postwar "Japanese miracle" is well known, including decades of growth and trade surpluses that at one point made Japan the world's second largest economy (today it is third). It is the world's largest producer of automobiles and a formidable financial power, despite the troubles of the bursting of the "bubble economy" and ensuing decades of stagnation. The richest country in Asia, Japan has long been a model for other countries to follow, as captured in the "flying geese" formation analogy.

Although Japan has an excellent information technology infrastructure, its steps toward e-government originally lagged behind other OECD (Organization for Economic Cooperation and Development) nations (Koga, 2003), forcing it to play "catch up" (Jain, 2002). Today, however, Japan has established an impressive *denshi seifu* (e-government) and *denshi jichitai* (e-local government) system. In mid-2016 Internet penetration stood at 91%, and its U.N. e-government readiness score was 0.8874, or sixth highest in the world. Its e-participation was a more modest 0.7368, indicating that some Japanese have yet to fully embrace the information society. Broadband is essentially universal in Japan, at very affordable prices (likely the lowest in the world) and with connection speeds 16 times faster than in the United States.

2.1.1 Development of Japanese e-government

Japan got a late start in developing e-government, with systematic attention beginning only in the late 1990s. In 1995, only 1% of local governments had access to the Internet. The Japanese government long exhibited a lackluster attitude toward government openness that threatened the power of its entrenched bureaucracy, often explicitly curtailing efforts to make access to state information easier. The Copyright Law of Japan, for example, extends copyright protections to public laws, regulations, legal judgments, translations, and webpages, preventing their full use or republication.

e-Government in Asia: Origins, Politics, Impacts, Geographies. http://dx.doi.org/10.1016/B978-0-08-100873-7.00002-7

Essentially the state has a monopoly over public information, which is regarded as "national property." Leadership in the area of e-government has been weak, fragmented, and poorly coordinated. As Jain (2002, p. 238) notes,

> *Japanese can progress with e-government only in an incremental, cautious fashion*
> *while the nation's political and administrative culture holds back on one-stop,*
> *nonstop government services to citizens, trying to prevent the erosion of the traditional*
> *hierarchy between elected representatives, public servants, and the citizenry.*

As in many countries with conservative cultures, e-government in Japan has met resistance, largely due to a rigid, overly cautious bureaucratic structure and lack of political will to change. Thus, paradoxically, Japan is financially and technologically well equipped to become a leader in e-government, but not culturally or politically. Political instability, including numerous prime ministers, and occasional corruption scandals have not helped.

Initial steps toward e-government included a "Master Plan for Promoting Government-Wide Use of Information Technology" in 1994 (which did not use the word "Internet"). In 1997 the plan was revised with the aim of making timely releases of government white papers and press announcements. The Electronic Disclosure Law in 1999 provided procedures for the release of public documents upon request. In 2000 the state established an IT Strategy Council, and the Ministry of Home Affairs issued guidelines to local governments for e-government implementation. Further steps included an alphabet soup of initiatives: e-Japan, u-Japan, and i-Japan. The highly successful and much lauded e-Japan Strategy I in 2001, which became the basis for all subsequent e-government programs, had as its goal to make the country the "world's most advanced IT nation within five years." Its successor, e-Japan Strategy II in 2003, offered ambitious goals that relied on both public and private efforts. It led to the start of 220 separate projects aimed at making the country into a worldwide leader in information technology adoption (Yonemaru, 2004), including the use of paperless documents and the promotion of mobile networking and ultrafast broadband use at home through tax breaks and subsidies (Bleha, 2005). In 2002, the Action Plan for Ensuring E-Government IT Security offered several relevant measures, including standardization of cryptography, enhanced IT security, improved emergency response systems, and programs to improve human capital (Kudo, 2010) (for details of the legislative history, see Asano, 2010). However, e-Japan eliminated many regulatory obstacles to Internet use and accelerated penetration rates considerably. In 2006, this was followed by the u-Japan program (u for ubiquitous, universal, user-oriented, and unique). In 2009, the i-Japan 2015 Strategy promoted digital inclusion and innovation (the "i" in i-Japan refers to these two words) through networked smart devices, emphasizing e-government, health care, and education; it also proposed a national e-post office box or digital locations for the storage of individual public records (e.g., social security). These initiatives are typical of the top-down mandates that have long characterized Japanese politics.

Japan undertook several steps to restructure the government around information technology. In 1997 the government constructed the Kasumigaseki wide area network, which connected all of the central government organs around the Kasumigaseki, the central government office area. As Hashemi et al. (2013) note:

> *In Japan, the national government is undertaking a major cloud computing initiative, dubbed the "Kasumigaseki Cloud" (named for the section of Tokyo where many Japanese government ministerial offices are located). By consolidating all governmental IT under a single cloud infrastructure, the Japanese government believes it will see not just reduced costs and operational benefits, but more "green," environmentally friendly IT operations. The Kasumigaseki Cloud is part of the Digital Japan Creation Project. This represents a governmental effort aimed at using IT investments (valued at just under 100 trillion yen) to help spur economic recovery by creating several hundred thousand new IT jobs.*

In the late 1990s and early 2000s, government webpages grew exponentially. By 2005, 96% of the government's administrative applications and reporting procedures were available online. The critical one for the national government is the e-Gov.go.jp website, designed to serve as a centralized gateway (*denshi seifu no so go madogu-chi*to) national e-government channels, which offers access to a plethora of statistics, legal texts, ministerial databases, and details about the national state, as well as links to all 47 prefectures. However, the central site is organized in terms of ministries, requiring users to know about the structure of the government before they can use it efficiently (Jain, 2002). However, national e-government websites are largely confined to the simple provision of forms and information, putting the country in the first stage of Layne and Lee's (2001) developmental sequence. Many local governments did not adopt interactive Web 2.0 technologies until the mid-2000s, or later, while as late as 2005 online payment systems were simply not available in many cities.

With the world's oldest population demographically, and vast numbers of people over age 65, Japan faces a particular challenge bringing e-government services to the elderly, many of whom are not comfortable with digital technologies. In the late 1990s, the government initiated e-health measures to promote the use of the web to obtain medical information. The Ministry of Health also set targets to digitize health data and subsidized the growth of electronic health records. Local governments followed suit. Ikeda prefecture placed pet animal-shaped robots in centers for senior citizens that interact like living animals but also acquire health information from users (Fujita et al., 2005). Ashikitamachi established a Play Rehabilitation Park for senior citizens to enhance their mental health through video games. As Obi et al. (2012, p. 4) note in the context of u-Japan, "These measures also aim to eliminate the negative perception of the elderly population toward online services as being less secure, private and reliable than traditional services."

2.1.2   Successes and failures in national e-government implementation

With cell phone usage ubiquitous throughout Japan, and the major means by which most citizens access the Internet, it comes as little surprise that the government has also promoted m-government (Madden et al., 2013), including the use of smart phones to pay taxes. The Japanese government considers the term "m-government" to be obsolete and favors "ubiquitous Japan," as in the u-Japan program. Japan has the highest rate of smartphone use in the world (as opposed to simply mobile phones), at 94%, so it is a natural fit for m-government applications, which have been deployed to provide and obtain information on tourism, disasters, health care, and child-rearing. The Vehicle Information and Communication System provides real-time information to and collects information from vehicles so that citizens can receive timely information services such as traffic congestion, road work, car accidents, availability of parking lots, and weather information.

Family registration systems (*koseki*) have a history in Japan that extends to the 7th century. Emanating from the Basic Resident Registers Act of 1999, the first phase of the so-called Juki-Net resident registry network began in 2002, but it did not become fully functional until August, 2003. The ambitions behind this system—to transform the paper records about citizens compiled at the municipal level into a digitized national network—were laudable, even if the ultimate outcome was not. Its core consists of personalized identity smart cards that use an 11-digit numbering system (as well as name, address, gender, and birth date) to facilitate the dispersal of government entitlement funding and allows them to move among cities without duplicating registration efforts. Proponents noted it eliminated the need to wait in line and pay fees at government offices, and that many banks and railroads issued similar smart cards.

Nonetheless, the Juki-Net system became the center of enormous controversy because it raised serious concerns about data privacy, including the specter of Orwellian control. These fears were confirmed when it came to light that some municipalities had leaked information about potential teenage military recruits to the Defense Ministry. Anti-Juki groups mobilized around the slogan, "Humans are not lumps of beef. The numbering of residents by the government is not acceptable" (Kita, 2006). Yet, even before the Juki-Net services started, Fukushima Prefecture's Yamatsuri town government pledged to refrain from joining the Juki-Net system; Yamatsuri is known for its unique town-building policy, including opposition to the central government's promotion of mergers between municipalities. Other local governments followed suit. Tokyo's Nakano ward announced its withdrawal on September 11, 2002, as did Kunitachi on December 26, 2002. Tokyo's Suginami Ward and Kokubunji also chose to keep away from the Juki Net. On August 5, 2002, a citizen filed a lawsuit against Osaka Prefecture's Toyonaka city government with the Osaka District Court, asking the court to prevent his or her personal data from being included in the Juki-Net system. On May 30, 2005, the Kanazawa District Court issued Japan's first court ruling that the Juki-Net system infringed on privacy rights. The Nagano prefectural government accused the Ministry of Internal Affairs and Communications of laxness, and at least five municipalities refused to participate. Yokohama initially gave residents the choice of whether to participate or not, but then succumbed to the national government's desires. Still, the Supreme Court ruled that Juki-Net was constitutional in 2008 (Horibe, 2012). More recently the Diet has considered a similar My Number system, accessed through customized portals, which would have improved safeguards, although it too has raised doubts about privacy, cost-effectiveness, and people's ability to control information about themselves. In the end, the Juki-Net identity card system collapsed: as of 2011, only about 5.6 million such cards were issued, a small fragment of the total population.

Other measures were much less controversial. In 2004, following a pilot study in Nagoya, the National Tax Agency (NTA) initiated the e-tax, in which income taxes for individuals and corporations could be paid online, through which it hopes to change the service into a more citizen-centric one (Chatfield, 2009). However, use of this service is voluntary and requires learning new software, often requiring multiple visits to government offices to do so. For those without their own computer, the NTA offers use of machines in its offices. Over time, use of the NTA system grew, and in 2007 more than 1.6 million people filed their taxes this way, still a small fragment of total taxpayers.

For a country long subservient to its business community, it comes as no surprise that Japanese e-government caters to firms and corporations. Indeed, Kudo (2010) describes its e-government programs as being business-led. Given the prolonged sluggishness of the Japanese economy following the burst of the famous "bubble" in the 1980s, e-commerce was often viewed as a means of stimulating productivity and efficiency, although Japan was slow to adopt credit cards. As Kudo (2010) points out, e-government was part of a wide-ranging set of regulatory reforms designed to pull the country out of its economic doldrums. Construction of a national high-speed fiber network was central to this effort. The government's adoption of paperless offices also motivated firms to move in the same direction. The Diet passed the Electronic Transactions and Contracts Intermediary Bill to expedite the growth of e-commerce. It also passed the Electronic Signature Law in 2001 as well as legislation pertaining to intellectual property, electronic payments, Internet crime and advertising, and moved the country's e-commerce laws to conform with international norms. Other examples include virtual fairs, where firms, NGOs, and governments can showcase their output in multiple languages; government support for corporate web-based project management systems; and the use of RFID tags to improve supply chain management. The telecommunications sector has benefited considerably from subsidies and the allocation of the frequency spectrum.

As in many countries, Japanese e-government has been touted as promoting transparency and reducing corruption. Certainly to the extent that it has enhanced accountability—the defining feature of modernity, according to Max Weber—e-government there has been successful, at least to some degree. Accountability is mitigated, however, by the government's widespread use of outsourcing to private firms, notably software houses and network companies. This issue is critical given that many Japanese are distrustful of the state, a problem compounded by weak privacy laws. As Kudo (2010, p. 73) notes, "there is a strong and deep-rooted fear held by the general public of the information society, the use of ICT in government, and e-governance itself."

Japanese e-government includes tentative steps toward Internet voting, which is restricted to local elections. Okayama Prefecture's Niimi city became Japan's first municipality to implement electronic voting for mayoral and city council elections in 2002. In electronic voting in Gifu Prefecture's Kani city on July 20, 2003, voting machines went out of order, forcing suspension of voting at all voting sites; the Supreme Court invalidated the election results and forced the election to be reheld (Asano, 2010). These troubles prompted some local governments to repeal electronic voting ordinances. As of June 2007, only eight municipalities had kept electronic voting effective. The government even instituted a ban on Internet-based election campaigns (Hori, 2011).

2.1.3   Obstacles to Japanese e-government

Despite the fact that it is a prosperous country, the implementation of e-government in Japan has encountered several obstacles. Foremost among these are the digital divide and the country's highly conservative political culture.

The digital divide remains an ongoing concern in Japan (Nishida et al., 2014; Pick and Sarkar, 2015), where it is known as the "information gap." Broadband (*burodobando*) penetration, for example, is significantly higher in central Honshu than other parts of the island or in Hokkaido, despite the government's "Program for the Complete Dissolution of Geographical Digital Divide Areas" (*Burodobando Zero Chiiki Kaisho Jigyo*), which aims to remove the remaining "broadband zero areas." Some rural communities lack even rudimentary IT facilities, in what Fitzpatrick (2010) calls "Japan's low-tech belly." As elsewhere, private telecommunications firms are loathe to invest in places that offer few economies of scale and often have lower-income populations. Nonetheless, the Japanese government has attempted to improve Internet service and accessibility in remote regions. In many rural areas local governments established telemedicine centers to improve access to health care. Arai and Naganuma (2010) studied the impacts of the national government's introduction of broadband cable in three remote, small, depopulated towns, Nishiokoppe (Hokkaido), the Kiso Region (Nagano), and Mie Prefecture noting that it offered television and Internet services that were difficult to obtain previously.

Political and cultural conservativism is also a problem. Public officials in small towns are often very conservative. In a study of Tôwa-chô, a small, agricultural town in northern Japan, Thompson (2002) found that local government officials grudgingly adopted e-government out of necessity and practicality as a means of cultivating ties with local residents. Some people are uncomfortable with the English language keyboard. An entrenched culture of *nigate-ishiki* (fear of embarrassment and uncertainty avoidance) discourages some from learning (Otani, 2003). Gender roles among traditional Japanese also inhibit elderly women. Moreover, many elderly Japanese in rural areas simply do not appreciate the benefits the Internet has to offer.

Despite its successes, Japan's progress on e-government continues to be slow. In 2011, Hori wrote that the government has been unable to make satisfactory progress toward the computerization of its administrative operations. The main reasons for slow progress are (1) failure to introduce a national identification number system that would serve as the foundation of e-government, (2) undue emphasis on hardware and failure to take the users' perspective into account, and (3) problems related to the government's approach to promoting computerization.... Consequently, almost no progress has been made in paperless and one-stop administrative services.... The outcome of all of this is that Japan now lags far behind other countries in the area of e-government.

This view is likely overstated, given Japan's high e-government readiness index. Nonetheless, as Takuya Hira, Japan's Parliamentary Secretary of the Cabinet Office, noted, "As we look back, the e-Japan initiative has operated too much from the viewpoint of the supply-side, and therefore, it was not always in sync with the needs and requirements of the Japanese citizens" (quoted in Orihuela and Obi, 2008, p. 77). Security remains a top concern: in 2006, military training schedules and other data at the Maritime Self-Defense Force leaked from an officer's personal computer into the Internet (Asano, 2010). In short, despite its late start, Japan gradually constructed a reasonably successful e-government system but not one without significant problems.

2.1.4 *Municipal and prefectural e-government in Japan*

Local e-government is widespread throughout Japan; nearly every prefecture has a council to examine and adopt plans for the phenomenon (Arai, 2007; Kubo and Shimada, 2007). The Local Governments Wide Area Network, completed in 2003, connects all municipal and prefectural governments to one another and the national state. Some communities enter into collaborative ventures with public and private entities, while others, such as Gifu prefecture, outsource the process to private firms. As with the national state, caution dominates: As Fujita et al. (2005, p. 177) note, "the majority of the municipalities are quite conservative and are not eager to be the first in applying a new scheme." On the other hand, Takao (2004) argues that Japanese localities are better positioned than the national state to use information technology to further meaningful reforms, including local participatory democracy.

Despite the centralized nature of the Japanese state, e-government implementation has been uneven among the nation's prefectures, with well-established systems in the greater Tokyo–Yokohama region and lesser degrees of implementation in Hokkaido and Shikoku. Under the guidance of the national state, Japanese cities have implemented e-government in a wide range of modes and levels of sophistication (Tanaka et al., 2005), ranging from almost nil involvement among some hamlets to intergovernment local area networks (LANs). In a country prone to earthquakes and tsunami, virtually all government webpages carry disaster mitigation information. Many cities carry information in Portuguese, which are aimed at Japanese–Brazilians (Arai, 2007).

There are 733 *denshi shimin kaigishitsu* (e-citizens' council rooms) hosted by municipal governments in Japan (Takao, 2004). Some cities, such as Fujisawa and Sapporo, took the lead in this regard, offering online community meetings, where residents can discuss government matters with officials and with one another. This phenomenon represents a maturation in Japanese e-government and a move beyond the simple provision of information. In some municipalities, governments have experimented with social networking services for community building and to provide disaster information (Schellong, 2008). Inadequate funding and shortages of human capital, i.e., skilled personnel, are significant obstacles in the adoption of local e-government (Fujita et al., 2005). People in some towns use e-communities to stay in touch with the distant villages in which they were raised.

Localities face different political circumstances than does the national state. For example, Chiyoda City, a small local government situated in the heart of Tokyo, confronted the issue of who is a resident, and therefore worthy of local e-government services. By day, filled with commuters, it swells to one million people; at night, it shrinks to 44,000. Commuters are excluded from the local ICT public network (Kudo, 2010), such as bulletin boards, electronic newsletters, and emergency notification services. In response to complaints about digital discrimination, Chiyoda instituted a local "social network system," a website that fills many of these functions. Participation in the network is minuscule, however.

Chiba Prefecture's Ichikawa in 2006 established a business plaza equipped with broadband to assist local firms. An e-government project called 360+5 has made many government services accessible online and installed Internet access kiosks at public locations as well as 600 convenience stores. It installed video cameras in public locations and launched an online Ichikawa Safety e-Net program, which allows citizens to report crimes and concerns through mobile phones. Roughly 100,000 people visit its Media City each month to access its library, audio–visual center, and informational programs for children and adults.

Mitaka, a suburb of Tokyo, is one of Japan's most innovative cities. It was one of the first in Japan to adopt high-speed broadband services and introduce them in the schools. It launched a SOHO City Mitaka program in the 1990s to create a corporate incubator, which now houses about 100 companies. It established a one-stop portal relatively early, in 1999, and has developed e-school programs for children. The Mitaka Child Care Network allows parents of young children to ask questions and consult with experts via the web. In addition, a public–private project called Mitaka City of Tomorrow is engaged in different e-citizen projects, including an online library and web-based educational programs. It is also a "worldwide hub for production of 'anime' cartoons, producing an estimated 75% of all anime seen around the globe" (Intelligent Community Forum, 2016).

Shiojiri, the center of Nagano prefecture, constructed a 130-km-long fiber network to provide broadband to 100% of its population. It proceeded to introduce its own municipal Internet service provider (ISP), which built a user base of 10,000 subscribers and offers free Wi-Fi spots throughout the city. It equipped its bus network with GPS and made real-time route information available to travelers via mobile phone. An incubation plaza has attracted 14 software companies.

Yokosuka, in Tokyo Bay, with 4.7 million inhabitants, published its Yokosuka Intelligent City Plan in 1986, and in 1998, announced the creation of the Yokosuka Research Park, which now employs 6000 people. In response to the national e-Japan program, Yokosuka invested heavily in e-government projects, including an electronic procurement system and e-bids for contracts. It has its own emergency management portal, which notifies residents via mobile phones.

Other examples abound. Yamato, just outside Tokyo, was the first city in Japan to invite citizen digital input on its master plan, in 1995, long before most cities had the capability to do so (Jain, 2002). Tourist centers such as Kamakura and Kyoto initiated sites aimed at foreign visitors quite early. Yatsushiro launched its Open-Gorotto project in 2004, to support community building, citizen participation, and disaster management, combining blogs, newsgroups, and multimedia libraries. In 2005, Ococo-Nagaoka began promoting networking services (www.sns.ococo.jp) that emphasized disaster preparedness in an earthquake-prone area. In Hyogo prefecture, which set up a prefectural webpage in 1996 when the web was in its infancy, the e-Hyogo program offers free broadband services and deployed information technology to streamline local administrative structures. Okayama pioneered a program to inform citizens about the quality of the local water supply using the web in its City Local Information Water Supply Concept; it also experimented with public terminals in households and community centers that allow visual communication with municipal personnel. Yokosuka used its fiber backbone to digitally integrate its fire authority, personnel authentication, e-procurement, and public comment procedures over the Internet; it also has a full service community e-card. Ikeda offers free open-access web GIS systems, location-based services, and provides information through mobile phones. The Ohotsk region, in eastern Hokkaido, established a website named "Ohotsk Fantasia" that houses the official webpages of all the local governments (Arai, 2007); originally focused on tourism, it became a one-stop portal and also formed the basis of subsequent efforts to bring the Internet to remote villages in the area. Yokohama undertook a Smart City project to manage its energy budget more efficiently; additionally, the FutureCity Project sought to deploy IT for several purposes, including minimizing carbon emissions, assisting the elderly, and promoting education and culture (Fietkiewicz and Stock, 2015). Finally, Kyoto offers information kiosks to encourage the use of public transportation.

2.1.5 Japanese e-government in perspective

Japan is a wealthy and sophisticated society with enormous potential to use e-government to maximum effectiveness. Unfortunately, its potential is not fully realized. A persistent digital divide and an overly conservative political climate, which discourages innovation, have hampered its development. Its adoption coincided with attempts to pull the country out of its persistent doldrums following the bursting of the bubble economy. There is, however, a rich array of e-government initiatives, with mixed success, at the municipal and prefectural levels. Some of its greatest successes have been in serving the elderly and in terms of disaster preparedness.

2.2 South Korea: world's best e-government in the Land of Morning Calm

Since it emerged from the devastation of the Korean war (1950–53), South Korea has emerged as a quintessential example of an Asian "tiger," a rapidly growing newly industrializing country. It established early successes in steel, shipbuilding, electronics, and automobiles, and more recently has moved into higher value-added sectors such as biotechnology. As a result, it has the world's eighth largest economy, an enormous middle class, and, despite several years under military dictatorships, has a well-functioning democracy.

With 51 million people, South Korea entered the knowledge-based economy and society with a vengeance. Starting in the 1990s, it developed a world class telecommunications infrastructure (including the highest rate of broadband penetration in the world, at roughly 98%). With 45 million Internet users in 2016, South Korea has a penetration rate of 92%, the highest in Asia (and higher than the United States). Seoul, the country's primate city (population 10 million), captures a large proportion of the country's netizens (Hwang, 2004). Smartphone penetration rates are very high, and m-government is popular. South Korea's e-participation index was a perfect 1.000, the highest in the world; perhaps no other country has embraced the Internet so enthusiastically.

2.2.1   The rise of South Korean e-government

After the Asian financial crisis of 1997, South Korea embarked on an ambitious, and largely successful, program to reinvent its public sector using e-government. As a result, it possesses an e-government system often rated as the world's most comprehensive and sophisticated (Shin, 2007; Taubman Center of Brown University, 2007). It gradually implemented e-government in a series of stages by forcefully overcoming bureaucratic inertia and resistance through strong and determined leadership and through the erection of a well-coordinated network of agencies involved in the effort (Song, 2002; Im and Seo, 2005). However, Park et al. (2013) caution that e-readiness indices do not necessarily lead to greater citizen use of e-government services.

A long series of policy directives paved the way for the country's success. In 1987, the government launched its Project for a Nationwide Communications Network, which planned to construct basic databases of the government's documents. In 1993, steps were taken to forge a nationwide fiber optics network, and in 1995 the government passed the Framework on Informatization Promotion Act. The first government webpage went online in 1998. In 2000 the Supreme Prosecutor's Office established the Computer Crime Investigation Department to enable the prosecution of cybertheft and identity fraud cases. In 2001 the government established the Special Committee of e-Government to promote interagency cooperation on this issue; it also passed the Promotion of Digitalization of Administrative Work for E-Government Realization Act, which, among other things, established the legitimacy of e-signatures and encouraged administrative offices to adopt business process reengineering. In 2003, the government released its vision for the future, entitled "World's Best Open E-Government." Lim and Tang (2008, p. 110) note, "The Korean government launched the "G4C (Government for Citizens)" portal system for administrative service transactions in 2002 and, in 2006, a public participation portal that enables citizens to engage in policy discussion and to present their ideas to public policy makers online." In 2006, this initiative was followed by the U-Korea Master Plan, which emphasized the transition to wireless e-government services. In 2010 the 2001 E-government Act was amended, and in 2011 the Smart Egov Plan was adopted. The Korean government has initiated 11 e-government projects aimed at integrating government online services, spending hundreds of millions of dollars to do so.

South Korea is unique in the degree to which it has emphasized transparency as a goal throughout the implementation of its e-government system. Citizens can make their views known to the national government through the online petition and discussion portal (www.epeople.go.kr). The presidential Blue House's *shinmoongo* system allows citizens to appeal judicial decisions and report corruption directly to the president's offices via its website. Users can choose whether to make their complaint visible to the public or not. Unlike the White House website, Korea's has an interactive forum and serves as a means of gauging public opinion (Lee and Hong, 2002). It is used by roughly 75,000 people annually. Both Seoul and Ulsan started e-government systems to solicit citizen input, initially using electronic bulletin board systems called "Citizen's Agora" (*Simin Gwangzang*; *Ulsansi-E-Baranda*). Most citizen suggestions concern issues with public service delivery (e.g., water quality, loud noises, parks) rather than policy. These systems also allow citizens to evaluate officials' responses to their comments on a five-point scale. Seoul also introduced its digital "Appeal to City Mayor" (*Sizang-Ege-Baranda*) in 1998. Residents are allowed to provide input only by using their real names, and it receives about 4200 comments annually, mostly about garbage disposal and green spaces; others concerned recycling programs and requests to modify their apartment buildings.

As befits a newly industrialized country, Korea uses its e-government system to cater to its business community. The Korea Online E-procurement System (KONEPS), which began in 2002, has dramatically reduced corruption in the allocation of public contracts. Roughly, 27,00 public organizations are required by law to place their information on the system, including contracts and suppliers. Registration is simple, and the process guarantees transparency. KONEPS is linked to 15 major commercial banks to assure electronic payment as well as associations of construction companies. It also includes an e-shopping mall from which public organizations purchase 97% of their inputs. As a result, waiting times for payments on contracts were reduced from an average of 14 days to 4 h (Iqbal and Seo, 2008). KONEPS won the United Nations Public Service Award, was selected by the OECD as one of the best examples for improving transparency, and won the Global IT Excellence Award from the World Congress on Information Technology in 2006.

Korea has also taken the lead in innovative technological advancements to e-government. The Big Data Initiative, launched in 2011 by the President's Council on National ICT Strategies (the highest-level coordinating body for government ICT policy), aims to converge knowledge and administrative analytics through big data. The Ministry of Health and Welfare initiated the Social Welfare Integrated Management Network to analyze 385 different types of public data from 35 agencies, comprehensively managing welfare benefits and services provided by the central government, as well as by local governments, to deserving recipients. The Korean Bioinformation Center plans to develop and operate the National DNA Management System to integrate massive DNA and medical patient information to provide customized diagnosis and medical treatment to individuals (Kim et al., 2014).

There are other notable highlights of the Korean system. The Electronic Customs Clearing Service streamlined import and export businesses by providing logistics through a one-stop portal. All tax activities and patent applications are processed online. The On-Nara Business Process System offers standardized government procedures. The National Computing and Information Agency manages the government's information systems and provides backup facilities. The Supreme Court Registry Office, with 13 district courts and 49 offices, adopted e-government to facilitate communications among its parts and yield better service delivery (Kim et al., 2007). This system allows for online recording of property records, requests for citizen services, and a statistical management system, while yielding reductions in staff hours and waiting times.

Korea's e-government is also notable for the high quality of its services. West (2007), in an analysis of e-government websites the world over, rated South Korea as having the best such webpages: three-quarters satisfied all the criteria for effective communication and optimal service delivery, including user personalization, audio and video clips, feedback forms, updates, and privacy policies. In 2003, the United Nations ranked Seoul's official website as the world's best municipal digital portal.

The country's e-government network has also been utilized effectively in the struggle against corruption. Following the traditional adage "no fungus grows in the light," the Seoul metropolitan government, for example, adopted a system called OPEN (Online Procedures ENhancement for Civil Application) (Cho and Choi, 2005; Kim et al., 2009). OPEN has been recognized by the United Nations and numerous countries as a model of what such a system can do. Initiated by mayor Kun Koh in 1998 in the wake of corruption scandals, and launched in 1999, it is part of a broader strategy to make the metropolis into the world's most hard-wired city. The Audit and Inspection Bureau manages the system and trains officials on how to use it. OPEN includes online systems to make administrative procedures open to the public, handle disputes concerning civil servants equitably, and allow citizens to monitor every step of applications for permits and licenses online. The system notifies users through SMS messages and emails. By 2007, more than 6.7 million people (15% of the country's population) had used it. The results include dramatic reductions in waiting times and complaints. Surveys showed that 84% of users thought it led to greater transparency. Some municipal officials complained, subtly, that their opportunities to enrich themselves at public largesse had been reduced. UN Secretary General Kofi Annan urged South Korea to offer the system to all member states of the organization, and it was upheld by the OECD as the very model of urban e-governance.

To combat crime, a project called "M-police" was implemented to assist police officers in capturing suspects and finding missing cars. The project enables the officers to retrieve detailed information on missing vehicles, driver's licenses, vehicles' histories, and pictures of suspects by using mobile devices. In Anyang City, parking inspectors collect parking information and print receipts on the spot using PDAs and small printers. The m-local tax management system, introduced in the cities of Uijeongbu and Kunsan, enables officers to access information on car taxes, obtain data on delinquent taxes, and immediately transfer data to the local tax database.

An important lesson from the Korean experience is the need for attention to stakeholders' trust and commitment and an understanding of the dynamics of organizational learning for e-government to be successful. As with all successful e-government models, it necessitated careful attention to stakeholders' interests rather than a rigid, top-down implementation. The design of the system included the perspectives and priorities of politicians, community groups, unions, public sector workers, and the lay public. Collaborative relationships were an essential part of this process to gain trust and commitment. The government's E-jiwon electronic records management system, for example, including vast digital archives, succeeded because of the institutional changes that accompanied it, not simply the technological advantages it offers (Lee and Lee, 2009). Getting public employees on board was also important. As Kim and Kim (2003) report, most government officials in Korea are satisfied with its e-government for various reasons: it facilitates communications among agencies; it improved efficiency and citizen convenience, resulting in fewer complaints; and it assured the privacy of citizen data.

An unusual feature of Korean e-government is video gaming. Many Koreans enjoy one of the 20,000 "PC bangs," local slang for Internet cafes; computer gaming is enormously popular (Schiesel, 2006), and games such as Starcraft have become a national obsession, with professional players. The South Korean government initiated and supports the Korean Games Development and Promotion Institute, an agency charged with encouraging and facilitating the gaming industry as a key strategic industry within that country.

Due to the international recognition of the high quality of its e-government system, South Korea has exported parts of it to governments around the world, earning substantial revenues as a result. Examples from 2011 alone include a data center for the Vietnamese government ($100 million); a disaster control information system for Mozambique ($25 million); an immigration control system for the Dominican Republic ($25 million); an electronic customs clearance house for Ecuador ($15.8 million); a wireless communication system for the Indonesian police ($40 million); security consulting for the Mexican government ($2 million); and a tax revenue information system for Laos ($28 million). Other clients include the governments of Mali, Morocco, Bulgaria, Brunei, Uzbekistan, and Kuwait (Song, 2010). Korea and Indonesia set up the Korea–Indonesia E-Government Cooperation Center in 2016.

2.2.2 Problems and resistance to Korean e-government

As in any country deploying e-government, the digital divide in Korea has been a concern. Internet access essentially falls into three categories: Seoul, other cities, and rural areas (Hwang, 2004). The capital's residents tend to show the highest rates of engagement with e-services such as banking. The growth of e-government was accompanied by a sustained public awareness campaign to promote Internet use, including subsidized access. To mitigate the country's digital divide, the South Korean government established a series of "information model villages" or e-villages. Increasingly, because Internet access is nearly universal, the Korean digital divide has become a "smart divide" (Lee, 2016) of which access to smart devices is the central feature. In 2012 the government of Seoul began distribution of second-hand smart devices to 200,000 low-income and disadvantaged populations as a means of encouraging Internet access and use of e-government services.

Despite these successes, e-government in Korea has occasionally suffered from a populist backlash (Jho, 2005), as in Japan. In part such protests reflect distrust of the state and the lack of formal privacy protection laws: for example, the Informatization Promotion Law of Public Affairs for E-government does not explicitly address misuse of confidential digital data by government employees. The most heated debates have occurred regarding the use of closed circuit televisions, the national identification card, and networks that made school data public. The Ministry of Government Administration and Home Affairs attempted to initiate an electronic national ID card that served as driver's license, credit card, and residence registration. Critics, however, objected to the surveillance capacity this card gave to the state and to the ensuing potential loss of privacy. Similarly, the National Education Information System attempted to link all of the country's schools so that information about budgets, personnel, and student data could be made online. The Korean Teacher's Union argued such a network also constituted an invasion of privacy and that it be abandoned and filed a lawsuit. Finally, when the Gangnam district of Seoul implemented CCTV cameras to observe public spaces, widespread protests led it to scale back the project.

2.2.3 Municipal e-government in South Korea

The enormous successes Korea enjoys at the national level are replicated at the municipal scale. As in many countries, political authority in Korea has devolved to the local level. As a result, local experiments in Korean e-government abound with varying degrees of success. Lim and Tang (2008) note that the quality of e-government websites varies among municipalities, with the most effective ones being run by a determined local senior management.

Seoul ranks at the top of the world's most-wired "smart cities," with a well-developed, networked infrastructure (Lee et al., 2014). In 2011, the government announced the "Smart Seoul 2015" program to maintain the city's status as a world model of e-government. The uses of information technology are ubiquitous and sophisticated. About 10,000 public buildings offer free Wi-Fi, which together serve 13% of the metropolitan region's area. Subway users can swipe credit cards to gain entry. Primary schools can use RFID tags to monitor students' locations and prevent kidnappings; they also ensure drivers comply with no-driving restrictions. Garbage trucks, bridges over the Han River, fire departments, and public parking lots all deploy GPS-enabled technologies to inform users of their locations. Similarly, the e-Seoul safety program uses RFID tags to monitor the locations of children and people with Alzheimer's; if the holder leaves a designated zone or pushes an emergency button it notifies authorities immediately. The city's Eco-mileage service serves roughly one-half million households in 2800 buildings: it promotes green initiatives and helps users save energy and cut down carbon emissions, including through purchase of certified green products and services. Power cables under the roads recharge electrical vehicles automatically. The city also pioneered a series of 10 smart work centers from which employees can do their jobs, resulting in shorter commutes. The distribution of smart meters in homes has led to reduced energy consumption. In the Eunpyeong district, completed in 2011, 45,000 people now live in smart homes in which they can obtain information on their living room walls. Closed circuit televisions automatically detect trespassers. A one-stop integrated service system allows residents to make appointments for one of the 30,000 public services online. An online spatial data system offers three-dimensional virtual tours of the city and allows planners to simulate developments. The city's u-Shelter bus stops offer maps, schedules, and routes to various smart devices.

A citywide smart payment system allows buyers to purchase goods and services with their smart phones without entering stores. The HomePlus virtual stores allow pedestrians on the move to make purchases using their phones and have them delivered via a mobile payments system.

Similarly, the Songdo business district in Incheon has emerged as another Korean smart city. Built from scratch on 1500 acres of reclaimed waterfront property, it exemplifies green and low carbon-based growth. The total population will rise to 80,000 when the project is completed, which is expected to be in 2018. Automated pipes suck in trash from kitchens and automatically recycle it (Arbes and Bethea, 2014). Its "telepresence" system allows residents to conduct video chats around the world. Home devices can be programmed via mobile phones. Sensors alert riders waiting for buses as to the arrival time. At the Cisco Innovation Center, a small "IoT (internet of things) cube" encourages software start-ups to develop new applications.

The government of the wealthy Gangnam district (population 600,000) in Seoul successfully adopted e-government services due to decisive but careful local leadership (Ahn and Bretschneider, 2011), leading it to become an internationally recognized "intelligent community." It is the site of numerous corporate headquarters as well as Tehran Road, South Korea's Silicon Valley. In 1997, it started a LAN connected to public kiosks, from which residents could pay taxes, and in 1999, they could apply for licenses and registrations. As more functions were automated, local government employment dropped by 25% over the next decade. More recently, Gangnam implemented an Internet Broadcasting of Senior Staff Meetings web application to allow residents to observe weekly meetings of senior personnel. The Cyber Local Autonomous Government Management System enabled citizens to make policy suggestions. An Online Citizen Survey that began in 2001 allowed residents to voice their approval or disapproval of how their local government was run and its policies. In 2003, it began a service known as online publication of official documents that posted 1900 government documents on its website. Its system for providing access to public documents was adopted by the national government in 2002. More than 200,000 residents belong to an e-mail service in which the Gangnam government asks for their opinion on public policies. An online system known as the Movement to Keep Basic Order allows people to report public disturbances and nuisances. Local social service staffs are equipped with wireless devices that enable them to check information, make reports, and request services while visiting clients. In 2006, Gangnam launched TV GOV, a set of interactive e-government applications on televisions that enables users to access government news channels; cultural and arts channels; and specialized information for seniors, women, and children. In 2007, it began offering a service that placed wireless motion detectors in the homes of the elderly and trigger an alarm if the sensor failed to detect motion for an extended period of time. A local program, the Regional Information Classroom, provides classes on how to use the Internet to over 400,000 senior citizens. The local library offers 330,000 electronic books and online classes on learning English, including interacting with native speakers. As the Intelligent Community Forum (2016) notes, "Today, 3000 Gangnam residents subscribe to Wibro, an advanced form of broadband that can be used even in a speeding car, while 8000 South Koreans are using a digital broadcasting service to watch TV on their handheld devices during the commute to work." In 2004, Saga City in Japan purchased Gangnam's style of e-government wholesale for $2 million.

Suwon, just south of Seoul, built an ultrafast broadband system that it used to integrate online programs such as taxation, real estate registration, public health and safety, transportation management, and city administration. A centralized gateway provides numerous online services and is visited by 10 million people annually. The Happy Suwon Broadcasting Station delivers news over the web. It hosts 20 educational centers that offer training in digital technologies, scholarships to low-income students, and extensive foreign language training. It also hosts a science festival and gamers' competition.

2.2.4   South Korean e-government in perspective

South Korea has the best e-government system not only in Asia but in the entire world. No better example of citizen-centric e-government could be found, and no other country exhibits the breadth and depth of Korea e-government programs. Its success results from a forceful leadership determined to harness the Internet to improve its economy and society. Koreans have reaped the benefits in numerous ways, notably in a more efficient and honest system with minimal corruption. Korea long ago moved well beyond simple dissemination of information to utilize Web 2.0 technologies that offer maximum citizen feedback, a sign of a healthy and well-functioning democracy. Not surprisingly, several other countries have turned to South Korea as a model, and it has exported its e-government system far and wide.

2.3   North Korea: world's worst e-government in the Hermit Kingdom

South Korea's evil sister is its northern counterpart. Like dehydrated water, e-government in North Korea might seem to be an impossible paradox. Arguably the world's most isolated state, the DPRK is an impoverished country of 24.5 million people ruled by the Kim dynasty for three generations. The country's per capita GDP in 2015 amounted to only $1800. Even as the government poured resources into the military, the country was gripped by periodic famines (Eberstadt, 2007). Numerous unappetizing adjectives have been used to describe the North Korean government, including secretive, hermetic, bellicose, bombastic, militaristic, provocative, confrontational, pugnacious, and aggressive (BBC, 2012; Choe, 2013; Hachigian, 2002; Yoon and Lau, 2001). That it is armed with nuclear weapons has long earned it a reputation as a rogue regime on the outermost margins of the world system.

The contrast in the status of cyberspace between North and South Korea could not be sharper. South Korea has one of the world's most sophisticated and well-developed Internet infrastructures. In sharp contrast, in the North, the Internet exists on the margins, utilized by a tiny elite of government officials and a few foreigners. In North Korea, Internet access for most people is illegal, and special permission is needed to be able to log in. Not surprisingly, the country's information infrastructure is extremely limited. Telephone landlines serve only 1.1 million people (Mansourov, 2011), mostly in government offices and state-owned enterprises. Cell phones serve roughly the same number but almost never offer Internet access. Computer hardware is in short supply, despite incipient attempts to develop a domestic information technology industry (Bae, 2001; Lee and Hwang, 2004).

Despite its isolation, the DPRK has taken hesitant steps into the information age (Yoon and Lau, 2001). Officially, the strategy for doing so is known as Single Leap, which aims to preserve its socialist political system while simultaneously developing a capacity in computer software development. These efforts have a surprisingly long history. Automatic telephone switching networks were introduced in the 1970s. In the 1980s the government established the Pyongyang Informatics Center, which developed word-processing and desktop-publishing capabilities. Simultaneously, it introduced a satellite ground station near Pyongyang using Intelsat and Russian satellites, and in the 1990s reached an agreement with Japan to share capacity on its communications satellites. In 1998 the government issued a personal data assistant, the Hana-21. The Ministry of Electronic Industry established a firm co-owned with China in 2002, the Morning Panda Joint Venture Computer Company, to produce personal computers, which generate roughly 100,000 units annually (Ko et al., 2007/2008). Fiber optics were first installed in North Korea with the Pyongyang–Hamhung line in 1995 via the port of Wonsan. All Internet connections outside of the country are made either through a fiber link to Netcom, a Chinese company, or via satellite to servers located in Germany. In 2000, international lines were initiated to connect Pyongyang with Beijing and Moscow, as well as between Chongjing and Vladivostok, where the lines crosses through the Khasan–Tumangang railway checkpoint at the border, a project completed in 2007. Fiber lines also connect DPRK military facilities on the Demilitarized Zone (DMZ) with Pyongyang. In 2013, the DPRK apparently opened a new satellite connection through China Unicom in Hong Kong, although the status of this link is unclear (Williams, 2013). North and South Korea are connected by several fiber lines, all of which are used for government-to-government interactions, including hot lines to monitor the DMZ. Yet others connect the Kaesong Industrial Complex to Munsan in South Korea. Internet penetration rates in North Korea are almost impossible to measure but are surely negligible; its e-participation score was close to 0, and its e-governance score was 0.3616, which is low, but not as low as many Central Asian dictatorships.

Software, not hardware, is at the core of the North Korean government's interest in information technology. The government developed Red Star Linux as the country's official operating system and hosts a browser, My Country (apparently modeled after Firefox), which also serves to foster independence from US software (Ko et al., 2009). As the BBC (2012) note, "the Red Star system correlates with the country's values." When the name of the country's leader, Kim Jong-Un, appears, its letters dwarf those of those around it. Today, the DPRK has seven research institutions focusing on information technology, the most important of which is the Korea Computer Center (KCC), a joint venture with Samsung that began in 2000 and is housed in Pyongyang's Mangyongdae district. KCC offers commercial Internet services through satellite uplinks to servers in Berlin, a service initiated in 2003 by German businessman Jan Holterman (Lintner, 2007). Others include the Pyongyang Informatics Center, the DPRK Academy of Sciences, and Silver Star Laboratories. The Education Ministry established computer training programs in a range of institutions ranging from elementary schools to universities. However, as Kim (2004) points out, this strategy has yet to generate synergistic effects throughout the economy, a situation that contrasts markedly with that of both China and South Korea. Moreover, many of its ventures into information technology are inspired by *juche* ideals of national self-sufficiency.

Information technology and software are arguably the most internationalized portion of the North Korean economy. For example, the country jointly owns the Hana Program Center in Dandong, on the border with China, and programmers from North and South Korea developed Dinga, a computer animation project (Ko et al., 2009). In 2001, the country's Kim Chaek University of Technology reached an agreement with Syracuse University to send students there for training in information technology. The KCC has worked to attract offshore software developments, including European back office operations doing business with Japan. The government has also passed laws protecting copyrights in software as a signal to foreign investors that it abides by international protocols. In 2001, North Korea joined the Society of Worldwide Interbank Financial Telecommunication (SWIFT), the international consortium that facilitates bank transfers, a step that necessitates a telecommunications infrastructure (Kim, 2011). The country has only one ISP with international links, Star Joint Venture Co., co-owned by the state's Post and Telecommunications Company and Loxley Pacific, based in Bangkok (Williams, 2013). The agreement between the DPRK and Loxley Pacific, signed in 1997, created the Northeast Asia Telephone and Telecommunications Company. Loxley Pacific also started the county's first cellular telephone network, Sunnet, in 2002, which has roughly 1.1 million users. In 2008, the state opened a third-generation (3G) mobile phone network called Koryolink, a joint venture of the Egyptian company Orascom and North Korea's state-owned Post and Telecommunications Corporation, which claims to have served 600,000 clients in 2011 (Kretchun and Kim, 2012), a number that may have surpassed one million in 2012 (BBC, 2013). Koryolink, which costs $14 per month and is thus unaffordable to the vast majority of North Koreans, does not allow calls outside of the country (Bruce, 2012). Nonetheless, it offers the opportunity for the country to leapfrog over its current, inadequate information infrastructure. The growth of prepaid phone cards has induced Chinese firms to construct cell phone towers along its border with North Korea. Almost all DPRK Internet users are confined to an intranet with no international linkages called Kwangmyong ("Bright Light"); it began trial services in 2001 and opened to a select group of users in November 2002 using a Japanese version of Windows and is managed through the Central Information Agency for Science and Technology (Williams, 2010). It offers a search engine, e-mail, and translation capacities for Japanese documents. While Kwangmyong itself is free, users (estimated to number roughly 10,000) must pay telephone access charges, which can be high. E-mail within the North was first offered by Chinese-based SiliBank via silibank.net, which has servers in both countries. A firewall between the intranet and the global Internet, installed by Gigalink Limited, screens e-mails and blocks outside attempts to penetrate the domestic system. Essentially, its usage is limited to the city of Pyongyang. Informally, it is known as the "170 Network," after its modem address (Williams, 2010). Pyongyang does have one Internet café, a joint venture with the South Korean firm Hoonnet, which opened in 2004, through which selected users may access the Internet. However, access charges can be as high as $10/hour, prohibitively expensive in a country where average per capita incomes are roughly $80/month.

Over the last decade, the North Korean government has quietly lifted some of its most onerous controls over cyberspace in the hope that information technologies would foster productivity gains from increased coordination and sharing of information among government agencies, while simultaneously excluding foreign influences (Bruce, 2012). Given the country's poverty and highly restrictive policies about information access, very few denizens of North Korea have access to a computer. A small handful of government officials, perhaps 2000 and mostly consisting of military officers and diplomats, use the North Korean Internet to send messages to the outside world (Hachigian, 2002; Zeller, 2006). Students at the Kim Il-Sung e-Library are occasionally allowed access to Google but only under strictly supervised conditions.

Very few websites have North Korea's domain name, .kp, created in 2007 (in contrast, South Korea's is .kr). The government maintains a block of 1024 IP addresses (175.45.176.0–175.45.179.255), most of which are never used. Most content is highly political in nature and promotes official state nationalist ideology. The government's primary digital propaganda arm, the Korea Central News Agency, runs off of a server in Japan (http://www.kcna.co.jp) and went live in October 2010. The DPRK's official website, Uriminzokkiri ("Our Nation"), found at uriminzokkiri.com, is based on a server in China, and hosts accounts on Twitter.1 (with 11,500 followers), Flickr, YouTube, and Facebook to improve the country's foreign image. Similarly, the DPRK Academy of Sciences acclaims its scientific accomplishments (www.stic.ac.kp). To promote tourism in the country, the state established a website called Arirang (www.arirangdprkorea.com) in 2002, which promotes a nationalist game known as *arirang*. It also opened Chosun Tour (www.dprknta.com) in Japanese to lure visitors from that country, while the DPRK embassy in Vienna opened www.dprkorea-trade.com to sell North Korean specialties online (Ko et al., 2009). Some sites, like that of Korea Info Bank, are explicitly erected to generate profits (Kim, 2011). Also popular are two Lotto sites, www.dk.lotto and www.jupae.com, which were developed by South Korean entrepreneur Kim Beom Hoon (McWilliams, 2003). Within North Korea, typically it is only resident foreigners but not tourists who are allowed access to such sites (Kim, 2004). South Korean ISPs routinely block access to North Korean websites (Deibert, 2009).

North Korea is one of the world's most severe Internet censors (Deibert, 2009; Deibert et al., 2008). For example, Reporters Without Borders, which monitors Internet censorship, rated the country the world's second worst in terms of press freedom in 2012 (following Eritrea), with a score of 141 out of a maximum of 142 (http://en.rsf.org/press-freedom-index-2011-2012,1043. html). This appellation earned it the dubious honor of being one of 12 "enemies" of the Internet. In defiance of these restrictions, some Koreans have established an informal "sneakernet" that smuggles CDs, DVDs, and flash drives across the relatively porous border with China

(Choney, 2013). Nonetheless, whereas in many countries the Internet has enabled populist movements (e.g., the Arab Spring) and facilitated mass political participation, in North Korea it has been used primarily to reinforce state control.

The North Korean government has periodically been implicated in different cyberattacks against corporate and government websites in South Korea and the United States (Sang-Hun, 2013a; 2013b). Distributed denial-of-service attacks against the South date back to 2003, if not earlier. In 2009, DPRK assaults emanating from servers in Georgia, Austria, Germany, and the United States shut down computers in the presidential palace in Seoul for several days. On July 4, 2009, hackers attacked servers in the U.S. Treasury Department and Secret Service (Mauro, 2009). In 2011, similar onslaughts crippled South Korean banks and newspapers. More recently, the government of Kim Jong-un openly stated that it sought online targets in its southern neighbor. On March 20, 2013 the DPRK apparently initiated waves of cyberassaults using malware against three South Korean banks, Shinhan, Jeju, and NongHyup, and three television broadcasters, KBS, MBC, and YTN, incapacitating 48,000 computers and paralyzing networks, although it attempted strenuously to cover up its digital trail and strongly denied involvement (Cho, 2013; Choe, 2013). The South traced 22 of the 49 IP addresses used in the attack to the North, specifically the military's Reconnaissance General Bureau, and noted that 30 of 76 malware programs used in the assault had been deployed previously. One hacker inadvertently revealed his or her IP address in Pyongyang (Schwartz, 2013). In March 2013, North Korean hackers disabled numerous ATMs in Seoul, unleashing a malware known as DarkSeoul designed to evade antiviral software. Similar onslaughts were reported against South Korea's presidential palace, military websites, and the U.S. Treasury Department and Federal Trade Commission (Sang-Hun, 2013a,b).

North Korean hackers use different means to cover their digital tracks, including IP spoofing, in which intruders trick target computers into believing attacks emanate from a trusted source, bouncing communications through multiple networks in different countries, and altering target computer event logs. These actions were likely undertaken by an elite team known as Lab 110, modeled after China's infamous People's Liberation Army Unit 61,398 and possibly trained by them, which has engaged in widespread hacking of South Korean and US government and corporate servers (Singer et al., 2013). The DPRK government erected a military academy in 1984, Moonshin Dong, which trains cherry-picked cyberwarriors in a five-year long training program in virus construction and penetration of military computer security systems (McWilliams, 2003). Originally located in Pyongyang, it was moved to the mountainous Hyungjaesan district, and it is officially known as the Automated Warfare Institute (AWI) or the University of the Gifted. Currently, it is estimated that the North maintains an army of between 500 and 1000 full-time specialists in cyberwarfare and allocates roughly $56 million toward such efforts (Kim, 2009; Mauro, 2009). South Korea has announced steps to form a similar unit to counteract such assaults.

North Korea launches cyberterrorist attacks against other countries, but it is also the victim of them. In early 2013, for example, the hacktivist group Anonymous infiltrated Uriminzokkiri, claiming to gain access to 15,000 passwords, demanding the end of the country's nuclear weapons program, and calling on Kim Jong-un to resign (http://rt.com/news/north-korean-infiltrationanonymous-249/). They also left the following message: "To the citizens of North Korea we suggest to rise up and bring [this]…government down!" it read. "We are holding your back and your hand, while you take the journey to freedom, democracy and peace. You are not alone. Don't fear us, we are not terrorist, we are the good guys from the Internet. AnonKorea and all the other Anons are here to set you free. We are Anonymous." Moreover, Anonymous also disabled DPRK websites for the North Korean Committee for Cultural Relations and the state-owned airline Air Koryo, which also has a Twitter account. Finally, caricatures insulting to the regime were posted on Flickr, the book and music outlet Ryomyong.com was shut down, and the entertainment site Aindf.com was defaced. Such phenomena point to the rising importance of cyberwarfare or cyberterrorism more generally as an inescapable arena of geopolitics and military conflict (Clarke and Knake, 2010).

2.4 Conclusion

Japanese and Korean e-government illustrates the phenomenon at its very best and very worst. South Korea is widely acknowledged as the world's leader in this regard, with an exceptionally broad array of innovative policies that have enriched the lives of its citizens immeasurably, and made Seoul perhaps the most-wired (or wireless!) city in the world. There can be no doubt that South Korea is a model for the rest of the world to emulate, and indeed much of it has tried to do so. Japan, too, despite a slow start, has forged a noteworthy e-government system, but its successes have been limited by a deeply conservative, entrenched bureaucracy unwilling to change at any cost. North Korea represents the other extreme: the Internet barely exists there and is used primarily for the tyrannical state to wage war on its own people and foreign institutions and governments.

China

3

Greater China, including the special administrative district of Hong Kong, as well as Taiwan (the Republic of China), offers a glimpse into how e-government can be harnessed for diverse political ends. On the one hand, the People's Republic has utilized it as a means of promoting growth and curbing corruption; Hong Kong and Taiwan, however, which are far more democratic in nature, have focused on the quality of everyday life. In both China and Taiwan, much of the most innovative uses of e-government occur at the municipal level.

3.1   The People's Republic: e-government in the Middle Kingdom

The world's most populous country (population 1.35 billion), with its second largest economy, makes the scale of e-government there of significant interest. China emerged from a period of international isolation in the late 20th century to become an economic and political behemoth. Fueled by an influx of foreign direct investment (FDI), it is the world's largest producer of steel, cement, textiles, electronics, toys, and numerous other products. It has enjoyed rapid rates of growth, averaging 7% annually, for decades, a process that has created a vast middle class with considerable purchasing power. Most of this growth has been concentrated along the Pacific Coast, leaving large parts of the interior underdeveloped. Half of China now lives in cities, which are often congested and suffer severe air pollution problems. The government is renowned worldwide for the severity of its oppression, censorship, corruption, and lack of human rights and democratic reforms.

Digital technologies and telecommunications have formed an integral part of the country's transition from socialism into an increasingly prosperous, globalized, and devoutly capitalist society. Since then, Damm (2007) notes, rising Internet penetration accompanied the development of a consumerist culture, increasingly severe social fragmentation, and a growing interest in identity politics. The state has long viewed information technology as essential to productivity growth and national competitiveness. For this reason, China's ventures into e-government have attracted considerable attention (Yong, 2003; Holliday and Yep, 2005; Ma et al., 2005; Chen et al., 2009; Zhao, 2010; Yang et al., 2012; Schlaeger, 2013). In 2016, China's Internet penetration rate was 52.3%; its 721 million netizens are the largest such national population in the world. In 2015, China's e-government readiness score was 0.5359, higher than most countries in the developing world but below that of the industrialized world. E-participation stood at a remarkably low 0.2105, indicating that the government's initiatives to construct e-government have outpaced most people's ability to utilize it. Since the 1990s,

e-Government in Asia: Origins, Politics, Impacts, Geographies. http://dx.doi.org/10.1016/B978-0-08-100873-7.00003-9

the state has laid over 2 million km of fiber-optic lines, forming a coherent nationwide grid. Global lines connect China to the world, including the enormously powerful TransPacific Express cable that crosses the Pacific Ocean to the United States.

The development of the Chinese Internet began in the late 1980s, at the behest of the Chinese Academy of Sciences. On September 20, 1987, Professor Qian Tianbai of Hsing Hua University sent China's first email titled "Crossing the Great Wall to Join the World." In 1987, the China Academic Network (CANet) and the Institute for High Energy Physics erected digital networks. Well-respected universities such as Fudan, Tsinghua, and Shanghai Jiatong became connected. In 1993, the State Education Commission established the China Education and Research Network (CERNET), with the goal of networking all of the country's institutions of higher learning. Government agencies such as the Ministry of Post and Telecommunications began digital networks. The Ministry of Electronics established a publicly owned corporation, Jitong, to encourage Internet diffusion. As incomes rose and the price of personal computers dropped, Internet use grew rapidly. Platforms such as Weibo and microblogging rose in popularity. Today China has embraced e-government in a variety of ways. Mobile phones are hugely popular as well: there are more than 1 billion users in the country, a 92% penetration rate; roughly one-third of the country's netizens rely on their smartphones for access.

With its own legitimacy highly dependent on sustained economic growth, the Chinese government sought to harness e-government as a means of promoting development, reducing administrative costs, and improving efficiency. Schlaeger (2013) notes the paradox of an authoritarian government attempting to become more service-oriented through the use of e-government. While the Internet offers Chinese citizens new avenues for civic participation, e-government may serve as a means of legitimating the regime in the eyes of the country's rapidly growing middle class, or providing stability in governance (Kluver, 2005). In this view, e-government is a little more than a means of salvaging a state that is badly outmoded and inefficient, a way of reducing corruption and creating a patina of transparency. Whether electronic government opens the door for a broader process of democratization in China remains to be seen, although to date it appears that so far e-government, or the Internet in general, has generated little substantive change in the country's political climate. The most optimistic statements in this regard tend to come from Western observers, not Chinese. Occasionally, groups such as Falun Gong make use of the web to challenge the state, and it has been harnessed to give voice to anger over environmental problems, disasters, and local corruption. However, the government expends considerable funds (514 billion yuan, or $77 billion in 2009) to "maintain social stability" (Schlaeger and Jiang, 2014). It could be that e-government remains little more than a thin veneer covering a deeply corrupt, often inept, and notoriously tyrannical state. Lollar (2006), for example, in a detailed examination of 29 government websites, found little evidence that they promote e-democracy. As Schlaeger (2013, p. 2) puts it, "E-government must therefore be seen as yet another type of propaganda, and there are multiple examples that support the interpretation that the Chinese government can successfully shape the Internet and e-government to suit their own interests." Content on government websites is controlled by the state's policy of "guidance of public opinion" (*yulun daoxiang*) and the Internet police. In short, Chinese e-government may simultaneously reinforce but perhaps also challenge the prevailing power relations that run through the state. Such comments indicate that e-government in dictatorial one-party states such as China differs markedly from that of democratic Asian states such as Japan or South Korea.

3.1.1   Origins and development of Chinese e-government

China's e-government approaches arose haphazardly and were badly fragmented by competing public bureaucracies. Deng Xiaoping noted that informatization would be a key part of national development in 1984. In Chinese, the term "e-government" (*dianzi zhengwu*) typically refers to government web applications, whereas "informatization" (*xinxihua*) refers to the broader ranges of information technology applications. Key to this strategy was the notion of technological leapfrogging and a perhaps exaggerated emphasis on information technology as the means to catch up with, or surpass, the West. Since then, the national government has spent more than 1 trillion yuan ($120 billion) on e-government and initiated wave upon wave of projects to encourage its growth and use. In many respects China's strategy sought to emulate the success of e-government in Western countries (Zhang, 2006), albeit tailoring it to the specific context of one-party authoritarian rule. Not only has e-government become widespread but also its use has shifted gradually from simple acquisition of information online to interactive services such as tax and bill payments and license registration.

Successive 5-year plans have trumpeted the need for developing and using a sophisticated information technology network. The first formal implementation occurred in 1994 (Chen et al., 2006), or roughly 15 years after the initiation of Deng Xiaoping's reforms that liberalized the economy and reintegrated China into the world system, although the CANet and the Institute of High Energy Physics network had undertaken steps even earlier. Fudan University, Tsinghua University, and Shanghai Jiaotong University were the first academic institutions to become directly connected to the Internet. In 1993, the State Education Commission formed the CERNET to link all the country's universities. Government websites grew rapidly, and comprise about 4.3% of all of those in the .CN domain (Zhau, 2004). The government is by far the largest owner of information resources in the country, with more than 3000 databases. By 2006, online portals were found in 100%, 93%, and 69% of provincial, city, and county government offices, respectively. An administrative structure to guide the growth of e-government was clearly needed. As Zhang (2002, p. 169) notes, "the origin of Chinese e-government can be traced to the establishment of the Joint Committee of National Economic Informatization in 1993." In 1996, it set up the State Council Informatization Leading Group, the nucleus of what would become the Ministry of Information Industry (MII), which has supervised subsequent developments.

In the 1990s, the Chinese government launched a series of parallel projects, which became the early core of e-government, collectively known as "the Goldens," as all contained the word in their title. The Golden Bridge (*jin wǎngqiáo*) project, which started in 1993, sought to link public and private networks by building a national infrastructure backbone of fiber-optic lines. The Golden Card (*jin ka*) project was aimed at fostering a national credit card system, unified payments system, and e-banking, a response to the country's fragmented banking system that often makes it difficult to clear transactions. More than 200 million cards were handed out in the next decade. It also encouraged the growth of ATMs and point-of-sale terminal networks. The Golden Bridge (*jin qiao*) focused on providing commercial Internet service to corporate clients, creating the infrastructure over which other networks would run. The Golden Customs or Gate (*jin guan*) project sought to connect foreign investors with banks and the customs department using electronic data interchange (EDI) (Holliday and Yep, 2005), which was also a means of curtailing smuggling and enhancing tariff revenues (which rose 22% in one year). The motive behind the Golden projects was to "unify the country by tying the center to the provinces and by allowing the government to act across ministerial and industrial demarcation lines" (Zhang, 2002, p. 170). Other Golden projects included Golden Sea or Golden Macro (*jin hong*, to set up centralized, networked databases on prices, investments, and resources to enable government bodies to communicate better regarding economic policy), Golden Taxation (*jin shui*, to enable banks to direct funds across the country and minimize tax fraud by adding digital codes to receipt to allow computers to compare sellers' declared revenues and buyers' expenses), Golden Intelligence (*jin zhi*, to allow teachers and researchers access to databases), Golden Agriculture (*jin nong*, to monitor agricultural supervisory committees and forecasting), Golden Enterprises (*jin qi*, to link 12,000 small- and medium-sized enterprises), Golden Health (*jin wei*, to distribute information technology to the medical community and encourage long-distance sharing of health information), Golden Housing (*jin jia*, to form a national property database), Golden Water (*jin shuǐ*, to create a national database used for water conservation), Golden Cellular (*jin feng*, to develop a national mobile phone system with roaming standards), Golden Trade (*jin shāngyè*, to promote e-commerce and intellectual property), Golden Finance (*jin jīnróng*, to enhance the management of national financial revenues), Golden Social Security (*jin bao*, to note changes in the national labor market), Golden Switch (*jin jiāohuànjī*, to accelerate domestic projection of digital switching technology), and Golden Audit (*jin shen*, to create a centralized auditing system). These grandiose visions were remarkably limited in scope, each to a prevailing sector of the state (Table 3.1).

Table 3.1 **The Golden projects**

	Year initiated	Purpose
Golden Bridge	1993	To promote Internet connectivity for large firms
Golden Customs/ Gate	1993	To connect foreign investors and enhance tariff revenues
Golden Sea/Macro	1993	To facilitate interagency economic communications
Golden Taxation	1994	To minimize tax fraud via online reporting of receipts
Golden Intelligence	1994	To connect researchers and teachers
Golden Agriculture	1994	To monitor agricultural supervisory committees

Table 3.1 **The Golden projects—cont'd**

	Year initiated	Purpose
Golden Card	1995	To create a national credit card and payments system
Golden Health	1996	To promote information sharing among health professionals
Golden Cellular	1996	To create a national mobile phone system
Golden Switch	1997	To generate a national switching system for telephone calls
Golden Housing	1997	To create a national property database
Golden Trade	1998	To promote e-commerce and intellectual property
Golden Shield	1998	To develop national linked crime databases
Golden Social Security	1999	To monitor changes in the national labor market
Golden Enterprises	2000	To network small- and medium-sized enterprises
Golden Tourism	2001	To promotion tourism products and services digitally
Golden Water	2001	To create a database of water resources for conservation
Golden Finance	2002	To improve management of national financial revenues
Golden Audit	2002	To establish centralized auditing of government agencies

In 1999, the Goldens were followed by a second state initiative, the Government Online Project (*Zhengfu Shangwang Gongcheng*), which sought to put most government functions onto the web, a strategy designed in part to overcome the sectoral differences of the various Golden projects. It was sponsored by China Telecomm, which saw an opportunity to lease its lines to government offices and thus subsidize website development, and more than 40 central government departments. Its website (http://www.gov.cn) was designed as the model for other public webpages to emulate. The initiative unfolded in three steps: first, to connect government offices to the Internet; second, to establish interagency compatibility; and third, still in the making, to make these agencies paperless. It focused on putting government documents on the web; promoted online databases, welfare payments, and bidding for government contracts; and sought to connect 80% of government agencies within a year (later this was postponed until 2005). One element, the National Population Information Network, sought to provide police departments with digitally collected information about all citizens older than 16 years, ostensibly as an aid to recapture escaped prisoners. The project offered guidelines, incentives, promotional resources, and informational centers, and was implemented on a trial basis in 100 cities. Government Online also encouraged active collaboration between the state and private information technology producers, including hardware and software manufacturers. It also drew advertising revenues from foreign and domestic firms (e.g., Microsoft, IBM, and Cisco). By the government's modest standards, the project was reasonably successful: within 2 years, 80% of government agencies had established websites, including numerous ministries (Agriculture, Culture, Labor, Railways, Foreign Affairs, etc.), national bureaus (Sports, Forestry, Surveying, Tobacco, Weather, etc.), and the People's Bank of China. By 2009, China had more than 45,000 government websites (Luo, 2009).

Government Online was followed by Enterprise Online, focused on e-commerce. In 1998, China's first government-to-business e-commerce website was established in Xiamen, which allowed government purchases to be tracked online. Enterprise Online, which started in 2000, was largely aimed at 1 million small- and medium-sized enterprises, and some large state-owned corporations. The initial stages encouraged the use of email and participation in online trade fairs. Subsequent ones sought digitized information on supply chains, Internet-based accounting and inventory control, and the creation of value-added services. However, many state-owned enterprises are averse to conducting e-business. The state's encouragement of economic activity online recognized that successful e-commerce requires a payment system that is convenient and secure. Finally, the state also planned a Households Online project, although the rapid growth of Internet usage driven by the private sector has largely rendered it obsolete.

In 2001, the State Council, the Communist Party's agency that undertakes such tasks, issued the China E-Government Application Model Project (*Zhongguo Dianzi Zhengwu Yingyong Shifan Gongcheng*). Since then, high-ranking leaders such as Jiang Zemin and Zhu Rongji have emphasized the role of e-government in high-profile speeches. In 2006, the government announced the State Informatization Development Strategy, which outlined national informatization goals for the next 15 years. In 2015, China announced its latest initiative, Internet Plus. As Mensah and Jianing (2016, p. 2426) explain,

> *The Internet Plus strategy seeks to integrate mobile Internet, cloud computing, big data and the Internet of Things with a focus on modernized manufacturing that will encourage the development of ecommerce, industrial networks, Internet banking and assist Chinese companies in increasing their international presence in the world.*

This new model reveals a novel level of sophistication, emphasizing mobile e-government services and the state's emphasis on the business community. It is also firmly geared to maximizing the effectiveness of China's external ties, notably along the emerging digital Silk Road routes crossing Eurasia as well as to Africa.

China has made rapid inroads in e-health, including digital medical records (Gao et al., 2013). Telemedicine has been a notable success story (Hsieh et al., 2001; Xiue and Liang, 2007). The process began as early as the 1980s, and grew rapidly. In 1998, the first Internet conference between health care professionals in Xian Medical University Hospital and Stanford University took place. Efforts were redoubled after the severe acute respiratory syndrome (SARS) epidemic of 2003. In 2005, the first telesurgery took place when a doctor in Beijing removed a brain tumor from a patient in Yan'an, the same year that it first occurred in the United States (Gao, 2011). Teleconsultations and telehealth education programs have become widely available (Zhao et al., 2010). Separate telemedicine networks are run through the Golden Health program, the People's Liberation Army (PLA), and the International MedioNet of China (Wang and Gu, 2009). The PLA "established a telemedicine network in the early 1990s that covers more than 100 bidirectional satellite stations in the army, military hospitals, and some rural army clinics" (Cheng and Mehta, 2013, p. 293). The MedioNet connects specialists in roughly 300 hospitals. Some hospitals offer text services that remind and inform patients about medicines (Ma et al., 2005).

These efforts have been supplemented by a the wider strategy to shift the nature of the state from direct supervision to macroeconomic management, gain control over corruption, unify technology standards, enhance responsiveness, increase productivity, and accelerate economic competitiveness under the National Informatization (*Guojia Xinxihua*) plan. Indeed, e-government is central to the effort to decentralize the tasks of public administration, and, paradoxically, to enhance the central government's oversight (Ma et al., 2005). The formal reasons for implementing e-government include attempts to transform the nature of government functions (i.e., clearly delineate agencies' obligations and duties), reengineer the structure of the state to become more lean and mean, and enhance transparency, openness, and responsiveness. Broadly, the intended result was to shift away from direct supervision of local agencies and publicize their functions and duties. The e-government campaign to reduce corruption aimed at diminishing the role of informal ties, i.e., *guanxi*, and the kickbacks that are a common part of the operation of the Chinese state. In 2013, the Ministry of Supervision received 15,253 online reports from citizens about government officials' malfeasance and negligence (Zhao et al., 2015).

Yet in practice the very force that the state wishes to harness to expedite economic growth is also the one that could challenge the monopoly on power and information held by the Communist Party. Access to e-government requires access to the Internet, which is increasingly difficult to control. This tension reflects the broader conflict throughout China between the older, nationalist center of power concerned with retaining its monopoly over information and the newer, privatized, and globalized centers that tolerate diverse flows of information. In short, China wants to promote and rein in the Internet simultaneously. This contradiction plays out in the implementation of e-government among the country's counties and cities. Seifert and Chung (2009) hold that whereas e-government in the United States was designed to inject business principles into governance and make the state more citizen centered, in China it is aimed largely at enhancing the central state's scrutiny of cities, in which bureaucrats in Beijing can keep track of municipal taxes, contracts, and expenditures.

Thus, e-government can constitute both two-way flows of information and power or one-way panopticonic surveillance, depending on national political and cultural contexts. E-government is not synonymous with democratization. Enhancing citizen power is feasible in well-established democracies with an independent media, but e-government can hardly be expected to perform such a role in one-party systems such as China, with its abysmal record of human rights, censorship, and authoritarian control. Even the goal of reducing corruption through e-government has been implemented more with an eye toward creating a good business climate for investors than promoting democratic governance.

3.1.2 Municipal e-government in China

Although most attention to China's e-government has been directed at the actions of the national government, a surprisingly diverse set of practices are found at a smaller spatial scale. At the municipal level, wide variations exist in the degree to which e-government initiatives have been adopted in Chinese cities (Lu et al., 2007; Fan and Luo, 2013). Whereas national e-government directives were delivered in top-down fashion from Beijing, at the local level these emerged more organically and unevenly. Inevitably, because information technologies are wrapped up with various configurations of power, the introduction of such measures changed the relative power of the central and local state (Schlaeger, 2013). Local governments are granted considerable autonomy in the degree to which they may implement e-government measures, with wide variations in the quality of websites and services (Shi, 2007). Some have reacted defensively out of fear that local corruption and mismanagement will be exposed. Others have very well-developed Internet infrastructures, with widespread broadband use. Not surprisingly, prosperous and globalized cities such as Beijing, Shanghai, Nanjing, and Shenzen have taken the lead (Tan, 2013).

The Shanghai metropolis, home to 23 million people, is perhaps the best-connected city in the country and the center of its producer services economy, and it has become China's most successful example of municipal e-government. It took rudimentary steps even before the national government embraced e-government, such as establishing an official website early (www.shanghai.gov.cn), which offers news and information about government affairs. The city united 19 local universities in the Shanghai Science and Education Network and formulated a centralized, carefully crafted strategy to utilize information technology as much as possible.

In 1998, eight local agencies submitted plans for smart cards that could be used for a variety of purposes (Chen and Huang, 2015). In 1998, in a vast undertaking overseen by the Shanghai Municipal Informatization Commission, the city began an all-inclusive digital social security smart card system that accesses a centralized database containing detailed personal information about holders (including fingerprints and medical insurance account numbers) (Lili Cui et al., 2006). Four types of cards are issued: blue, for users older than 16 years; red, for those older than 70 years; golden, for retired officials; and green, for students younger than 16 years. Users can access terminals in a variety of places, including hospitals and government offices, and through them can perform numerous functions: apply for home loans and drivers' licenses; register employment status, marriages, and divorces; apply for unemployment subsidies; make housing payments; and claim medical expenses. The project proceeded in three stages: the first, starting in 1998, brought together a project team and developed the infrastructure and regulatory framework, and publicized it to the city's residents. The second, in 2001, laid down guiding principles and practices, detailed the roles of different agencies, and initiated training programs. The third, beginning in 2003, popularized the cards and began mass dissemination. By 2005, more than 9.3 million cards were used by 70% of the target population. Careful planning went into this project, which drew on local pools of engineers to provide technical support. Partnerships between the city's public and private sectors were established. The city's e-government services have become indispensable for firms operating there.

In 2013, the Shanghai Government Data Service Portal was opened, and it provided an enormous array of small but important services online: payments of utility bills, fines, tickets, and taxes; applications for licenses; scheduling of appointments with public officials; registration of sales and purchase of houses; marriage and divorce records; and birth and death certificates. One component, the AIRNow-I project (*kōngqì zhìliàng rìbào yùbào*), which began in 2010, provides information on air quality (a major concern in Chinese cities) and allows citizens to upload data via mobile phones, a form of citizen science. It was soon emulated by other cities in the Yangtze River Delta region. Shanghai has succeeded in other realms as well: Shanghai Medical University is China's leader in telemedicine.

Shanghai's e-government caught the eye of the government in Beijing and became a model for the rest of the country; at the urging of the central government, its system was designed to be replicable in other contexts. As a result, its social security administration system is being emulated throughout large parts of China. The city has provided guidance and expertise for several other provinces and metropolitan areas through collaborative agreements. In the process, Shanghai's model has been gradually altered to reflect technological changes and the diffusion of skills among the population, which enables them to use it.

Beijing, a sprawling metropolis of roughly 12 million people and the nation's capital, got an early start in e-government. It was the first Chinese city to initiate an online office work system for public employees. In 1999, it fostered the Digital Beijing project, including the Capital Public Information Platform (*Shoudu Gongyong Xinxi Pingtai*), which offers access to databases about population, traffic flows, and public offices, and allows civil service examinations to be taken online. The Zhongguancun Park of Science and Technology, which began in 2000 in northwest Beijing and grew to include 6000 corporate tenants, streamlined its administrative procedures through its Haidian Digital Park, through which firms can file statistics, taxes, and financial reports through a "one-stop shop" portal. As a result, turnaround times for government approval dropped from 2–3 months to 10–15 days (Zhang, 2002). The city's Municipal's Public Security Bureau launched online ID (*shen fen zheng*) applications for its residents. It also established the Beijing Municipal Public Security Comprehensive Digital Broadband Network Project largely aimed at integrating the voice, data, and video surveillance systems. The Beijing Administration for Industry and Commerce uses an online service platform named Red Shield 315 to offer 20 tax application forms online, as well as forms for registration and annual inspections, corporate identification verification, new Internet business approval, and domain name registrations. Such projects aim to lure investors by making it easy to complete the necessary forms and navigate the often Byzantine bureaucracy of the Chinese state. On days of extreme air pollution or flood possibility, the police department government uses Weibo to notify residents under the Safe Beijing program (Rubenstein, 2012).

Tianjin (population 1.1 million) has enjoyed successful e-government implementation as well, with 600 public sector functions online. A high-speed broadband network links the majority of the city's people. A Distance Tax Collection System allows taxpayers to check their accounts. The Port Information System expedites customs clearances for ships' cargos in Tianjin's port. Its Digital City industrial park has attracted a cluster of software and biotechnology companies. The Tianjin Binhai New Area combines the port, industrial, and free trade zones and offers numerous educational programs.

The Shenzhen metropolis, with a population of 10 million in 2015, is the rapidly growing capital of Guangdong and a vital economic hub of the Chinese economy. It adopted e-government several years after other large cities in China had already begun the process (Tan et al., 2013). A major center of trade and FDI, Shenzhen, developed systems for online administrative approval, corporate registration, tax collection, and community services. The city's Municipal Land Administration Bureau posts land use classifications and applications online. As Ma et al. (2005, p. 30) notes, "E-government in Shenzhen focused on the projects such as the online official approval system (*Wangshang Shenpi Xitong*), electronic tax declarations (*Diazi Baoshui Xitong*), online company registration (*Wangshang Zhuce*), and community information services (*Shequ Xinxi Fuwu*)." The municipal government connected 88 public offices and departments with intranets and wireless data networks.

Nanha, in the Pearl River Delta, developed a Government Network System of fiber-optic lines that connect the public with the offices of public safety, family planning, electricity distribution, taxation, weather forecasting, services for the elderly, public procurements and construction projects, and land auctions. Nanhai's system is regarded as one of the most successful in China, despite resistance from middle managers (Luo, 2009): Beijing heralded it as an "E-government Model City." The local state used e-government to streamline its bureaucracy, merging several agencies and flattening its administrative structure. The municipality established the City Administrative Services Centre, which centralized 22 public services (e.g., registrations, tax collections), which reduced administrative costs and improved interoffice interactions.

Chengdu, the capital of Sichuan, has built a unified "smart city" e-government platform utilizing the city's cloud computing center. It offers a variety of social services and emergency notifications, and has been deployed to monitor hazardous chemical spills, traffic control and accident detection, trace tainted foods, and observe groundwater levels and quality. Government service centers use closed-circuit television (CCTV) cameras to monitor employees with direct contact with the public to assess productivity and quality of service delivery (Schlaeger, 2013). Similarly, the police use a CCTV system called Skynet to monitor streets.

Other local and provincial examples abound. The government of Guangdong province moved aggressively into online records, contracts, and signatures. The city of Xian offers online tax reporting, payments, and tax statements. Nanjing, the capital of Jiangsu province, started Digital Nanjing; the Nanjing Public Safety Bureau posts service standards, procedures, and prices online, as well as phone numbers for claims and complaints. Ningbo offers online approval for permanent residency under the *hukou* system, reducing waiting times from 40 to 15 days. Its official website, China Ningbo Web (*Zhongguo Ningbo Wang*), launched in May 2001, largely carried news from the municipal Party propaganda department and the newspaper *Ningbo Daily* (Zhang, 2002). Suichang County, in Zhejiang Province, established a rural e-commerce portal to encourage local farmers and artisans to sell their goods online. Korla, in Xinjiang or the Uyghur Autonomous region, implemented a Smart Korla Development Master Plan, an unusual case of successful e-government in the country's periphery.

The national government's annual *Chinese Government Website Performance Assessment Report* monitors the effectiveness of municipal websites in terms of their transparency, effectiveness, and service provision. Shi (2006), however, found serious problems in accessibility to e-government websites there, and many are not updated regularly. Many Chinese are simply unaware of the existence of e-government webpages or their usefulness (Xiong, 2006). Zhao et al. (2015) examined numerous public webpages to assess their transparency and found that most simply provided information; only a small minority offered interactive capabilities.

Finally, many Chinese cities have turned to social media to disseminate information (Zheng, 2013; Buyong and Shaoyu, 2014). For example, many local police departments use Twitter and microblogs, which have become important avenues for communications between the state and citizens (Ma, 2013). Local propaganda agencies use them to monitor public opinion and as mouthpieces to encourage support for the state. As Schlaeger (2013) points out, information about the government is not the sole property of the government itself. Many Chinese discuss issues of local governance on chat rooms, microblogs, and bulletin board systems. The potential of these venues to undermine the state's monopoly over information is considerable, although given how fastidiously the Chinese government monitors its own people, there are considerable risks to expressing dissident opinions. Conversely, social media allow people to provide information to the state: citizens have used social media to report outbreaks of SARS, children killed in earthquakes, and instances of contaminated milk (Yongnian and Wu, 2005).

After the Sina Corporation started SinaWeibo in 2009, local governments began to use microblogs enthusiastically: by 2013, there were more than 176,000, one-third of which were run by security agencies. The Yunnan provincial government was the first to adopt microblogging, in 2009. Schlaeger and Min (2014) analyzed numerous government microblogs to explore whether they offered opportunities to encourage reforms or reinforce the existing political status quo, and concluded that they serve as spaces of experimentation for improving both governance and government control, including managing social conflicts. They note (p. 190) "that research on Chinese state–netizen relations tends to emphasize confrontation while the more mundane and conciliatory use of social media by local governments in Chinese netizens' everyday life is often downplayed or trivialized."

3.1.3   Obstacles to Chinese e-government

China's deeply centralized political system presents serious obstacles to the successful implementation of e-government initiatives, including conflicting priorities, poor interagency communications, and offices with bloated staff numbers. In a sense, e-government tests, and sometimes ruptures, the bounds of China's old cadre system (Liou, 2007). State secrecy laws are often woefully out of date and irrelevant for the modern, rational administrative systems that e-government fosters. Fears of the Internet's political potential loom in the background: Hachigian (2001, p. 118) notes that the Communist Party has long been concerned about "how to prevent this commercial gold mine from becoming political quicksand." Luk (2013) points to several obstacles to e-government adoption in China, including an overly skeptical attitude of government officials toward information technology and the lack of sufficient financial resources and technical skills. E-government is an abrupt departure from traditional ways of conducting governance, and thus is not always welcomed by those who fear they have something to lose. China's conservative administrative structure has changed little as a result of e-government. This leads municipal authorities sometimes to supply the government in Beijing with false data. Ma et al. (2005, p. 24) argue

> *As a consequence of a deeply centralized and often inefficient management system, China has faced critical problems including bloated administrative structures, overstaffing, confusion between government and enterprise management, and the often unhelpful intervention of the central government in the economy. Contradictions arose and became ever more significant as administrative reform lagged behind economic reform.*

Similarly, Holliday and Yep (2005, p. 243) argue that "Perhaps the largest constraint on the development of e-government in China is that while it entails new modes of service delivery and information dissemination, it also goes beyond that, requiring a recasting of the mindset of the Chinese bureaucrats." Such comments illustrate that simply introducing web-based technology is not enough: e-government necessitates organizational change, as well as new outlooks and culture. E-government is decidedly as much political in nature as it is technical.

As Gao et al. (2013) note, despite its history of centralized planning, China's e-government system is quite fragmented. Rather than an undifferentiated whole, it is more realistic to view the state as a galaxy of agencies and offices with competing demands. Control over the Internet rests in the hands of a dozen different authorities. Turf battles among different ministries, each of which views the Internet as its exclusive domain, have led to struggles over budgets and hampered the formation of well-coordinated policies. For example, the Xinhua news agency and the China International Travel Services have battled over the revenues from international firms such as Reuters. The State Administrative of Radio, Film, and Television and China Telecomm sustained conflicts over the development of broadband cable services, and the resulting revenues. Conversely, e-government does not only reflect, but also affects, the government's administrative structure (Liou, 2007).

Kluver (2015) notes that e-government is a technical solution to problems that are deeply social, institutional, political, and cultural in nature. For example, while Golden Tax certainly reduced tax fraud and enhanced public revenues, it barely put a dent in China's massive tax evasion, which is nearly universal and reflects norms that hold that taxes are inherently illegitimate. The Chinese state suffers from a credibility gap and widespread mistrust, and no digital system can rectify that problem.

Other problems persist. Public awareness of and participation in e-government programs remains low (Shao et al., 2015). Many municipal governments lack the financial resources to purchase adequate computers and networking equipment. Often, personnel in government offices lack the technical skills necessary to establish and maintain web-based systems. Implementation schemes frequently run over budget and behind schedule. Different agencies often have different objectives and priorities in this regard (Zhang et al., 2015). Finally, e-government networks, like all Internet-based ones, are vulnerable to hacking and fake information. Despite its investments in information technology, China's information technology (IT) infrastructure is under-developed and unequal. Broadband diffusion lags behind other Asian countries, and connection speeds are often painfully slow: in 2016, China's Internet speed ranked 91st in the world, with an average broadband connection of 9.46 megabits per second (Wong, 2016).

There is a large literature on the diffusion of information technology in China and the country's digital divide (cf. Hughes and Wacker, 2003; Song, 2008; Chen et al., 2010), which takes several forms. The most serious is between wealthy urban areas and impoverished rural ones (Fong, 2009). A second manifestation is that between the prosperous southern and eastern coast and lagging northern and eastern inland provinces (Tang, 2000), a division exacerbated by the country's globalization. A third form is differentiation among villages and stratification among the peasantry (Guo and Chen, 2011). Even the quality of government websites varies geographically, with those in the interior generally less sophisticated and interactive than those on the coasts (Zhao, 2004). The country's social and spatial inequalities are thus replicated in cyberspace. Social inequalities in Internet access and use are also persistent. As in most countries, Chinese netizens tend to be young; the elderly are often unaware or are intimidated by digital technologies.

The Chinese state has sought to increase Internet access in remote rural areas (Harwit, 2004; Chen and Lai, 2010) and has promoted the mobile Internet there (Loo and Ngan, 2012). Key to this effort is the Village Access Project (Xia and Lu, 2008), which began in 2004 to provide telephony in rural areas. Many migrants to urban areas, whose numbers may exceed 100 million, particularly those without *hukou* permits to live there, lack Internet access or literacy in information technology and thus cannot utilize e-government services (Wang and Chen, 2012). However, some Chinese planners see e-government as a means of decreasing the urban–rural divide as the Internet spreads into remote villages, including electronic classrooms. As Mo et al. (2013) point out, the One Laptop per Child program has helped to provide computer skills to disadvantaged children of rural migrants. With funding from the United Nations Development Program, the Ministry of Science and Technology funded a series of rural telecenters in rural Wu'an (Soriano, 2007; Zhang, 2007). Sichuan addressed the issue with a public–private partnership that portrayed serving the unprofitable rural market as a civic duty for telecommunications carriers (Liu, 2012, 2016). And, as Rubenstein (2012) notes, "In 2010, the Ministry of Agriculture began an outreach program aimed at rural farmers that distributes information on weather, drought, and agricultural science via text message." But the problems of rural informatization are severe and persistent (Qiang et al., 2009; Oreglia, 2014), with low incomes and rates of computer literacy.

To some extent, the digital divide is mitigated by the widespread use of mobile phones (Loo and Ngan, 2012), which have become affordable for the vast majority of the population. Particularly popular is Little Smart, or *xiaolingtong*, a low-end, inex-pensive mobile phone service that operates only within one city in which the user is registered (Cartier et al., 2005).

Indeed, the Chinese state has never paid much attention to the needs of the "information have-nots" or "have-less" (Cartier et al., 2005; Qiu, 2009). It has not encouraged the growth of cybercafes, which in many countries form a primary segueway into cyberspace for those unable to afford a personal computer, although more than 1,100,000 exist in the country. Its obsession with political control does not help: many e-government services are provided through one-stop-shop government affairs service centers (*zhengwu fuwu zhongxin*) monitored by security cameras, which inhibit use.

3.1.4 Chinese Internet censorship

It should, of course, be recalled that China is among the most severe Internet censors in the world (Warf, 2010). Indeed, the government manifests a clear paranoia about the liberatory power of the Internet, which may give the population access to information other than that controlled by the state. Fear of the state leads to widespread self-censorship. The government, the world's largest and most corrupt kleptocracy, leaves nothing to chance, however.

The government deploys a vast array of measures collectively but informally known as the "Great Firewall," which includes publicly employed monitors and citizen volunteers, screens blogs, and email messages for potential threats to the established political order. There are numerous components to the Great Firewall that operate with varying degrees of effectiveness. International Internet connections to China are squeezed through a selected group of state-controlled backbone networks. Popular access to many common web services, such as Google and Yahoo!, is heavily restricted (MacKinnon, 2008; Paltemaa and Vuori, 2009). The national government hires armies of low-paid commentators, commonly called by the derogatory term the "five-mao party," to monitor blogs and chat rooms, inserting comments that "spin" issues in a light favorable to the Chinese state. Some municipal governments take censorship into their own hands: Beijing, for example, uses 10,000 volunteer Internet monitors (Wines, 2010). However, a large share of censorship occurs via Internet companies themselves (MacKinnon, 2008), which monitor chat rooms, blogs, networking services, search engines, and video sites for politically sensitive material to conform to government restrictions. Websites that help users circumvent censorship like anonymizer.com and proxify.com are prohibited. Users who attempt to access blocked sites are confronted by Jingjing and Chacha, two cartoon police officers who inform them that they are being monitored. Instant messaging and mobile phone text messaging services are heavily filtered, including a program called QQ, which is automatically installed on users' computers to monitor communications. Blogs critical of the government are frequently dismantled, although for the most part the government outsources this function to blog-hosting companies (MacKinnon, 2008). In 2006, for example, Microsoft's MSN Spaces blog-hosting site agreed to conform to government "guidelines" in return for freedom from censorship at the ISP level. In June, 2009, the government attempt to require manufacturers to install filtering software known as Green Dam Youth Escort on all new computers, but retreated in the face of a massive popular and corporate outcry; a lawsuit from a California firm, Cybersitter, alleging that China stole its software (Crovitz, 2010); and the fact that Green Dam inadvertently jammed government computers (Lake, 2009). In response, Falun Gong released a program to circumvent it called Green Tsunami.

The Great Firewall system began in 2006 under an initiative known as the "Golden Shield," a national surveillance network that China developed with the aid of US companies Nortel and Cisco Systems (Lake, 2009) and extended beyond the Internet to include digital identification cards with microchips containing personal data that allow the state to recognize faces and voices of its 1.3 billion plus inhabitants. The envy of authoritarian governments worldwide, the Golden Shield has been exported to Cuba, Iran, and Belarus. Indeed, in many respects, China's state-led program of Internet development serves as a model for other authoritarian governments elsewhere.

The Chinese government has periodically initiated shutdowns of data centers housing servers for websites and online bulletin boards, disrupting use for millions. Email services like Gmail and Hotmail are frequently jammed; before the 2008 Olympics, Facebook sites of critics were blocked. In 2007, the State Administration of Radio, Film, and Television mandated that all video sharing sites must be state owned. Police frequently patrol Internet cafes, where users must supply personal information to log on, while website administrators are legally required to hire censors popularly known as "cleaning ladies" or "big mamas" (Kalathil and Boas, 2003).

At times government censorship can generate problems with foreign investors. The government for years blocked access to *The New York Times*, until its editors complained directly to President Jiang Zemin, but left the website for *USA Today* unmolested (Hachigian, 2002). In the Chinese case, Google, the world's largest single provider of free Internet services, famously established a separate, politically correct (by China's government standards) website, Google.cn, which censors itself to comply with restrictions demanded by the Chinese state, arguing that the provision of incomplete, censored information was better than none at all (Dann and Haddow, 2008). In early 2010, responding to the ensuing international criticism, Google announced it would no longer cooperate with Chinese Internet authorities and withdrew from China. Untroubled, the Chinese government promotes its home-grown search engines such as Baidu, Sohu, and Sina.com, which present few such difficulties.

Finally, the Chinese state has arrested and detained several Internet users who ventured into politically sensitive areas. Although it cannot monitor all websites in the countries, the state pursues the intimidation strategy popularly known as "killing the chicken to scare the monkeys" (Harwit and Clark, 2001). *Reporters Without Borders* reported in 2008 that China had incarcerated 49 cyberdissidents, the most in the world. For example, cyberjournalist Hu Jia, winner of the European Sakharov Prize for Freedom of Thought, was sentenced to 3½ years in prison in 2008 for "inciting subversion of state power." Human rights activist Huang Qi received a similar sentence that same year for posting criticisms of the Sichuan earthquake relief efforts. Librarian Liu Jin received 3 years imprisonment for downloading information about the organization Falun Gong, which China treats as terrorists. China's best known blogger, Zhou Shuguang, was prohibited from traveling to Germany to judge an international blogging competition. Others have been prosecuted for posting or downloading information about Tibetan independence, Taiwanese separatism, or the Tiananmen Square massacre. No avenue exists to repeal censorship decisions.

Such measures have helped to limit the use of the web by democracy and human rights advocates, Tibet separatists, and religious groups such as Falun Gong. They also help proactively to sway public opinion in favor of the state. However, given the polymorphous nature of the web, such restrictions eventually fail sooner or later. By accessing foreign proxy servers, a few intrepid Chinese netizens engage in *fanqiang*, or "scaling the wall" (Stone and Barboza, 2010). Using its programmers in the United States., Falun Gong has developed censorship-circumventing software called Freegate, which it has offered to dissidents elsewhere, particularly in Iran (Lake, 2009). Chinese censorship and its resistance thus form a continually changing front of strategies and tactics: As one Chinese blogger put it, "It is like a water flow – if you block one direction, it flows to other directions, or overflows" (quoted in James, 2009).

3.1.5   The People's Republic in perspective

With the world's largest population of netizens, e-government in China affects more people than anywhere else. The country exemplifies how e-government can succeed when it is powered by top-down initiatives, such as the multiple Golden projects and Government Online. China's programs appear above all to be designed to encourage economic growth. Thus, front and center are efforts designed to facilitate the growth of e-commerce, including tariff and tax collection, promotion of FDI and tourism, financial management, and intellectual property. Such measures surely placate the middle class, an undertaking that their planners no doubt hoped would help to legitimize the rule of the Communist Party. There is a rich array of municipal and provincial e-government programs as well that touch on the lives of Chinese urbanites in many ways, including contact with police departments, tax declarations, telemedicine, and microblogs. China has done little to confront the digital divide and underserved rural areas; for example, it lacks a robust series of rural telecenters such as found in India. Finally, China is one of the world's most aggressive censors of the Internet, testimony to the fear that the ruling party has widespread access to information not channeled through the state.

3.2   Hong Kong: the Fragrant Harbor excels

Hong Kong, long a British colony but under Chinese control since 1997, forms a Special Administrative Region in China, where the influence of Beijing is not as all-encompassing as in most Chinese cities. It is home to the world's largest port, through which half of China's trade passes, and is a major center of financial services. Wealthy, globalized, and technologically sophisticated, with roughly 7 million inhabitants, it is not surprising that Hong Kong has developed a formidable e-government system. More than 80% of its residents use the Internet, far more than China (52%), and mobile phone penetration stands at 125%, making m-government far more feasible than in the rest of China; for example, the government warned residents of the SARS epidemic through text messages, and agencies were held accountable for misreporting data (Mol, 2009).

Under the leadership of the Information Technology and Broadcasting Branch (ITTB), the city has positioned itself as a global leader in the use of information technology and is sometimes called the "world's most wired city". More than 90% of firms and households have broadband connections. Because it is officially part of China, the United Nations did not include Hong Kong in its e-government readiness survey. Nonetheless, it is a model of a comprehensive and well-integrated e-government system. The city was adept not only at using e-government to automate many state functions but also to restructure them and make them more user friendly, including for the business community (Holliday and Kwok, 2004), complementing rather than duplicating private sector efforts. For example, it offers information kiosks with Internet access in railroad stations, supermarkets, shopping malls, and government offices.

Policies to encourage the growth of e-government in Hong Kong proceeded through a series of Digital 21 Information Technology strategies at successive moments. The first, in 1998, sought to develop an electronic service delivery infrastructure. The second, in 2001, sought to move government services online. The third, in 2004, emphasized improving customer relations. Finally, the fourth, in 2008, sought to formulate citizen-centered modes of service delivery to encourage participation in e-government. A part of the Digital 21 Strategy included financial (e.g., cash rebates, fast-food coupons) and nonfinancial (e.g., priority and personalized services) incentives to users who make use of certain online services.

Hong Kong's success in e-government is manifested in several ways. It initiated an Electronic Transactions Ordinance in 2000, paving the way for paperless government offices. The ITTB created an e-government coordination office to change bureaucratic cultures resistant to e-government, to provide technical help, and to provide guidelines for how to optimally disseminate information over the web. The e-government coordinator meets regularly with external consultants.

The city aims, and has largely succeeded, at being the world's leader in e-commerce, much of which is facilitated by the government's overtures to the business community. In 1998, it launched a 26-ha "cyberport" to lure high-tech firms with an incubator, advanced telecommunications links, hotel, conference center, media laboratory, and cyber library. The Electronic Transactions Ordinance, enacted in 2000, gives firms legal backing to digital signatures, and thus security to Internet commercial transactions. The Trade and Industry Department regularly courts firms and investors digitally, has offered EDI since 1997 for license and certificate of origin applications, and freely dispenses information about licenses, permits, approvals, and taxes. The Hong Kong Trade Development Council cybermarket matches businesses and provides contact information. The Virtual Small and Medium Enterprises Information Centre hosts a one-stop Website that seamlessly links government agencies and licensing authorities, trade and industry associations, and various professional bodies. The Business Advisory Service offers webinars on investment and running businesses. InvestHK, the agency charged with attracting local investment, answers questions, organizes online investment forums, and markets Hong Kong abroad, all performed only online. The city is also a model of e-procurement, or government purchases online (Gunasekaran and Ngai, 2008), making expenditures transparent and minimizing kickbacks. It is adept at e-stamping, or secure, Internet-based ways of paying duties to the government (Luk, 2009). To assist small- and medium-sized enterprises, it erected an Information Technology Training and Development Centre to provide online training.

E-government services are also aimed at the population, i.e., G2C programs. Particularly notable is its electronic service delivery (ESDlife) initiative (Poon, 2002), a key part of the government's Digital 21 strategy, which began in 2002. ESDlife is an innovative joint venture between the state and the private sector, which makes the government a user rather than the owner. ESD life offers one-stop access (www.esdlife.com) to roughly 40 government services, including marriage registration, volunteer registration, reservations at leisure and sports facilities, and filing tax returns. It is used by 3 million people per month (Holliday and Kwok, 2004). Similarly, the Hong Kong Hospital Authority uses intranet to provide health information and booking services, clinical guidelines, a medical database, and training programs. Hong Kong residents are legally required to carry identification cards, whose information links to this system seamlessly. During the SARS outbreak, the government sent warning via text messages to 6 million people. The Drainage Services Department conducts inspections using mobile phones. The Hong Kong Police Force offers an online reporting center to report crimes. The city's judicial system offers online guides to the courts, including dockets. To address the city's digital divide, Hong Kong established the Community Cyber Point project, which offers Internet access in post offices, libraries, and community centers. Some of these include Braille and text-to-voice translation services. The traffic department, which operates a network of closed-circuit television cameras, allows people to check congestion levels online and calculate the most efficient path through its Route Advisory System.

3.3   Taiwan: the Republic of China leads the way

On the island of Taiwan, the government of the Republic of China has pursued an aggressively capitalist course, with US backing, since 1949. With 23.5 million people, Taiwan's export-oriented economy includes impressive industries in electronics, industrial machinery, and petrochemicals. As a country with a much higher per capita income than China, and a relatively democratic government, Taiwan has both the resources and the political context to implement e-government in a democratic fashion.

Taiwan's success in implementing e-government stands in sharp contrast to China. Its 2015, e-government readiness score was 0.82, not far behind Asia's leaders, South Korea and Singapore. Internet penetration in 2016 stood at almost 84%, and mobile smartphone usage is very high. Its e-participation score was 0.89 (higher than Japan's), the third highest in Asia (after South Korea and Singapore). In short, a well-educated, technologically savvy population made the country well primed for the introduction of e-government.

Taiwanese e-government unfolded legislatively in a very different context from that of the People's Republic. Unlike the highly secretive Chinese government, the government in Taiwan has passed a variety of Freedom of Information Acts, modeled on those in the United States, that facilitate the public's rights and opportunities to obtain data about their state. For example, in 2011, the Taipei municipal government established an open data portal (data.taipei.gov.tw), and by 2013 the national government followed suit (data.gov.tw).

With roots that can be traced back to 1998, the Taiwanese e-government was rolled out in four phases: the first sought to disseminate information technology through public offices (a goal accomplished by 2002); the second aimed at shifting roughly 1500 services online; the third emphasized interoperability among various agencies; and the fourth, still under development, took as its goal the creation of a one-stop center or common platform (http://www.gov.tw/) that could address a variety of needs. All government agencies use electronic document storage and exchange.

The development of Taiwanese e-government was given its current institutional form through the Electronic Government Program, which was passed by the executive branch in April 2001 (Lee et al., 2005). It proceeded in several overlapping stages. Its origins, in 1998–2000, developed fiber backbones and electronic certification procedures. The second, in 2001–04, linked government agencies together. The third, 2002–07, moved 1500 services online. The fourth, 2008–11, sought to enhance citizen participation through Web 2.0 technologies. Taiwan's success in this regard is in part attributable to a centralized information system that crossed stubborn administrative boundaries (Yan et al., 2012). The country also placed considerable emphasis on e-government services accessible through mobile devices, or "m-government" (Hung et al., 2013). The Research, Development and Evaluation Commission of the Executive Yuan put a priority on making websites useful and accessible.

The best known example of Taiwanese e-government program is its online tax filing and payment system (Hung et al., 2006). It uses blogs to keep users up to date about changes in rules and regulations, and users can share tax-filing tips and experiences. Users of this system reported higher levels of satisfaction with the government than those still reliant on traditional forms of payment (Fu et al., 2004). In addition, to protect Taiwanese business executives operating in China, the government has expedited the use of online contracts (Liao and Jeng, 2005). Other applications include online automobile registration, job-matching sites, electronic procurement of contracts, access to tariff applications, and utility services. The government's Certification Authority assures quality control.

Information security is another important aspect of Taiwan's e-government, mandated by the Executive Yuan (Huang and Farn, 2016), including security audits, protection of vulnerable databases, feedback and adjustment protocols, and safeguards for critical elements of the information infrastructure. Local tax bureaus oversee the construction of backup systems. This system also contains guarantees for the protection of personal data.

Because citizen involvement is essential to good e-government, Taiwan has opened digital channels for residents to voice their opinions and complaints. The mayor of Taipei, for example, has a special email system for this purpose, although his office is cognizant that the digital divide limits this avenue to those with Internet access (Chen et al., 2006). Indeed, the wide variations in adoption of e-government tools among the country's national and local governments reveal an intragovernmental "digital divide" (Chen et al., 2006). Some locales have excelled: for example, Taoyuan County undertook U-Taoyuan, a large e-government initiative that provides comprehensive services to the local aviation and logistics industry. The county government uses RSS feeds to disseminate updates and promote new services; mashups offer essential information to targeted communities. Blogs and discussion for a new facility involve the local community, and the government provides updates through RSS feeds.

Although it is a relatively small country, nonetheless, geographic variations in Internet access and the quality of e-government exist in Taiwan. Hsieh et al. (2013) found that e-government was most accessible and widely used in the northernmost and southernmost parts of the island, i.e., the cities of Taipei and Kaohsiung. More remote regions, in contrast, offered fewer of the most popular e-government services. The government is well aware of the digital divide there and has taken active steps to mitigate it (Yu and Wang, 2004).

Several Taiwanese cities and counties have taken steps to introduce e-government in various ways. Changhua County implemented a fiber optic system and offers free instruction on the Internet to tens of thousands of residents. Hsinchu City, with a science park that employs 150,000 people, was the first in Taiwan to implement e-learning platforms—the e-Book Schoolbag and e-Book Reader. Its Intelligent City Project Office produced a local smart card that allows residents to ride busses, check out library books, and pay parking fees. Kaohsiung took the lead in implementing 4G mobile phone applications for e-government, including virtual tours of its arts center. Each head of its 891 neighborhoods is trained in using social media to alert residents to emergencies and promote conservation. New Taipei City has universal broadband access and 10,000 Wi-Fi hotspots. A cloud-computing development called U-Town has attracted 2300 businesses and created 80,000 jobs. Yunlin County uses public blogs to connect agricultural producers with one another, where they share farming techniques and solutions to problems. Taipei has a CyberCity program, including an electronic document system open to the public, e-schools, and more than 400 e-government applications. Free Internet kiosks were established at 800 convenience stores. An e-health care initiative has integrated the data systems of 300 municipal hospitals. Taitung County created a real-time decision support system that examines previous typhoons to help predict incoming storms. Taoyuan created Digital Opportunity Centers in remote areas and uses networked sensors to detect air and water pollution violations. In short, municipal e-government in Taiwan exhibits a wide variety of innovative and successful programs.

3.4 Conclusion

Greater China—the People's Republic, Hong Kong, and Taiwan—illustrates two sharply divergent paths to e-government. The People's Republic of China has largely harnessed it for purposes of promoting economic growth, state surveillance, and legitimating the Communist Party, forming one of the world's worst digital panopticons. It is notable how little of China's e-government is concerned to make the process citizen centric. Opportunities for feedback are limited, and the state heavily censors the Internet. In contrast, Hong Kong and Taiwan, have deployed IT to enhance the quality of people's lives, making them safer and more convenient. Such sharp differences testify to the deeply political nature of e-government and how it is entwined with relations of power: far from being some neutral technology, its uses everywhere are conditioned by local cultural, social, and political contexts.

Southeast Asia

4

Southeast Asia, including Indochina and the numerous island states to its south, is a large and highly varied region comprising countries with diverse economies, cultures, religions, languages, and colonial histories. It includes states as different from one another as impoverished Laos and Myanmar on the one hand and wealthy Singapore on the other. Several of these nations followed Japan and South Korea to become newly industrialized countries (e.g., Thailand, Malaysia, Indonesia) whereas others remain relatively isolated within the global economy, and thus disadvantaged.

Although Southeast Asian states generally lag behind leaders such as South Korea and Japan, nonetheless e-government has made steady progress in this region (Holliday, 2002). In part these efforts reflect an initiative in 2000 from the Association of Southeast Asian Nations (ASEAN, now the Asian Economic Community), followed by a 2015 Action Plan, to promote the use of information technology (IT), encourage the growth of e-commerce, and reduce the digital divide. The rapidly emerging economies of the region reveal considerable variations in e-government readiness and implementation, ranging from Singapore, one of the world's leaders in e-government, to countries such as Timor L'Este (East Timor), where e-government is still nonexistent. A brief summary of relevant Internet access statistics is provided in Table 4.1. The growth of knowledge-based economies poses special dangers for those without Internet access, leading to concerns across the region about the digital divide (Tipton, 2002). Most e-government programs in the region consist of websites that simply provide information (Holliday, 2002), although this is changing rapidly.

4.1 Vietnam: Leninist e-government in action

After decades fighting French, Japanese, and American occupations, Vietnam established a rigid, single-party communist dictatorship in the 1970s that in many respects imitated that of China, with strict socialist controls and severe political repression. However, gradually, starting in the 1980s a series of steps, such as the *doi moi* reforms, led to a quasimarket-based economy. It also began to loosen the government's grip and open the country to the world economy, including joining ASEAN and the World Trade Organization in 2006. Its economy is still largely agricultural, but it has developed burgeoning industries in garments and food production. While a relatively poor country, its population of 90 million is well educated.

Vietnam ranks relatively low in terms of IT usage. Its 2015 e-government readiness score was a mediocre 0.5217, and Internet penetration stood at 51%. There are only five Internet service providers (ISPs) in the country, including Vietnam Data Communications, a subsidiary of the state monopoly, Vietnam Post and Telecommunications. Mobile phone usage is common and constitutes one of the main avenues for accessing the

e-Government in Asia: Origins, Politics, Impacts, Geographies. http://dx.doi.org/10.1016/B978-0-08-100873-7.00004-0

Table 4.1 **Internet and e-government statistics for Southeast Asia, 2016**

Country	2016 Internet Penetration	2015 e-Government Readiness	e-Participation	Mobile phone Penetration
Brunei	71.0	0.625	0.4737	110.1
Cambodia	25.7	0.2902	0	132.8
Indonesia	34.1	0.4949	0.2105	128.8
Laos	19.9	0.2935	0	67.0
Malaysia	68.1	0.6703	0.5	148.8
Myanmar	19.2	0.2703	0	54.0
Philippines	52.6	0.513	0.2105	111.2
Singapore	82.0	0.8474	0.9474	146.9
Thailand	60.1	0.5093	0.3158	144.4
Timor L'Este	27.0	0.2365	0	119.4
Vietnam	51.5	0.5217	0.1053	147.1

Internet. It is also one of the world's most severe Internet censors. E-participation was rated at a mere 0.1053, indicating a society not yet positioned to reap the fruits of the Internet. Five ISPs serve the country.

Vietnam got a very late start in implementing e-government, and did so precisely as reformers began the gradual shift to a more market-based society. Early efforts were supported by the French government (Thao and Trong, 2015). At the behest of the e-government steering board, ministerial websites were completed, but not until 2003. In 2002, it formed the Ministry of Post and Telematics to oversee IT development in the country. In 2010, the government passed Act Number 43, which promoted the shift of government services online. The state has attempted to create an e-customs facility, with limited success.

At the simplest level of e-government—web pages that provide information—Vietnam has made several gains. All 64 provinces developed their own websites, to various degrees of functionality. Virtually all public offices are connected to the Vietnam Wide Area Network (CPNet), built in 1997 in the LotusNotes environment, which supports e-mail, searches of journals, and exchanges of documents. Vietnamese e-government is most evident in cities such as Hanoi, Saigon (Ho Chi Minh City), and Danang (Tsai et al., 2009). It is there the government has taken tentative steps toward online registration and licensing. Hanoi allows online registration of births and deaths. Hanoi and Saigon introduced the "tale of two cities" project (Desai and Magalhaes, 2001), portals that inform potential investors of how to start a business there. However, many government websites are not user-friendly, are not updated sufficiently frequently, and provide few opportunities for user feedback. They are thus "supply driven" rather than user driven. In 2006, the government launched the official Vietnam government information portal (www.vietnam.gov.vn) using Oracle technology. The

Vietnam digital government webpage (http://egov.org.vn/2016/en/homepage/) is relatively sophisticated, with announcements of conferences and seminars. Despite considerable investment, e-government in Vietnam has fallen far below popular expectations (Khanh et al., 2015).

Vietnam has suffered its share of disappointments in e-government. Its first major foray was a disaster. In 2001, Vietnam launched the widely heralded Project 112, at a cost of $220 million, to integrate government software across the country, train personnel in IT, and link government agencies through a shared network of linked databases. However, the project never really got off the ground and never confronted the country's severe digital divide between cities and rural areas. Project 112 disappointed its government backers (Obi and Hai, 2010) and collapsed in 2007 when several high-ranking administrators were arrested on charges of receiving kickbacks from software companies (AmCham Vietnam, n.d.). In 2012, the project was discontinued. To be fair, however, failures of e-government projects are not uncommon in the developing world (Dada, 2006), where they are particularly painful given the limited resources at their disposal.

More recently the country has enjoyed modest successes. In 2007, the state began the ICT Development Project with World Bank funding. It yielded several fruits, such as allowing the Ministry of Foreign Affairs to issue visas online inside of Vietnam and at 95 overseas diplomatic offices. Similarly, Microsoft's CityNext project funded the growth of interactive municipal websites in the country as well as e-health programs and a cloud computing e-government platform. In 2014, Vietnam took steps toward establishing an e-procurement system modeled after that in Chile and installed by South Korean experts in an exchange brokered by the World Bank. The same year Danang developed Vietnam's first municipal e-government system with input from South Korea, offering 1500 services online, such as license applications, land use registration, water quality monitoring, and free wireless Internet. In the same vein, Hai Phong City launched an e-government program in 2015 that allows residents to use secure user names, pay fees, and submit comments. The city also has a networked environmental management system that provides online data about air quality, which is also displayed on a large digital bulletin board in the central market (Mol, 2009).

Vietnam's lack of success in e-government reflects, among other things, the country's relatively low rate of Internet penetration; for many people in rural areas, IT is simply unaffordable. Nguyen and Shauder (2007) concluded that vast swaths of the populations were simply unprepared to use the Internet effectively. Large shares of the population have never heard of e-government or used available services (Obi and Hai, 2010). As Việt Nam News (2013) notes, "Government online services fail because of problems with internet connections, font errors, documents and systems, lack of online announcements, and feedback and support." IT standards are often not the same, limiting interoperability. Moreover, the government generated insufficient technically skilled personnel, inadequate funding, poor protection of intellectual property, and lacked clear, decisive leadership. Many policies focused on implementing hardware without due consideration of staff and users' needs.

But Vietnam's problems have another, deeper cause. In totalitarian states, governments fear the potentially democratizing effects of the Internet and the access to media channels outside of officially sanctioned ones that it offers. Vietnam's Leninist state has long pursued a rigid path of Internet censorship (Pierre, 2000), or what is sometimes called the "Bamboo Firewall" in homage to China. Surborg (2008) notes that the government uses its censorship tools selectively to maximize its flexibility in its control of cyberspace. The Ministry of Public Security rigorously monitors web pages for content it deems offensive. Despite the liberalizing efforts known as *doi moi*, the Vietnamese Communist Party keeps a firm grip on cybertraffic, particularly Internet sites considered to be "offensive to Vietnamese culture" (Human Rights Watch, 2002). The state uses a complex system of firewalls, access controls, and strenuously encouraged self-censorship. Websites that express views on human rights, religion, or the views of the Vietnamese diaspora are routinely blocked, as are those that carry Radio Free Asia. In 2003, the government lashed out at Reporters Without Borders after the organization listed the country as one of the world's 15 worst censors of the Internet. The country's sole ISP with a license for international connections, Vietnam Data Communications, is a subsidiary of the government telecommunications monopoly. Domestic content providers must obtain special licenses from the Ministry of the Interior and lease connections from the state-owned Vietnam Post and Telecommunications Corporation. E-mail is regularly monitored by searches for key words. Vietnam has imprisoned those who dare to use the Internet to speak out against the government: bloggers such as Phan Thanh Hai, Paulus Lê Sơn, Lu Van Bay, Pham Minh Hoang, and Nguyễn Văn Hải have been repeatedly arrested, all for calling for democracy. A 2010 law requires owners of cybercafes to install software that monitors users' actions. Owners who permit searches of unauthorized websites by their clients face fines of five million dong, roughly US$330 (Kalathil and Boas, 2003).

In short, Vietnam's strategy appears to offer the patina of transparency without democracy. It is thus caught in the classic "dictator's dilemma," i.e., it needs the Internet and the benefits it offers but is fearful of the emancipatory opportunities it inevitably generates.

4.2 Cambodia: the Khmer Republic moves toward electronic governance

A small and impoverished state (population 14 million) devastated by years of warfare, including the American invasion in the 1970s and horrendous Khmer Rouge genocide, Cambodia has struggled to find a footing in the global economy. Overwhelmingly rural and agricultural, it has incipient industries in garments and back offices. Literacy stands at only 69%.

One might not expect Cambodia to have any e-government presence whatsoever. In 2016, its Internet penetration was only 25%, well below the world and Asian averages. However, 94% of Cambodians claim to have a cell phone, of whom 39% use smartphones (Phong and Sola, 2015). As the bulk of the population lives in rural areas, the digital divide is severe (Wijers, 2010), and rates of e-literacy are low. As of 2011, it had 37 ISPs and 229 Internet cafes. Oddly, Prime Minister Hun Sen decreed that 3G mobile phones would not be allowed to support video calls. Like many poor Southeast Asian states, its e-participation index was not measurable.

Cambodia is in the very earliest stages of e-government. In 2000, the government established the ICT Development Authority, which was charged with the creation of information networks there. The government has since issued a series of plans to promote ICT use, with limited success. The latest plan, the New National ICT Policy of 2015, includes calls to promote IT literacy, improve the rate of use by women, and reduce the digital divide (Kevreaksmey et al. 2015). Sang et al. (2009) identify multiple challenges policy implementation, including lack of an IT infrastructure, poor management, inequality in access, and insufficient digital privacy and security. In 2001, the state initiated the e-government project to build a Wide Area Network to service 27 government ministries in Phnom Penh, with plans to extend it in phases to cities lower in the urban hierarchy. An incipient fiber backbone system tentatively connects the major cities. In Ratanakiri province, an innovative project links remote villages to the Internet via a Wi-Fi access point mounted to motorbikes; the e-mail system allows the provincial hospital to use the system for referrals to Massachusetts General Hospital/Harvard Medical School in Boston, with digital cameras for long-distance diagnoses (Borzo, 2004).

Most Cambodian e-government consists of simple one-way flows of information via websites, the most primitive form. The National Information Communication Technology Development Authority built a website (www.nida.gov.kh) in 2000 to offer information to the minority of citizens with Internet access. However, IT adoption is very uneven among government agencies due to varying leadership styles and availability of qualified personnel (Cambodian National Information Communications Technology Development Authority and Japan International Cooperation Agency, 2009). Even ministries with websites often do not update them sufficiently. However, this situation may be changing: the Ministry of Foreign Affairs launched e-Visa, which allows for tourist visas to be obtained online.

The country's most significant venture into e-government is the Government Administration Information System (GAIS), which started in 2000 and was designed to include an electronic document exchange system as well as registration systems for real estate transactions, residents (for keeping track of jobs, school attendance, and tax payments), and vehicle registrations, including taxes, registrations, and safety inspections (Sang et al., 2009, 2010). It also includes bulletin boards and electronic document management tools. However, as yet the system does not enjoy widespread use, and measures to guarantee transparency and accountability have fallen short.

Internet censorship in Cambodia is minimal, although the government does occasionally block some blogs, ostensibly on moral grounds. The constitution protects free speech, although this is not always the case in practice. The state has blocked access to the hosting service Blogspot. It also periodically monitors cybercafes, including surveillance cameras, and has threatened to close cafes too close to schools. Some NGOs have complained about limitations on Internet service as well.

4.3   Laos: small and poor, but making progress

Laos is a small (population 6 million), impoverished, landlocked state that holds the dubious distinction of being the most-bombed country in human history. One of the poorest in Asia, it relies heavily on subsistence agriculture. The government remains a rigid communist dictatorship.

Laos's 2015 e-government readiness score was merely 0.2935, Internet penetration in mid-2016 stood at 19.9%, but cell phone usage reached 80%, including cheap phones using pirated software, and mobile Internet use has been growing. A fiber backbone stretches over the country, built in phases. The Internet is administered by the National Internet Committee under the prime minister's office, and censorship is minimal. Most of the telecommunications operators are state owned, but there are two private ISPs. As with many highly undeveloped states, most people live in rural areas with little to no Internet access, and technical skills are rare. IT equipment is uncommon and Internet service is also quite expensive. The government lacks a clear IT strategy, and its implementation has been slowed by in-fighting among ministries and agencies. However, it launched its own satellite, LaoSat-1, in November 2015. Like Cambodia and Myanmar, its e-participation is so low as to be not measurable.

Despite these structural impediments, Laos has taken tentative steps toward e-government implementation. The Lao E-government Action Plan in 2006 implemented the Lao National E-Government Project. An optical fiber network runs throughout the capital. In Vientiane, it erected a national e-government service center to coordinate digital communications among agencies, and founded 16 provincial e-government service centers throughout the land. The National Bank of Laos has slowly moved toward e-banking. The National University of Laos began distance-learning courses for students in remote villages. The Ministry of Public Security implemented a national electronic citizen ID card system. The Lao Decide Info project has online databases for census, housing, agriculture, and mining and hydropower. It has initiated steps for interactive websites, although this capacity is largely lacking to date. In 2013, the government allowed businesses to submit applications for operational and trade licenses online. The same year, the Lao Ministry of Post and Telecommunication's National Internet Center launched the Lao Computer Emergency Response Team, a unit focused on battling cybercrime. Laos also joined the Greater Mekong Sub-region Information Superhighway Network, which also includes China, Vietnam, Thailand, Cambodia, and Myanmar, and whose purpose is to promote IT adoption in the region. It also established cooperative agreements with India and South Korea toward that end.

4.4   Myanmar: can the Burmese state adopt the Internet?

Formerly Burma, Myanmar has long been one of Southeast Asia's poorest and most isolated countries. A corrupt, repressive government, the State Peace and Development Council inhibited economic and social development through mismanagement, although since 2011 it has taken small steps to becoming more open and democratic. Sanctions have been eased and foreign investment has grown. As with many Southeast Asian countries, the population is overwhelmingly rural. Given this context, the telecommunications infrastructure is poorly developed; its 2015 e-government readiness score was an abysmal 0.2703, and in 2016 Internet penetration was only 19.3%. Shortages of equipment and technical skills are endemic. Myanmar has no coherent national IT strategy or e-government policy, and e-participation was essentially zero.

Against all odds, e-government has taken root in Myanmar (Oo and Than, 2008). As early as 1996, it passed the Myanmar Computer Science Development Law. Under the junta, with little to no Internet access or IT experience, programmers developed a font so that they could communicate in their language, the *zawgyi* standard, which is not Unicode compliant; as a result it inhibited integration into the computer systems of multinational corporations and the broader global Internet. The Ministry of Science and Technology developed and implemented several IT master plans. By 2003, some ministries had developed their own web pages, and over the next decade almost all 32 had done so. The state passed the Electronic Transactions Law in 2004 to lay the legal basis for the digitization of government programs, including electronic records and signatures as well as punishment of computer crimes (Blythe, 2010).

Under the military junta, the government of Myanmar, according to the OpenNet Initiative (2006, p. 4), "implement[ed] one of the world's most restrictive regimes of Internet control." The junta barred 84% of sites "with content known to be sensitive to the Burmese state" (p. 4). It also excluded e-mail sites such as Hotmail and Yahoo because they cannot be monitored for political criticism, and pornography. The 1996 Computer Science Development Law required that all network-ready computers be registered with the Ministry of Communications, Posts and Telegraphs. To implement its censorship, the government purchases software from the U.S. company Fortinet to block access to selected websites and servers. At times, the state resorted to blunter instruments: when it sought to silence demonstrators in 2007, it switched off the country's Internet network altogether for 6 weeks.

With the collapse of the junta in 2011, the pace of change accelerated. The government set up an e-National Task Force to draft cyberlaws and sought to increase the number of IT professionals. It partnered with the Asian Development Bank in 2013 to develop a systematic plan for e-governance. Many municipalities have developed their own web pages. Most public websites were developed by Myanmars.net, a longstanding Burma-based web developer. The state initiated an e-procurement system (Xinhuanet, 2004), and the government now accepts online applications for visas. More recently it developed the Myanmar Basic E-government System project with a $10 million from the Daewoo International Corporation and KCOMS Company of South Korea. The government also partnered with InfoSys, Microsoft, and Cisco to develop the necessary hardware and expertise. The e-passport project uses an RFID tag to verify a person's identity with technology from the Malaysian Image Retrieval Identification System. The government has also used IT in selected parts of the education sector (Mar, 2004). Burma/Myanmar has only two ISPs and both outlets charge high prices for e-mail accounts. Some cities, such as Yangon and Mandalay, have gingerly approached the use of IT through their respective development councils. Some agencies have even begun to make their web pages citizen centered (Misra and Das, 2014).

4.5   Thailand: Siam moves ahead

One of the second generation "mini-dragons" or "new tigers," Thailand has since the 1990s experienced rapid and sustained economic growth, as the perpetual traffic jams in Bangkok attest. A large, skilled middle class, high rates of literacy, and considerable disposable income attracted significant sums of foreign investment. All told, Thailand was ripe for the creation of an IT infrastructure and e-government. In 2016, its Internet penetration rate was 60.1%, and its 2015 e-government readiness index stood at 0.5953. E-participation was rated 0.3158 but improving. In terms of e-government variables, Thailand thus stands ahead of countries such as Cambodia or Myanmar, but behind states such as Singapore and Malaysia. Broadband is available in all the large cities but much less so outside of them.

Thailand got an early start in e-government. In 1986, it established the National Electronics and Computer Technology Center, reorganized in 1991 as the National Science and Technology Development Agency. In 1993, Chulalongkorn University initiated Internet connections. Its e-government initiatives date back to 1994, when the Sub-Committee of Promotion of Utilization of Information Technology in Public Organization began to push for the computerization of public offices and the promotion of IT training for employees. Soon thereafter the state promoted the use of electronic data interchange among public agencies. In 1996, the government announced its first National IT Policy, called IT2000, which accelerated development of the government's information network (a high speed virtual private network), the SchoolNet program to introduce the Internet into schools, and the legal infrastructure that makes digital transactions safe, private, and secure. Relevant legislation included an Electronic Transactions Bill, an Electronic Signature Bill, and a Computer Crimes Bill. In 2001, this effort was updated as IT2010, or "IT Policy 2.0," the country's vision of a future information-based society. On the heels of ASEAN's 2000 declaration that IT and e-government were regional priorities, the e-Thailand program was born, which emphasized rapid response, rural coverage, and round-the-clock service. Since 2007, the e-government interoperability framework has guided the slow initiation of digital communications among different government agencies (Kawtrakul et al., 2011; Funilkul et al., 2011).

The state has worked assiduously with private firms to develop a well-integrated telecommunications structure. In addition to the country's fiber network, Thailand has four satellites in geostationary orbit, launched by the Shin Corporation, that provide television and Internet services to remote rural areas. One, iPSTAR, offers broadband service. A number of Wi-Fi hotspots can be found in hotels and airports. The Government Information Technology Service (GITS) established a cloud computing center for use by Thai government agencies.

Thailand's e-government initiatives have earned a modicum of success. For example, the Royal Thai government's primary webpage, www.thaigov.net, was designed as a one-stop, citizen-centric portal. Besides links to ministries, it offers daily news feeds, a public forum, and an array of services, including digital payments and procurements. In 2001, the Thai Customs department eliminated manual processing of import and export documents (Wescott, 2001). The e-Revenue program has gradually shifted a large share of corporate, personal income, and value-added tax payments online through its website (www.rd.go.th). One of the brightest spots of Thailand's e-government concerns health care. All of Thailand's 92 provincial hospitals have access to the Internet. All 9000 district health centers have dial-up Internet access. The Ministry of Public Health launched its first telehealth pilot program in 1994. The state also erected e-health services that can be accessed by smartphone, a program aimed largely at the elderly. Its distance-learning initiatives currently connect 22,738 primary schools, 152 tertiary educational centers, 413 vocational institutes, and 37 IT campuses (Rattakul and Morse, 2005), although the digital divide has hindered development in rural schools. The Government Information Technology Service (GITS) provides Internet access for all public offices, while the Office of Information Technology Administration for Education Development serves its universities. The state's e-procurement program has proceeded relatively smoothly. The National Spatial Data Infrastructure provides geographic information systems services for the government.

In other areas, however, the country has suffered setbacks. For example, consider the Smart ID cards that contained the owner's personal demographic and economic data, and were intended to substitute for telephone, debit, and credit cards. Initiated in 2002 at a cost of 800 million baht ($23 million), the program was implemented first in Bangkok and subsequently in the outer provinces (Krairit et al., 2004). It failed utterly due to its haphazard, insufficient security, unsystematic implementation, and uncontrolled enrollment, and was halted in 2007 (Gunawong and Gao, 2010). Similarly, efforts to implement an e-parliament suffered because most ministers preferred information on paper rather than digitally. These failures have a real human cost. For example, following the 2004 tsunami, rescue efforts were hampered by interoperability problems among government agencies.

Finally, the digital divide in Thailand is severe, although mobile phones offer a plausible route to alleviate it (Srinuan et al., 2012). To improve IT literacy, the state launched a "People's PC" initiative in 2003, and installed kiosks in convenience stores such as 7-Eleven and True Shops. The TOT Corporation Public Company provides free Internet service for Thai citizens. Chulalongkorn, Chiangmai, and Kasetsart universities all offer free web training to acquire IT skills.

While it is a democracy, the Thai government is not above authoritarian impulses and engages in periodic Internet censorship, primarily through its Ministry of Information and Communication Technology. Most of its efforts have focused on blocking pornography. The number of blocked websites jumped markedly after the military coup of January, 2006. Messages to users attempting to access blocked sites made it appear like a network failure. Upon declaring a state of emergency, the state shut down numerous ISPs. When YouTube posted a silly 44-second video ridiculing King Bhumibol Adulyadej in 2007, the government temporarily banned the website entirely throughout the country and deported the producer, a Swiss national, back to his country. Following the 2014 coup, censorship underwent another rise. Websites that oppose the coup, and those that support the southern Muslim insurgency, are routinely blocked, as are video-sharing sites like Camfrog.

In short, while Thailand's e-government programs are competent, they are uninspiring. The country has not shown decisive leadership on the issue, municipal programs are virtually nonexistent, and with a few successes (e.g., schools, health care), it has introduced only a few programs out of the possible range of applications.

4.6 Malaysia: e-government exemplar for the Muslim world

A well-regarded model of a Muslim democracy and growing economic powerhouse, Malaysia has enjoyed rapid growth, rising incomes, trade surpluses, and an expanding middle class. One of the second generation newly industrializing countries, it has witnessed considerable economic and political changes, including the growth of a robust electronics sector as well as petroleum.

In 2015, Malaysia's e-government readiness score was a respectable 0.6703, and in 2016, Internet penetration stood at 68.1%. Broadband penetration is at roughly 20%, and cell phones, including smart ones, are very popular. As befits a rapidly growing economy, its e-participation rate was 0.50.

Malaysia has a long track record of successfully pursuing IT as a national development strategy. It established the National Information Technology Council in 1993. The Communications and Multimedia Commission formulated and implemented IT policy objectives and the regulatory framework for the relevant industries. Rarely has e-government been so explicitly harnessed to national development goals as in Malaysia. Its introduction in the 1990s coincided with a wholesale reform of government that launched the country into an aggressive path of globalization, with considerable success. E-government forms a core part of Malaysia's ambitious Vision 2020, a strategy to become a fully developed economy by the year 2020 that centers in large part on the adoption of IT (Ghani et al., 2012). Malaysia's government online efforts come under the umbrella of the Administrative and Modernisation Planning Unit, which mandates that all agencies must have an e-government strategy. In 1994, the state created the Civil Service Link to disseminate information to the public, which was subsequently upgraded and renamed the Malaysian Civil Service Link. To lay the legal groundwork, the Malay government passed a series of laws in the late 1990s, including the Communications and Multimedia Act (1998), the Digital Signature Act (1997), the Computer Crimes Act (1997), the Copyright Amendment Act (1997), the Telemedicine Act (1997), and the Personal Data Protection Act (2004).

In 1996, the government launched the famed Multimedia Super Corridor (MSC), essentially an enormous technology park that stretches for 50 km from Kuala Lumpur to two new cities, Putrajaya and Cyberjaya, connecting them with a high speed broadband fiber cable. Cyberjaya, a 7000 ha development, was started in 1999 as an e-commerce center. These became the nucleus of a cluster of IT corporations that went far toward transforming Malaysian society, economy, and government. As part of this project, the next year, 1997, saw the dawn of formal e-government legislation, known simply as e-government, as one of the MSC flagships, which revolved around several interlocking goals: generic office environment, to promote a collaborative, paperless public workspace; electronic procurement through three modules (the enterprise-wide information management, communications, and collaboration systems); the project monitoring system, to coordinate managerial functions of numerous statutory bodies on diverse public projects and to facilitate the exchange of best practices; the Human Resource Management information system, to enhance government employee functionality; the Electronic Labour Exchange renamed JobsMalaysia, launched in 1999, which is an online job matching site used by 35,000 people annually; e-Syariah, to upgrade services in the 102 Syariah courts and the effectiveness of the Islamic Affairs Department; and e-Land, to make the National Land Administration more accurate. e-Land includes the e-Tanah project of the Ministry of Natural Resources and Environment, begun as a pilot project in Penang, which oversees land registration and sales to facilitate land transactions (Kaliannan et al., 2007). e-Syariah, begun in 2002, became fully functional in 2005 and centers on a portal that allows attorneys, prosecutors, plaintiffs, and defendants to file suits and affidavits online, get hearing dates, and view court decisions; current plans call for a future ability to allow plaintiffs and respondents to meet via teleconferencing.

Malaysia has a successful track record in using the Internet to deliver public services; indeed, e-Services was one of the initial flagship projects when e-government was introduced (Hussein et al., 2010). In the early 1990s, the Public Service Network transformed post offices throughout the country into one-stop payment centers, a precursor of e-Services. The full-fledged e-Services initiative, begun in 2002 and also known as eKL, was implemented in phases following a three-month long pilot program in the urbanized Klang Valley. The initiative adopted the widely used "one government, many agencies" principle to integrate public services, including online delivery of drivers' licenses, court summons, and tax and utility bill payments. The Rilek services program offers Internet access to the public with touch screens at information kiosks, where they can pay fees, fines, and utility bills with a credit card. An experimental mobile e-government service, the MySMS initiative, used a single number, 15,888 (Thunibat et al., 2011). The Agriculture Ministry sends short messaging service (SMS) notes to farmers to warn them of rising water levels and impending floods. The state also offered several telehealth programs, often aimed at rural areas, including: the Lifetime Health Plan (advice for healthy living); Mass Customized Personal Health Information & Education (health information tailored to people's demographic specifics); Continuous Medical Education (which provides health information to health care professionals); and Teleconsultation, which allows citizens to speak with professionals online. All of these are accessible at hospitals and 41 public health clinics. Other successful examples include its Road Transport Department (e-insurance, e-road tax, and e-license renewal), immigration (e-passport and e-visa), the Royal Malaysian Police (e-summons), and the Kuala Lumpur City Council (e-complaints) (Abdullah and Kaliannan, 2006).

In 2001, the state began to issue the Government Multi-Purpose Card, known as MYKAD, the world's first multipurpose smart identity card (Yeow and Loo, 2010). It includes nine applications, consolidating personal identification, banking, driver's license, passport, health, and transit information. It can thus be used at stores, schools, buses, and hospitals. MYKAD reduced the processing time for passports from eight weeks to two days (Siddiquee, 2005).

One of Malaysia's success stories concerns taxes (Dorasamy et al., 2010). Integrated electronic tax preparation, filing, and payment were introduced in 2006 by the Inland Revenue Board (IRB, or in Malay, *Lembaga Hasil Dalam Negeri*) (Azmi and Bee, 2010). Security includes a 16-digit PIN number; when security loopholes were discovered, the IRB moved quickly to close them. Although the initial use fell below expectations, in 2009, a total of 1.25 million people filed taxes digitally. Surveys indicated that the most likely users were young, female members of the Chinese minority (Ambali, 2009). In an effort to increase participation, the IRB added a new feature to the e-filing system, *e-bayaran* or e-payment, in which taxes can be paid through banks. The online system was shown to have lower error rates than paper submissions and has raised compliance levels.

Malaysia's e-government includes the interests of the powerful business community. Port authorities and the customs department are integrated through electronic data interchange to process applications for imports and exports. A major success is called e-Perolehan, a website (www.eperolehan.co.my) launched in 1999 at a cost of RM35 million ($12 million), in which registered companies can submit bids for government contracts, advertise their wares on the web, and receive government payments digitally. It has received significant amounts of scholarly attention (Kaliannan et al., 2007; Siddiquee, 2008; Sambasivan et al., 2010; Aman and Kasimin, 2011; Hui et al., 2011), more than any other aspect of Malaysia's e-government. It comprises a novel and highly successful form of e-procurement aimed largely at small- and medium-sized enterprises (SMEs) and has lowered the state's operational and administrative costs. Given the size of the government's procurements—more than 23 billion ringgit in 2007 ($5.7 billion)—this is no small issue. More than 120,000 firms are registered. The system reduced the time between application for registration and approval of supplies from 36 days to 20 days (Siddiquee, 2005). However, firms must purchase a smart card to use it, train employees, and periodically upgrade their software. Nonetheless, e-procurement of government contracts has steadily become the norm (Santhanamery and Ramayah, 2014), even if growth rates did not meet expectations.

There have been roadblocks on Malaysia's path to e-government adoption. For example, the culture's emphasis on egalitarianism, fatalism, and individualism at times impeded the implementation of relevant policies (Seng et al., 2010). Public awareness of e-government remains low. Bureaucratic in-fighting was another obstacle, which diminished trust, teamwork, and knowledge sharing. While government websites in Malaysia are generally functional, they occasionally suffer from broken links and accessibility problems; these are compounded at the state level (Isa et al., 2011). Lack of trust among its residents has slowed enthusiasm for e-government programs (Lean et al., 2009). However, Malaysia resorted to the use of public-private partnerships to overcome these barriers (Kaliannan et al., 2010), in which private firms invested in public projects but the state retained responsibility for the delivery of core services. One example is the aforementioned e-Perolehan procurement program. Finally, mobile e-government is hampered in part because many state web pages are not designed to accommodate them well (Thunibat et al., 2011).

At the local level, Malaysian e-government has enjoyed considerably less success (Khadaroo et al., 2013). Local governments face significantly greater obstacles than does the national one. Many are short of funding and the requisite IT skills, and some have outsourced to unreliable software vendors. Not all of the 144 local governments have websites, and many still rely on paper transactions. Some outsource the task to the Ministry of Local Government. Others have adopted more interactive features, such as e-complaints, e-compounds (for impounded vehicles), e-assessments, e-communities, e-forums, and e-taxes. Lack of collaboration among local governments inhibits sharing of information and best practices.

Given the wide discrepancies in standards of living between peninsular Malaysia and the two provinces on Borneo, Sabah, and Sarawak, it is no surprise that the country suffers from a significant digital divide (Genus and Nor, 2007). The government's National Strategic Framework of Digital Divide lays out a comprehensive approach to promoting IT use in rural and disadvantaged areas, including rural telecenters and broadband diffusion. One of its most important e-government initiatives is e-Bario, named after a remote, isolated village in Sarawak. Led by university researchers, the state initiated Internet access in local schools and a publicly accessible telecenter; because electricity is unreliable, the system used diesel generators. Another is KedaiKom ("community building"), a collaborative program between Malaysia Communications, the Multimedia Commission, and ISPs. Launched in 2002 in Kedah, Melaka, Pahang, Perak, and Perlis, it provided 58 telekiosks (Ibrahim and Ainin, 2009). Finally, promoting the Internet in rural areas requires more content in Malay, rather than English.

Censorship exists in Malaysia to varying degrees. Unlicensed printing presses and pornography are strictly banned. Despite state promises not to censor the Internet, starting in 2014, the government began filtering politically sensitive websites, and at times has harassed bloggers and cyber-dissidents. News blogs must be registered with the Ministry of Information, and blogs that have reported allegations of corruption have been shut down. Some Facebook pages and Youtube videos have likewise been blocked.

To summarize, Malaysia has made significant strides in e-government, particularly at the national level. It is arguably the best example of e-government in the entire Muslim world. Most public services have moved online, with notable successes in taxes and procurement. As Mohamed et al. (2009) note through empirical surveys, most Malaysians are satisfied with their e-government's timeliness, accuracy, and content. The digital divide remains a pressing problem, and mobile e-government, or m-government, is still in its infancy.

4.7   Singapore: "any public services that can be delivered online must be digitized"

A cosmopolitan, multiethnic city-state of slightly more than four million people, Singapore is one of the world's premier e-government success stories. As one of the "new tigers" that followed the Japanese model of industrialization, succeeding in garment production and other low-wage industries, it moved steadily into high value-added services. It enjoyed rapid rates of economic growth for several decades, and today it is the second wealthiest country in Asia, a financial services and telecommunications hub for the Asia–Pacific region, and hosts the world's second-largest port.

Having a well-educated and informed public also paved the way for its e-government programs, among the best in Asia and the world. In 2016, Singapore's Internet penetration rate was 81%, third highest in Asia (following South Korea and Japan). Its 2015 e-government readiness score was 0.8474, slightly below South Korea's (0.9283) but ahead of Taiwan (0.82) and Japan (0.8019). Its e-participation rate was a near-perfect 0.9474, second highest in the world (next to South Korea). Waseda University (2009) ranked Singapore's e-government as the best in the world in 2009, although more recently South Korea has seized that honor. It has since received numerous international awards, such as Stockholm Challenges (2008, 2010), the Commonwealth Association of Public Administration and Management Innovations awards (2006, 2008, and 2010), and United Nations Public Service awards (2006, 2007, 2008, and 2010) (Ha, 2013). The government is not modest about its successes: the Infocomm Development Authority (IDA) claims to have built a "world-class e-government" that enables citizens to "be involved, be empowered, and be a pacesetter." Because it has implemented a highly successful e-government, Singapore has been the focus of significant scholarly attention (e.g., Siew and Leng, 2003; Chan et al., 2008; Baum et al., 2008).

Singapore clearly moved to capitalize on the digital revolution as a means to improve its government at an early moment. Its e-government initiatives began as early as 1980, with the launch of the Civil Service Computerisation Programme and then, in 1981, of the National Computer Board. Its progress then advanced in several waves, including the National IT Plan (1986–91), the IT2000 Master Plan (1992–99), and Infocomm (or Singapore) 21, which began in 2000 with a series of forums and surveys; it proceeded to accelerate the development of government web pages and e-government in the hopes of creating an "intelligent island" (Ke and Wei, 2004). In the 1990s, the Singapore One (One Network for Everyone) project, launched in 1997, created the world's first nationwide broadband network, and it reaches 99% of the population. In 2000, it unveiled its E-government Action Plan, budgeting $932 million over the next three years to implement it (funds are approved through the Ministry of Finance). Since 2002, e-government initiatives have been coordinated by the IDA. The government initiated a Remaking Singapore project in 2002 that solicited citizen input as to how to improve competitiveness and the functioning of the state. In 2006, the iGAP 2010 initiative, funded with $2 billion, coordinated planning for the next five years. In 2011, it started the E-government Master Plan, with the explicit aim of providing "government-with-you" (Baum and Mahizhnan, 2014). The most recent initiative is eGov 2015. The system is highly centralized: all of the government's e-services follow identical security, electronic payment, and data exchange procedures. Today, more than 1700 government services can be delivered online (Ke and Wei, 2004; Ha, 2013); essentially, "any public services that can be delivered online must be digitized" (Ha and Coghill, 2006, p. 107). The central government portal (www.ecitizen.gov.sg) offers access to a wide array of services. The state also invested heavily in security measures to protect online transactions from hacking, identity theft, and cyberterrorism. In 1998, in a bid to increase IT and Internet literacy, the government organized a five-day mass hands-on training event called Surf@Stadium.

Singapore's e-government system works well for several reasons. First, it possessed strong, proactive leadership with a clear vision of the need for e-government, with well-specified goals and sufficient financial resources. From the beginning, its designs were inclusive and citizen-centered (Ha, 2013). The stated objectives of e-government are CARE: Courtesy, Accessibility, Responsiveness, and Effectiveness (Ha and Coghill, 2006). Cultivating trust was central to its success (Srivastava and Teo,

2009). Engagement of users—state employees, firms, and the public—was essential (Pan and Chan, 2008). Pan et al. (2006) note that the Singapore IDA invested heavily in training programs and cultivated considerable goodwill. The government's promotional campaign featured "Q-busting," i.e., the prevention of queues at government offices through e-government. As Sriramesh and Rivera-Sanchez (2006) point out, Singapore is also well educated and has a corporatist, communitarian culture. Also, the state was careful to identify potential stakeholders in designing and implementing it (Tan et al., 2005), including public servants, corporations, academics, and labor unions. The state solicited input from a variety of interests to gain a holistic interorganizational perspective, helping to align stakeholders with the state's objectives. Managers were encouraged to facilitate collaborative learning, and to hold meetings where best practices could be exchanged. When implementing e-government, it held a prolonged public relations campaign, including IT literacy education and a series of online fairs. However, there are faults in this system too: Singapore lacks privacy laws for electronic transactions (Ha, 2013), although many public websites state privacy policies. Notably, the state rejected a proposed Freedom of Information Act.

Since 1999 a one-stop ecitizen portal (http://www.ecitizen.gov.sg), the world's first to be provided by a government (Netchaeva, 2002), provides a single point of access, through which citizens can check traffic, download publications, register births and deaths, search for jobs, pay fees, fines and taxes, check retirement benefits, register to vote, and obtain health care advice. With more mobile phones than people in Singapore, access to the portal is effortless. As Sriramesh and Rivera-Sanchez (2006) report, it receives about nine million hits per month; 75% of Singaporeans have used it and 80% of them report satisfaction. Users can sign up for a personal password, SingPass, to protect their credit card information. It has become the model of many such portals around the world.

Does e-government promote democracy in Singapore? Nominally a parliamentary democracy, it also has a long history of authoritarian control. E-government, however, has amplified transparency in government decision making and increased the public's trust. Nonetheless, the state can use digital technologies to retain tight control as noted by Netchaeva (2002, p. 472):

> *Singapore was the first country in the world which used the Internet to conduct a population census.*

But at the same time the administrative structures demand registration of all citizens and keep the public under rigid control. If a citizen does not turn up at the polls, his or her name will be struck from the register and his or her right as a citizen to vote lost.

Singapore certainly makes it possible to use the Internet to provide citizen feedback: anyone can voice their views at www.feedback.gov.sg without being traced. However, Sriramesh and Rivera-Sanchez (2006) assert that Singaporeans tend to be apathetic and suffer from a cultural trait known as *kiasu* (conformity) that inhibits such participation. Moreover, they argue (p. 725) that "The government of Singapore does engage in e-consultation but as mentioned previously, it is not clear to what extent this feedback actually influences policymaking."

One of the stars of Singapore's e-government is its state-of-the-art Electronic Tax Filing system (Tan et al., 2005), which it implemented in response to significant uncollected revenues in the 1980s. While it started as a telephone-based service in 1995, the Web soon allowed this system to move online. In 1998 e-filing began, allowing Singaporeans (even those overseas) to pay through the Internet. The government's investments in the requisite technology were recouped within five years. The digital system not only reduced paperwork, but necessitated fewer staff as well. Large corporations and government bureaus were encouraged to submit information about their employees to expedite the process. It includes a system that allows taxpayers to communicate with the tax authority and with one another, including questions and complaints; this feedback is often used in upgrading and improving the system. In 2008, 87% of potential tax returns were filed this way (Dorasamy et al., 2010). One motivation for filing taxes electronically is that filers get immediate acknowledgment.

In other ways, too, Singapore's e-government was unique. It was among the first countries in the world to implement a national e-library, and an e-citizen center (http://www.ecitizen.gov.sg). The government launched a "Connected Homes" test bed for home networking and community services and a MySingapore website giving citizens access to a broad array of services. The e-litigation service reduces the complexity of legal filings and encourages court attendance; lawyers can also appear in court via videophones (Ha and Coghill, 2006). The Singapore Immigration & Checkpoints Authority offers discounts to those who apply for visas and passports digitally. The Ministry of Manpower introduced iJOBS, an online job matching site. The Singapore Sports Council implemented iBook, an online service for booking for sports facilities. The IDA recently facilitated a pilot project for the distribution of new Indian films via satellite to secure servers in Indian movie theaters.

Singapore has been especially innovative in using social media, particularly Facebook, to engage citizens in dialogues (Soon and Soh, 2014). For example, it deployed social media extensively to alert residents during the Severe Acute Respiratory Syndrome outbreak of 2004 (Pan et al., 2005). The Immigration & Checkpoints Authority gives permissions for exit permits to go overseas by SMS, while other agencies send text messages to pay parking tickets and national service obligations (Trimi and Sheng, 2008).

E-government has been highly useful to Singapore's business community. The state introduced electronic commerce plans as early as 1996 (Wong, 2003). Under the e-Business Industry Development Scheme, it introduced subsidies to encourage firms to enhance their e-commerce capacities. Subsequently, the government passed the Cyber-Trader Act, the Electronic Transactions Act, and the Compute Misuse Act. Other laws protected entrepreneurs, venture capitalists, start-ups, and patent holders. In 1997, it established Tradenet, an electronic clearing house that seamlessly unites firms, the Customs Department, the Trade Development Board, and air and seaport authorities (Teo et al., 1997). The active participation of the island's business community, which anticipated the benefits, was central to the success of these initiatives (Chan and Al-Hawamdeh, 2002; Tung and Rieck, 2005). Because multiple stakeholders were included in the design and implementation of e-government initiatives, such measures enjoy widespread trust among different segments of the population (Lim et al., 2012); as with e-commerce, trust is central to the effective adoption of e-government, and trust, like all social constructions, varies greatly over time and space. The portal, gebiz.gov.sg, allows firms to conduct many functions online, including electronic registration, tax payment, submission of contracts, and license renewal, update, or termination. It has cut red tape considerably; the time needed to incorporate a company dropped from two days to two hours (Sriramesh and Rivera-Sanchez, 2006). Similarly, the One-Stop Public Entertainment Licensing Center cut processing times "from 6 to 8 weeks to about 2 weeks" (Ha and Coghill, 2006, p. 113). The government's website http://www.gebiz.gov.sg/ allows firms to conduct business with the state easily. Firms and entrepreneurs can apply for patents online through http://www.epatents.gov.sg/.

Empirical analysis confirms that the digital divide is an impediment to e-government in Singapore (Ke and Wei, 2006). To alleviate this issue, Singapore provided 27 self-service Citizens Connect kiosks. The state partnered with private firms to implement the PC Reuse Scheme, which recycles personal computers to those in need. It also pumped S$25 million into a program to encourage late adopters to get online (Pan et al., 2006). However, a linguistic divide persists: a former British colony, Singapore provides all of its e-government services only in English, a potential obstacle in a country where the majority of residents speak Mandarin, Tamil, or Malay.

In 2004, to address national security and infectious disease concerns, the Singaporean government launched the Risk Assessment and Horizon Scanning (RAHS) program, which collects and analyzes large datasets in the hope of predicting terrorist attacks, epidemics, and financial crises (Kim et al., 2014). Its Experimentation Center (REC), which opened in 2007, focuses on new technological tools to support policy making for RAHS and enhance and maintain RAHS through systematic upgrades of the big-data infrastructure. A notable REC application is exploration of possible scenarios involving importation of avian influenza into Singapore and assessment of the threat of outbreaks occurring throughout Southeast Asia. The government also launched the portal site data.gov.sg to provide access to government data gathered from more than 50 ministries and agencies.

While Singapore is a world leader in IT and e-government, it is also widely known for being authoritarian and censoring the Internet regularly (Rodan, 2000; Gomez, 2002). Its primary vehicle in this regard is the Singapore Media Development Authority (MDA), which has regulated Internet content under the guise of monitoring a broadcasting service since 1996. All ISPs are automatically licensed by the Singapore Broadcasting Authority, which routes all Internet connections through government proxy servers. Licensees are required to comply with the 1996 Internet Code of Practice, which includes a definition of "prohibited material," i.e., content that it deems "objectionable on the grounds of public interest, public morality, public order, public security, national harmony, or is otherwise prohibited by applicable Singapore laws" (OpenNet Initiative, 2007, p. 3). Moreover, "the government has at times taken unannounced strolls through several thousand personal computers with internet connections, subsequently explaining such actions as sweeping for viruses or pornography" (Kalathil and Boas, 2003, p. 78). Self-censorship is also encouraged as a means to stifle political expression. The use of lawsuits under stringent defamation laws is also common, and can reach well beyond the island's perimeter. For example,

Jiahoa Chen, a Singaporean student at the University of Illinois, was forced to shut down his caustic.soda blog under threat from the government-run Agency for Science, Technology, and Research. As a result of these measures, Singapore's government has achieved near-total control over its Internet environment with minimal loss of political legitimacy.

4.8   Indonesia: cyberjaya in cyberspace

With 250 million people, Indonesia is the world's fourth–most populous country and the largest Muslim nation. A vast, diverse archipelago consisting of 17,500 islands, Indonesia is Southeast Asia's behemoth. Following the traumatic coup against Sukarno in 1965, the country was opened up to global economy in a wave of neoliberalism and military dictatorship. Recently it has inched toward democracy and enjoyed significant rates of growth, forming yet another "tiger." Long dependent on oil revenues, it has diversified its economy as foreign investment has fueled the growth of garment production and electronics. Nonetheless, corruption is a serious problem and deeply entrenched poverty persists.

Private initiatives to create an Internet in Indonesia date back to 1994, when the first ISP, IndoNet, began. Today, however, Indonesia lags behind many of its neighbors in e-government. Its e-government readiness score was 0.4949, well behind Malaysia and Singapore, and its Internet penetration rate was only 34.1%. Most of Indonesia's 88 million netizens live in large cities and gain access through cybercafes, which tend to be clustered in tourist and business districts. However, cell phone usage is ubiquitous, and mobile Internet services are available in large cities. Its telecommunications infrastructure includes the Dumai Malacca Cable that runs under the Malacca Straits to Malaysia and its home-grown Palapa satellite network. Broadband is available only in large cities. Its e-participation index was a relatively low 0.2105. The country's limited success is, in part, due to endemic corruption, lack of political will, and shortages of qualified personnel (Rose, 2004; Rahardjo et al., 2007).

Early attempts to apply IT to the Indonesian state include the Archipelago-21 project in the 1990s, which was discarded during the financial crisis of 1997–98. E-government got a very late start in Indonesia, where it was introduced by Presidential Instruction No. 6 in 2001, which stressed the need for affordable IT services, strategies for their development (e.g., training), and offered guidelines to local governments for its adoption. This was followed by Instruction No. 3 in 2003, which emphasized the construction of the necessary technical and administrative infrastructure. A coordinating body consisted of government officials, academics, representatives of the business community, and members of social organizations. By the end of the year, hundreds of government agencies had opened their own websites, although maintenance and updating have been a longstanding problem. In 2004, the Department of Communication and Informatics followed up with guidelines for quality standards, project implementation, and a blueprint to implement them. In 2006, Presidential Decree Number 20 established the Council of National Information and Communication Technology (*Detiknas*). Subsequently e-government unrolled in several phases, including pilot projects and an e-government task force. Many of these efforts were developed in collaboration with the Indonesia Telecommunications Company (PT Telkom).

The national government's websites usually only offer cursory information, and only in a small number of cases have interactive capacities. Rahardjo et al. (2007) found that government web pages that received citizen feedback tended to improve considerably in terms of their functionality and appeal. The Indonesian Digital Library Network (http://idln.itb.ac.id), which began in 2001, is a collaborative effort of local universities, national government agencies, and foreign donors. One of the most popular websites is Lapor (*Layanan Aspirasi dan Pengaduan Online Rakyat*), initiated by President Susilo Bambang Yudhyono in 2011, which allows citizens to report instances of corruption or infrastructure problems via SMS (lapor.go.id) and receives 1000 reports per day (Lukman, 2013); a team then checks the complaint of wrongdoing for accuracy (at least in theory) and notifies the complainant of actions taken. More recently, President Joko Widodo repeatedly vowed to implement an e-government system that would strengthen monitoring, improve accountability, and reduce corruption. His administration did establish a one-stop integrated service to obtain investment permits and licensing, computerized school exams to prevent cheating, and e-blusukan, which enables the president to engage in contact with citizens via teleconferences. The e-Livestock program registers individual cows from birth to slaughter. As in many countries, Indonesia moved in 2008 toward e-procurement for government contracts (*Sistem Pengadaan Secara Elektronik*), a system overseen by the Government Good/ Service Procurement Policy Organization. The state also introduced electronic tax filing in 2014, although it has not enjoyed much popularity. It has experimented with the Sistanas system that would allow e-balloting. It created an Instanet with 18 institutional members to expedite information among agencies.

Very recently, i.e., since 2014, the government has experimented with more novel ideas, including a state-sponsored hackathon, Code for Vote, to test the mettle of e-elections software; an elections app to disseminate data; various smart cities initiatives; and an Open Data Club, consisting of information-sharing via WhatsApp (Huang et al., 2016; see their map of e-government initiatives in the country). The government used Twitter to alert citizens of the impending eruption of Mt. Sinabung in 2014 (Chatfield and Reddick, 2015).

Following a long tradition of highly centralized political control, Indonesia moved decisively to grant provinces greater autonomy, starting in 1999, which made local e-government initiatives all the more significant (Rose, 2004). To facilitate this process, the national state in 2003 published a handbook of e-government (http://www.kominfo.go.id). Siskom Dagri is the national government network that connects the government in Jakarta with district governments. However, local efforts have been highly uneven, as a result of local contingent conjunctures of administrative capacities (Nurdin et al., 2015). By 2004, less than half of Indonesia's 385 regional governments (*kabupatens*, cities, and provinces) had their own websites; those that did were located mostly in Java. Few are interactive, and often lack contact information for local officials. None had dialogue rooms. Municipal websites hardly fare any better (Prahono, 2015).

There are some bright spots in Indonesia's local e-government, however. Surabaya, the second-largest city, has initiated an e-procurement system, reducing its costs by roughly 25%. Jakarta introduced two location-based e-government apps: Qlue, which allow citizens to file geotagged complaints with the municipal government (and has been downloaded 80,000 times), and Crop, used by ground-level officials who respond to the closest complaint. Jakarta has also used social media to inform citizens; it opened Twitter and Facebook accounts in 2012. The Yogjakarta government started the Jogja Cyber Province Initiative to manage IT implementation in government offices. In a study of Yogyakarta, Tangerang, and Kutai Kartanegara, Nurmandi and Kim (2015) identified human capital as the central factor in the implementation of successful municipal e-procurement programs. The Takalar (Sulawesi) and east Kutai (Kalimantan) districts moved some services online in 2000, reducing the time needed to obtain permits and identification cards. Kutai Timur had the best of 400 local government websites in the country (Rose, 2004), with a one-stop portal (http://www.kutaitimur.go.id.utaitimur.go.id) called SIMTAP (Information Management System of One-Stop Services), where 12 public services, including identity cards and building permits, may be obtained. Investment permits can be obtained in 36 min. Similarly, the new city of Gorontalo took admirable steps to enhance transparency with its web pages. All too often, however, these initiatives are underfunded and lack sufficient human resources and leadership. For example, only 19% of localities use geographic information systems.

The brightest spot in local e-government in Indonesia is the Regency of Sragen, in central Java, which has been particularly successful with its one-stop portal approach, Kantor Pelayanan Terpadu (KPT, One-Stop Services). The so-called Sragen Cyber-Regency developed a wireless network and web page that includes a public forum, news services, tourism information, statistical data, search engine, licensing service, teleconferencing ability, complaint center, and civil registry office. It issues 52 types of licenses online. It has conducted Indonesia's first, and only, Internet elections, for village chief. Its system has been imitated, with varying degrees of success, by the Regencies of Lebak, Katingan, Sika, Mataram, Balangan, Dumai, and Sika. In 2006, Sragen won an e-government award for achievement in 2006.

Indonesia's implementation of e-government has been slow and haphazard, and hampered by several obstacles. The telecommunications infrastructure is underdeveloped, and its regulatory framework could be much improved. The necessary initiatives rarely receive sufficient funding. The government has not invested much in human capital or technical skills. Many regional officials simply do not take it seriously (Wahid, 2004; Rose, 2004), exhibiting what Anwaruddin (2012) calls a failure of e-leadership. There is little overall strategy, resulting in duplicated efforts. Local officials are often highly conservative and distrustful of e-government. Security problems persist. Corruption makes the allocation of budgetary expenditures inefficient.

Recognizing it needs assistance, the Indonesian government has reached out to Singapore and South Korea for assistance; the Korea-Indonesia E-Government Cooperation Center opened on March 2, 2016, and will run until the end of 2018. Indonesia also adopted Korea's electronic patent system, its national financial management system in 2009 ($43 million), and its public security management system in 2015 ($72 million).

The country's enormous digital divide is also a major obstacle in Indonesia's efforts to implement e-government (Hermana and Silfianti, 2011), particularly the schism between Java and the outer islands. The geography of government websites mirrors that of the population: half are located in Java, another indication of how the real and virtual worlds are interpenetrated. To address the digital divide, the government established a series of information kiosks. Educational efforts can also mitigate the digital divide: Rye (2008) discusses two small Internet-based distance-learning master's degree initiatives in Indonesia, both offered by Universitas Terbuka (Open University Indonesia), which offered students on remote islands access to higher education services they would not have otherwise have had.

The government does engage in modest Internet censorship, albeit with a light touch. In 2008, it passed the Law on Information and Electronic Transactions, which enables certain forms of censorship, including pornography, anti-Islamic content, gambling, and incitement of hatred. Access to Youtube and Reddit sites has been blocked periodically. When a Facebook account called to have a cartoon contest portraying Mohammed in 2010, the government requested that the account be closed. Bloggers accused of defamation of public officials have been harassed.

To summarize, Indonesia lags behind its neighbors in implementing e-government. Although a few notable local examples exist, there has been little systematic and coherent strategy for using the Internet to serve citizens. The usual suspects—inadequate funding and lack of human capital—are accompanied by corruption and indifference. The digital divide persists, particularly in the low Internet adoption rates in the outer islands.

4.9   Brunei: oil-rich sultanate takes steps

Brunei Darussalam is a small (population 420,000), immensely rich sultanate in northern Borneo that in many respects resembles the Persian Gulf sheikdoms. Its enormous oil revenues give it one of the highest per capita incomes in the world. Its 2015 e-government score was 0.625, higher than Indonesia but below that of Malaysia, and Internet penetration was 71%. Like many very wealthy countries, Brunei has more mobile or cell phones than people. E-participation was rated 0.4737, relatively high for a developing country but behind neighbors such as Singapore, Malaysia, or Taiwan.

Brunei has also taken steps toward implementing e-government initiatives (Kifle and Cheng, 2009; Rahman et al., 2012). In 1995, an initiative called TEMA ("TEknologi MAklumat," Malay for "Information Technology") was launched in 1995 to raise IT awareness among civil servants. In 2000, His Majesty Sultan Hassanal Bolkiah called for the establishment of e-Brunei, and allocated roughly $1 billion annually for its implementation. Planning for the project, however, did not get underway until 2003, when the e-government Program Executive Council was established. The slow start reflects the lack of clear objectives and the country's unfamiliarity with IT, leading the Sultan to express his disapproval at the tepid rate of adoption. Rather than impose a top-down model, the state solicited ideas from various ministries in a bottom-up fashion. By 2007, a series of projects were under way: biometrically scanned passports to expedite movements through airports and borders; e-MIPR (e-Ministry of Industry and Primary Resources); Islamic information kiosks; and e-billing and e-maintenance management programs. In 2008, Brunei founded the E-government National Centre, and in 2009, it launched a five-year E-government Strategic Plan, with the aims of modernizing the civil service and making the state more user-friendly. The "Internet for Schools" project achieved Internet connections in all of the country's public schools, including religious ones.

4.10 Philippines: texting as e-government

Another vast archipelago of 7100 islands, the Philippines, with its history of Spanish colonialism, Catholicism, and American occupation, occupies a unique cultural niche in East Asia. With more than 100 million people, the country is sizable, but poor, and has enjoyed little of the rapid economic growth found in most of Southeast Asia. Agriculture still accounts for a third of its economy, although it has seen some growth in garments and electronics production, as well as call centers. Literacy is a remarkably high 93%. A vast diasporic population is the source of significant remittances.

Its 2015 e-government readiness index was 0.513, roughly on a par with that of Indonesia, but its 2016 Internet penetration rate was 52%. However, mobile phones are widespread and text messaging is wildly popular. E-participation was evaluated at 0.2105, identical to Indonesia.

Efforts to use IT in the Filipino government began remarkably early, with the establishment in 1971 of a National Computer Center. Although the government identified e-government as a strategic priority, it committed few resources to the project. In 1994, the state established the National Information Technology Council, which initiated steps toward the adoption of computers. The enactment of RA 7925 in 1995, the Public Telecommunications Policy Act of the Philippines, was another milestone that liberalized that sector. In 1998, it launched IT21, a plan for the 21st century, as well as the Electronic Commerce Promotion Council. This was complemented by Administrative Order 232, which instructed local offices to begin digital networking with one another. The Central Visayas Information Sharing Network, established in 1998, began to offer news, statistics, business guides, and local updates very early, well before the Internet had become entrenched in Filipino society.

The origins of Filipino e-government may be said to lie with the Republic Act 8792 or the Electronic Commerce Law of 2000, which gave legal recognition to electronic documents, signatures and transactions. Similarly, the Government Information Systems Plan in the same year guided the computerization of public offices and the implementation of e-government measures. The Information Technology and Electronic Commerce Council was given wide latitude to encourage the growth of an information-based economy and society. However, the country lacks a single, coherent strategy in this regard, leaving different agencies to pursue e-government on their own. More recently, the ICT Roadmap (2006–10) laid out the government's strategy to deal with the digital divide there through a series of community e-centers. In 2011, the plan *du jour* was the Philippine Digital Strategy. In 2013, it unveiled its

E-government Master Plan calling for a digitally empowered, transparent government. In June 2016, the Department of Science and Technology launched the Government Network (GovNet) to expedite this process.

The Filipino state has enjoyed several e-government successes. The Department of Management and the Budget established the Government Electronic Procurement System as the official channel for soliciting and approving bids on government projects (Lallana et al., 2002), increasing transparency in the process and reducing corruption. To address similar problems of corruption in the process of importing and customs declaration, the state adopted a single electronic form that calculates payments due, a cashless system that reduces opportunities for bribe-taking as face-to-face meetings between inspectors and cargo agents were eliminated; as a result, waiting times for cargo were reduced from eight days to four hours. The Department of Budget and Management's Bottom-up Budgeting interactive website allows for citizen input into the process. The state has also started distance-learning programs, although these are aimed primarily at basic education (Ramos et al., 2007).

The Philippines has often been called the "text messaging capital of the world," with 100 million texts sent daily, generating a higher number per capita than any other country. Given the popularity of text messaging there, it would be odd if the government did not avail itself of the medium. Indeed, the country in some respects appears poised to skip e-government altogether and leapfrog directly into m-government, becoming something of a world leader in the process. Text messaging has long played a key role in Filipino cultural and political life: in 2001, President Estrada was deposed in an SMS-organized campaign he called a "coup de text," when just 15% of Filipinos had mobile phones. With the introduction of the TXTGMA service in 2001, Filipinos all over the world were able to bring their concerns directly to President Gloria Macapagal Arroyo. Today, half of all government agencies use SMS to keep in contact with the public. The Civil Service Commission launched an SMS service called TextCSC that allows citizens to complain about corrupt workers and slow service delivery; it is the most widely used public SMS service in the country. The Bureau of Internal Revenue launched an electronic payment confirmation scheme using SMS messages on mobile phones to guard against "fixers" who issue fake receipts to taxpayers. Known as e-broadcasting, the system provides taxpayers with direct confirmation within 38 h that their payment has been received by authorized banks. The Department of the Interior has a centralized emergency and crime reporting service called Text 117. Citizens can voice their concerns and questions to the Department of Environment and Natural Resources through the DENR@YourService project. When the state floated a proposed tax on text messages, the public responded with a virtual NGO called TxtPower, which led a successful campaign to defeat it. Starting in 2002, citizens have been able to help enforce antipollution laws by reporting smoke-belching public buses and other vehicles via SMS or online (http://www.bantayusok.com) due to the Bantay Usok project of the Land Transportation Office; it receives about 6900 SMS messages per month. Oversees Filipino workers can seek assistance from the Department of Foreign Affairs via the SMS service TXTDFA, and the Center for Migrant Advocacy initiated an SOS SMS program for overseas workers facing emergencies. Starting in 2002, the National Police allowed citizens to report suspicious activities and crimes by criminals and police officers via SMS. The national JobHunt program sends SMS messages to applicants when a relevant position becomes open. The Bureau of Internal Revenue offers a raffle to selected texters. In other respects, however, the country has to play catch-up: for example, there is no system for m-payments.

Another success story from the Philippines concerns telemedicine. In 1998, the University of the Philippines established the National Telemedicine Center, which manages referrals from 40 doctors in remote areas around the country (Marcelo, 2009). Some of its major accomplishments include the Community Health Information Tracking System (CHITS), founded in 2004, a disease surveillance system used in 12 community health centers; the E-Learning for Health Project, which offers a series of short videos on issues such as poisons, strokes, tuberculosis, and influenza; the BuddyWorks Community Partnership, which established broadband connections in remote sites so that difficult medical cases could be referred to experts; and the SMS Telemedicine Project, which allows doctors and patients to communicate via mobile phone messages.

In 2002, the Filipino government began the Jumpstarting Electronic Governance in Local Government Units (e-LGU), to encourage them to develop web pages and develop a system of 700 community e-centers to provide Internet access. Set to run for three years, it was seen as a means of enhancing efficiency and generating revenues. At its end, in 2005, essentially all local governments had web pages, although many were not updated regularly and few offered interactive services. Siar's (2005) analysis showed that most were lacking substantial information, including relevant contact information, what services they offered, or online forms. Only a tiny handful attempted online management of property records or business permits and licenses. However, Bulacan Province was touted as the leading local government in this regard, and was rewarded with a Galing Pook award in 2002 for its efforts to promote digital inputs from citizens.

The digital divide in the Philippines remains severe, particularly between urban and rural areas. As blogger Suerte-Cortez (2016) notes, this has serious implications for e-government there:

> *In northern Luzon, people face a two-hour commute over rough roads just to check their e-mails. When they get to a local internet cafe, they are faced with slow and unreliable connections and unexpected power outages. E-governance seems far away when reliable connection happens once a month. ... Web access remains a challenge in remote areas of the Philippines, and a significantly large amount of the population is excluded from e-governance.*

Cognizant of this problem, the Filipino government has responded as best it can, including the 700 community e-centers established under e-LGU noted earlier; privately operated, they are nonetheless cheaper than Internet cafes. The Pan Asian Networking program established four multipurpose telecenters on Mindanao. Virtually all public schools have Internet access via the Gearing up Internet Literacy and Access for Students (GILAS) program. Other measures include subsidies for rural Internet connections, Internet terminals in public libraries, the distribution of free (open source) software, and distance-learning programs in some rural villages. The country's heavy reliance on mobile phones may also play a role in fostering Internet growth.

In short, the Philippines presents a unique example of e-government. Mimicking the successes of other ASEAN countries in some respects, it is also unique to the extent to which it relies on SMS texting. Hampered by corruption and a frequently stagnant economy, the government has nonetheless successfully adopted several e-government programs, although there is still much progress to be made.

4.11   Conclusion

Given the enormous diversity among Southeast Asian countries, it is unsurprising that e-government varies considerably there as well. Examples range from barely developed (Myanmar, Laos) to mediocre (Thailand, Indonesia) to very good (Malaysia) to among the world's best (Singapore). Internet use is growing rapidly throughout the region. In general, the more open and democratic the government is, the more likely it is to use e-government, although the causality in this case may be bidirectional. These observations indicate that e-government is tailored to specific national and cultural contexts, and serve as a warning against simplistic "one-size-fits-all" interpretations.

South Asia

5

In comparison to the vibrant and energetic implementation of e-government in East Asia, South Asian efforts have been less well developed. To some degree this status reflects its huge, often impoverished populations, low rates of literacy, and truncated internet penetration rates (see Fig. 1.1). The region uniformly ranks very poorly in terms of e-readiness (Fig. 1.2). Many governments lack the human capital (i.e., trained personnel) and institutional capacity to generate even the modest e-government services. A summary of relevant statistics is provided in Table 5.1.

5.1   India: Bharat is the world's leader in telecenters

Huge, with 1.3 billion people, the world's second most populous country and largest democracy reveals a staggering diversity of cultures, religions, and languages. Two-thirds of the population live in rural areas, mostly as farmers, and constitute the largest national population of poor and hungry people in the world (living on less than $1 per day). One-third of the population is illiterate. Long mired in poverty, India since the 1990s has become increasingly liberalized and globalized, with significant economic progress, particularly in the western parts of the country. India has become the world's largest film and software producer. The country is thus one of gargantuan diversity and disparities.

India has a long history of flirtation with information technology (IT), culminating in the success of IT hubs such as Bangalore, the "Silicon Valley of Asia." It set up a National Informatics Center in the 1970s, and has had numerous initiatives to computerize both public and private offices since (Gupta, 2012). International donor agencies, nongovernmental organizations (NGOs), and the World Bank have often been involved in these efforts. In 2015, India's e-government readiness score was a mere 0.3829, e-participation was rated at 0.3829, and in 2016 internet penetration was 36%, but rising rapidly. With more than 462 million netizens in 2016, India has the second largest population of internet users in the world. The state-owned incumbent telecom operator, BSNL, has gradually attempted to extend fiber cables to almost every *taluka* (county town) in India, although connectivity in many rural areas remains poor. In addition, roughly three-quarters of Indians have a mobile phone, primarily those in cities, but most are not internet connected and m-government is essentially nonexistent in the country.

As in many countries, e-government in India came about through a series of legislative initiatives. In the 1990s, the National Informatics Centres Network connected district level and rural government offices to state capitals and the national administration in New Delhi. The first explicit step toward e-government was the Information

e-Government in Asia: Origins, Politics, Impacts, Geographies. http://dx.doi.org/10.1016/B978-0-08-100873-7.00005-2

Table 5.1 **Internet and e-government statistics for South Asia, 2015**

Country	2016 Internet penetration	2015 e-government readiness	E-participation	Mobile phone penetration
Bangladesh	33.1	0.2991	0.0789	80.0
Bhutan	38.6	0.2942	0.0263	82.1
India	36.5	0.3829	0.1842	74.5
Maldives	68.7	0.4994	0.0263	189.4
Nepal	19.9	0.2664	0.0263	81.1
Pakistan	17.8	0.2823	0.1316	73.4
Sri Lanka	27.4	0.4357	0.0789	103.2

Technology Act (ITA) of 2000, which provided a legal framework to facilitate electronic transactions, including privacy laws and electronic signatures; this was followed by approval of the National E-Governance Action plan in 2003, as well as a Freedom of Information Act. The Department of Information Technology proposed a National e-Government Plan (NeGP) in 2006 with the goal of creating the institutional mechanisms to implement such programs nationwide. NeGP included 26 Mission Mode Projects to be implemented at the central, state, and local government levels, such as digital tax returns, insurance, customs, visas, e-procurement, and a national citizen database. The Ministry of Information Technology played a key role in the formulation and adoption of these plans. As a result, every state in India has an IT policy in place. As Hirwade (2010, p. 254) notes, "In September 2007, the Indian government approved a city-specific ambitious programme covering 323 cities in the country to provide e-government services." Nationally, the government has established an ongoing series of task forces, institutes, committees, and ministries to encourage public use of ITs. In 2011, the government formulated a framework for the use of social media in government organizations (Banday and Mattoo, 2013). Finally, as Thomas (2009) notes, India has long had a right to information movement that culminated in the Right to Information Act of 2005.

Most Indian e-government projects have been aimed at mitigating poverty in rural areas, whose residents live in semifeudal conditions, and there is a vast literature on the subject (e.g., Singla, 2005; Harris and Rajora, 2006; Krishnan, 2010). Private Internet Service Providers focus largely on cities, where incomes are higher and they can reap economies of scale.

5.1.1   National e-government programs in India

India is famous for its bloated government bureaucracy, characterized by corruption and inefficiency, rude personnel, chronic absenteeism, shabby offices, and long waiting times. E-government has allowed many Indians to escape these problems. Monga (2008) notes that whereas visiting government offices there used to be a harrowing experience, increasingly transactions can be conducted digitally. Indeed, as Haque

(2002, 232) argues, "the government tends to portray e-governance as the panacea for all ranges of problems confronting India." While not a panacea, e-government has helped to improve the dysfunctional bureaucracies, reducing bribes, and saving users time by eliminating many trips to offices, as well as delivering services that are perceived to be more fair (Bhatia et al., 2009).

National e-government initiatives include a series of web portals. The government's national website (India.gov.in), launched in 2005 and one of the biggest in the world, offers access to 5000 other websites (Verma et al., 2006) and 1576 online services, of which 89.5% are aimed at citizens, 3.4% are aimed at companies, 3.2% are aimed at other government agencies, and 3.9% are aimed at government employees (Hirwade, 2010). It divides services into four categories: Obtain, Apply For, Check/Track, and Book/File/Lodge. In short, it is decisively citizen-centric. The website of the Indian Parliament (alfa.nic.in) offers essential information regarding the House of People (Lok Sabha) and the Council of States (Rajya Sabha), including their committees, budgets, web addresses of all ministries and states, publications, profiles of parliamentary members, and opportunities for citizen feedback. The Department of Agriculture and Cooperation's website (www.nic.in/agricoop) includes information relating to its various programs, prices of agricultural products, weather conditions, and announcements. The Supreme Court of India maintains a website (supremecourtofindia.nic.in) that displays the constitution, profiles of judges, and an option for citizen feedback. The Directorate of Public Grievances website (dpg.bharatsarkar.nic.in) allows citizens to send their complaints against any government agency. According to the Department of Communications and Information Technology, the Indian government offers roughly 258 programs online (www.mit.gov.in). In 2014, the government created Vekaspedia (*vekas* is Sanskrit for "development"), an online information guide (http://vikaspedia.in/index) in 23 languages. The effectiveness of these sites has yet to be ascertained. Because many such websites were designed by IT professionals and did not put users' needs first, Bhattacharya et al. (2012, p. 247) hold that "These portals often face challenges with multilingualism, presentation of features, plurality of services, interoperability and communication."

The government has slowly edged toward e-procurement, including e-tendering and e-reverse auctions. However, Verma (2006) is scathing about the quality of the process:

Electronic notification of tender opportunities is provided through the use of internet as the worldwide web. Most government departments and their corporate agencies, both at the federal level and the provincial levels, have their own websites where such information is made available, although there is lack of frequent updation (sic) of these sites, and there are very often problems of disorganisation in the availability of information, since there is very little standardisation in terms of product types. Also, since there is virtually no progress on maintenance of suppliers' lists, notification by email is virtually non-existent. Thus, a supplier of a particular product would have to scan all possible websites of various procuring agencies, both at the federal as well as the provincial level, to know the venues for sale of his product, and this information is not available to him in an automatic, timely or organised manner. Most of these government websites are really unprotected, and digital verification and authentication of downloaded tender papers is not possible.

Even so, the national e-procurement model has been followed by Delhi, Karnataka, Chhattisgarh, and Indian Railways.

The Indian government has made several strides in adopting e-government in other domains. The India Healthcare Delivery project was set up to reduce paperwork for auxiliary nurse midwives, who provide most health services in rural areas. The post office allows direct e-credit of Monthly Income Scheme returns to the investor accounts. The Indian Customs Department was long regarded as one of the most corrupt in the country. However, the introduction of electronic signatures and payments of duties increased transparency and reduced processing times. "Now 95% of all documents are filed online and 100,000 people visit the customs Web site daily to file papers or to check their status" (Patak and Prasad, 2005, p. 445).

The national state has also adapted IT to revenue collection. E-filing of income taxes, introduced in 2004, is optional for individuals but mandatory for firms since 2006 (Bhattacharya et al., 2012). Most Indians who file electronically are young professionals (Ojha et al., 2009). Tax preparers can file on behalf of clients if they have valid electronic signatures. The Department of Revenue's Central Exercise program allows online collections of excise and service taxes, and is accessible round-the-clock via its website (http://exciseandservicetax.nic.in; Sahu and Gupta, 2007). Excise taxes can be filed electronically through the Electronic Commerce/Electronic Data Gateway program, with three centers in Mumbai, Delhi, and Chennai. The Ministry of Corporate Affairs created the MCA21 Mission Mode Project to reduce paperwork and expedite e-commerce initiatives.

As the world's largest democracy, Indian elections are huge and elaborate affairs. The internet has become sufficiently important in India that it figures in electioneering (Gadekar et al., 2011). One new political party in particular – Lok Paritran – has used the web to great effect for fund-raising (www.lokparitran.org). The Election Commission set up a website where information on candidates can be accessed easily (www.eci.gov.in). Gowda et al. (2006) note that voter registration roles have become computerized, reducing errors and fraud, and many registrations are done online. In Bangalore, a get-out-the-vote program called Citizens Initiative (www.citizensinitiative.org) spreads awareness among college graduates, although e-registration was dwarfed by traditional methods. Electronic voting machines were introduced nationwide on a trial basis in the 2004 general elections, saving paper and eliminating the problem of invalid votes. They are stand-alone units to avoid attacks by hackers, running off of batteries in the case of power failures.

Other measures include the use of IT to combat crime and corruption. The National Crime Record Bureau "has also developed a number of e-government initiatives, such as the Police Station Management System, Prison Statistics, Jail Management Software, Prosecution Branch System, National Bomb Squad System, Forensic Science Laboratory System and The Motor Vehicle Information Counters" (Kolsaker et al. 2007, p. 101). India has used e-government effectively to combat corruption. The Central Vigilance Commission operates a website, launched in 1999, which allows citizens to lodge complaints against officials without disclosure and publishes a list of revenue service officers who have been charged with corruption or punished (Patak and Prasad, 2005), a process dubbed "e-shaming." It did, however, raise concerns that some innocent officials could be wrongly smeared.

Several other e-government programs are worth noting, particularly those housed under the Digital India program. The DigiLocker service, launched in 2015, offers residents personalized electronic spaces for storing documents. The Modi administration created the attendance.gov.in website to record of the attendance of government employees. MyGov.in is a platform to share ideas concerning policy and governance. The eKranti plan called for enhanced delivery of services online. Finally, the National Scholarship portal is a one-stop Website for applications and disbursement of university scholarships.

5.1.2 E-government in Indian states

Most Indian e-government programs unfold at the state level, giving rise to an uneven topology of implementation across the national landscape. Most of these are aimed at alleviating rural poverty, including telemedicine, microfinance, and aid to farmers. While there are also corporate-led initiatives, the focus here remains on publicly funded or operated ones. The simplest level of such initiatives consists of websites: the analysis of 200 websites of 25 state governments in India by Ray et al. (2006) revealed wide variations in their degree of user-friendliness, with most simply providing information and allowing forms to be downloaded and few allowing two-way interactions or citizen input. A more sophisticated and powerful set of programs involves rural telecenters, the centerpiece of India's informatization policy (Pick et al., 2014).

Karnataka is one of India's leading states in the implementation of e-government. It declared 2001 the "year of e-government," and in 2003 created the position of e-government secretary. Among other things, the state created the ITPolice program to comprehensive integrated application platform across 15,000 police stations, allowing rapid access to data about crimes, individual criminal histories, traffic accidents, forensic labs, and finances. Other components include eBeat, which uses Radio Frequency Identification Device tags to ensure police are on their scheduled routes, the Automated Finger Print Identification System, and GIS-Based Crime Analysis and Reporting Engine, a geographic information system to analyze crime patterns. Karnataka also implemented Khajane in 2002, which connected all 215 of its local treasuries through a satellite network, allowing automatic payments to contractors and pensioners, controlling expenditures, and making sure budgets are not exceeded. It also instituted Karnataka Valuation and E-Registration (KAVERI) that allows online registration of property sales and purchases and deeds in 387 Sub-Registrars' Offices (Bhatnagar and Singh, 2010).

Arguably the most famous instance of Indian e-government is Karnataka's Project Bhoomi ("land"). Funded by the state Revenue Department, Bhoomi, which started in 2001 and was launched in 177 *taluks* (subdistricts), allows internet delivery of 20 million land titles for 6.7 million rural farmers. Efforts to computerize land records in the region date back to the 1990s, but Bhoomi accelerated registration considerably (Bhatnagar and Chawla, 2007). The system operates as a public–private partnership, in which firms run the front end through kiosks in exchange for service fees and the registration department issues the certificates for the record of Rights, Tenancy and Crops (RTCs). Bhoomi allowed farmers to access the relevant data via 800 internet-connected kiosks ("Bhoomi centers") for a fee of 15 rupees (23 US cents) and print the records off themselves. Kiosks are run by operators who must use their thumbprint and biometric scan to achieve access, thus leaving an audit trail, improving accountability. Farmers can print RTCs for a cost of 15 rupees. More than 12 million people used the system by 2006, and 700,000 continue to do so monthly (Harris and Rajora, 2006). Bhoomi is widely believed to have reduced corruption significantly. Prior to Bhoomi, all "mutation requests" to change RTC titles were written on paper and handled by accountants in 9000 villages, which could take up to 2 years. In the process, it greatly reduced opportunities for bribe taking (average bribes ranged from 100 to 2000 rupees). As Bhatia et al. (2009, p. 72) point out, "It is difficult to ascertain all the reasons for the sharp reduction in bribery in the Bhoomi project. But it appears that the introduction of a first-in-first-out system for handling service applications and an increase in transparency contributed to this success." This constitutes an excellent example of IT-enabled disintermediation. Users report going to fewer government offices and conducting their business more rapidly than previously. Bhoomi is estimated to have saved 1.32 million days in waiting time and 806 million rupees in bribes (Andersen, 2009), and has generated revenues for the state government. The project succeeded because of strong leadership (i.e., a dedicated and overworked department head) and the mobilization of political support beforehand. But Bhoomi is not without problems. Walsham (2010, p.14) notes several shortcomings:

> *Firstly, the Bhoomi system computerised only one document in the overall land registration process, leaving a range of other documents on land title, cadastral maps etc. unaffected and unavailable to the scrutiny of citizens. Secondly, the computerised RTC certificates benefit land-owning farmers only, since landless farmers often have an unofficial sanction to the lands they farm, and do not interact with the Bhoomi system. Thirdly, transparency should not always be seen as beneficial, since the authors noted that the visibility of the RTC records enabled land sharks in some cases to better target vulnerable farmers.*

In addition, electricity outages occasionally left some kiosks unusable. Some worry that making it easier to obtain RTCs made poor farmers vulnerable to land sharks (Guha and Chakrabarti, 2014).

Bangalore, the capital of Karnataka, is a world-class center of software development and call centers. It is no surprise that it too has created a unique system of e-government. In 2002, it started PROOF (Public Record of Operations and Finance), an online site that discloses public financial activities and enhances transparency; Bangalore was the first city in India to do so. In 2004, it unveiled the website of the Bangalore Mahanagara Palike (www.blrbmp.org) that is responsible for civic development within an area that offers information ranging from roadwork to the budget to a place for filing grievances (Raman, 2008). Bangaloreans can also participate in local administration through an initiative called WardWorks, giving input on priorities for the local budget. Bangalore One (or B1), a project to provide G2C services in cities, operates a chain of one-stop Citizen Service Centers.

In Gujarat, several initiatives have unfolded. The government developed Gujarat State Wide Area Network. Gyan Ganga, a project to bring the benefits of the IT revolution to the rural masses, operates as a public–private partnership between the Gujarati government, its IT development arm Gujarat Informatics, a private firm, n-Logue, and local ISPs (Thomas, 2009). It provided 212 one-stop telecenters that offered e-health, e-government, and e-education services. However, despite some successes, the project suffered serious, near-fatal problems – insufficient training of kiosk operators; lack of content development and insufficient number of e-services; low participation by women – that damaged its credibility and popularity. In the Godhra district, Gujarat also created Mahitishakti ("power of information") in 2001 in 80 information centers that provide maps, medical information, legal aid, online applications, grievance redressal, photo galleries, and access to 200 forms. The Gujarat government also installed 10 computerized check posts on highways to monitor truck traffic, including video cameras to capture their registration number, a database of their unladen weight, and a system for automatically levying fines for carrying loads over the legal limit, reducing possibilities for bribery. Tax collections from the system tripled over the next 2 years. The e-Dhara Kendra program computerized land records and changes called mutations, where the data are stored at central server situated at the state capital Gandhinagar.

In Andhra Pradesh (population 80 million), where 40% of the population is illiterate, the SmartGov project saw that 214 deed registration offices were computerized, eliminating the need for corrupt middlemen for people to obtain services. The regional government also developed two telecenter programs, Rural e-Seva and Rajiv Internet Village Centers (Rajivs; Kuriyan and Ray, 2009). The e-Seva ("electronic service") project (www.esevaonline), modeled after Akshaya, was originally named the Twin Cities Network Services Project after the cities of Hyderabad and Secunderabad. It began in 1999 and was subsequently renamed and expanded. E-Seva consists of a series of 275 community one-stop kiosks scattered throughout Hyderabad, Secunderabad, and the Ranga Reddy district, each of which serves roughly 30,000 people using LINUX software and dial-up telephone connections. Kiosks allow locals to pay electricity, water, and telephone bills online; reserve and pay for bus tickets; obtain birth and death certificates; and apply for passports. Services are offered within 2 minutes. As a result of e-Seva, the time needed to acquire a passport was reduced from 45 to 3 days. E-Seva was "the first major initiative in the country to employ information technology as a tool to improve services for citizens" (Kalsi et al. 2009, p. 216), and conducts more than 50 million transactions per year. The Rajiv Internet Village centers program includes two corporate partners, who pay the state for access to e-government information, although districts provide subsidies. Through 8000 kiosks, citizens can access 135 services online, including those listed previously (Kaliannan et al., 2010; Bhatnagar, 2006; Bhatnagar and Singh, 2010). It allows residents to do their business without visiting numerous offices and confronting the inevitable corruption. The system was organized through public–private partnerships with the telecommunications operator Bharat Sanchar Nigam, in which private firms provided the hardware and software in return for transactions fees. Andhra Pradesh and Tamil Nadu also established a system of e-*challans*, in which traffic tickets could be paid through e-Seva centers; a website allows motorists to track if their vehicle has any offences registered. It is operational in Ahmedabad, Chennai, Hyderabad, Bangalore, Lucknow, Delhi, and Vijayawada.

Andhra Pradesh has also taken the lead in Indian e-government in other ways. In 2000, it also established an e-procurement marketplace that links government agencies and vendors, and created a system to make police transactions more transparent (eCOPS) that "permits a complainant to file a complaint at the nearest police station as convenient, irrespective of jurisdiction" (Kolsaker et al. 2007, p. 102). It created Samaikya ("coming together for a good cause" in Telugu) Agritech, a digital outreach program with 18 telecenters to service rural farmers, which provide information on weather, prices, and best practices. Similarly, the Health Information Systems Project (HISP) in Andhra Pradesh, which started in 2000 with a pilot program in a district called Kuppam, has been moderately successful in using the internet to disseminate public health information and create a web-enabled database (Sahay and Walsham, 2006; Madon et al., 2007). Andhra Pradesh also launched a Wide Area Network, with voice, data, and video communications, which allows citizens to pay utility bills and property taxes, purchase certificates and apply for licenses, and acquire information regarding building permits and property registration (Schware, 2000). Finally, Andhra Pradesh also created the Computer-aided Administration of Registration Department (CARD), which began in 1998. CARD uses a local area network to allow online registration of property deeds, sales, and purchases in 387 access points throughout the state, speeding up and simplifying the procedure. By 2006, more than 5 million people utilized it, and it had registered 4 million land titles and 2.16 million encumbrance certificates. It is credited with reducing corruption. Walsham (2010, p. 9) cautions that "ironically, CARD reforms had made corruption easier since staff no longer had to find and copy documents by hand, freeing them up to concentrate on extracting additional money from citizens." The state's success is attributable to several factors, including decisive leadership, the involvement of multiple stakeholders, and a willingness to persist over time.

The city of Visakhapatnam in Andhra Pradesh established the Saukaryam ("facility" in Telugu) in 2001, the first project in the country based on a public–private partnership in e-government. Citizens can use broadband-enabled kiosks to check and pay their tax dues, apply for building plan approval and track its status, get birth and death certificates instantly, and register complaints (Patak and Prasad, 2005). The rules and procedures are prominently displayed on the Saukaryam website. The system is used by 3000 citizens daily, and the website has more than 25,000 registered users. However, the system was plagued with corruption and fraud due to inadequate software security safeguards, resulting in 13 arrests in 2011 and the program's temporary suspension.

Andhra Pradesh's success has not escaped attention. The CARD system was copied in Maharashtra and Punjab. Madhya Pradesh followed Andhra Pradesh's example by creating a similar system: Drishtee is a rural distribution and promotional network for consumer goods and basic services based on kiosks (Kaushik and Singh, 2004). It provides 309 kiosks in six Indian states, including Haryana and Punjab (Chaudhri and Dash, 2006). Haryana launched the District-level Integrated Services of Haryana program, and Chandigarh, capital of Punjab and Haryana, created project Sampark, developed in collaboration with IBM, which established a series of Sampark centers through which residents can pay taxes and utility bills, get bus passes, apply for passports, and register as domestic servants.

One of India's best known initiatives was the Gyandoot ("purveyor of knowledge" in Hindi) project, a low-cost government to citizen initiative launched in 2000 in the poor, drought-prone, and tribal-dominated Dhar district of impoverished Madhya Pradesh. Over time, it set up 40 solar-powered intranet-connected kiosks (*soochanalayas*) in local government buildings in villages that functioned as weekly markets for their hinterlands. Each kiosk was designed to serve 20–30 villages, or approximately 30,000 people; some were run by the village, others by private operators (*soochaks*). Run by educated local youth who earn fees, they allowed online access in Hindi to 20 public services: email; government applications; filing of complaints; printing of land records; applications for driver's licenses; matrimonial services; information on agricultural prices; an auction site for sales and purchases of land, equipment and animals; matrimonial advertisements; horoscope services; online discussion forums; and a public complaint line for reporting broken irrigation pumps, unfair prices, absentee teachers, and other problems. In the first year, more than 6000 complaints were filed. Again, by avoiding middlemen, including local officials, it reduced bribery and corruption (Bhuiyan, 2011). Kiosks are located in air-conditioned offices and are highly popular with the public. Citizens received responses within a maximum of 7 days. Empowered poor people began receiving stipends in a more timely manner, and farmers received higher prices for their crops. The project pioneered the use of rural telecenters in India and served as a catalyst for improving computer awareness. Gyandoot won the Stockholm Challenge IT Award in 2000, and was judged a best practice by the IMF, World Bank, and the Asian Development Bank.

However, the very poor, illiterate, members of low castes, and women (for reasons of *purdah*) rarely utilized the kiosks, often out of simple ignorance, and overall usage rates were low. Insufficient electricity and periodic power cuts, inadequate dial-up internet connectivity, high prices charged by operators, insufficient updating of crop prices, low revenues for *soochaks* (Cecchini and Raina, 2004), and declining use led the program to end within 5 years. Moreover, local bureaucratic resistance was intense, and district councils were often reluctant to provide funds. Such observations cast doubt on rosy expectations that IT alone can unleash catalytic changes in rural areas. Indeed, trade-offs between financial stability and providing services to the poor in such contexts may be inevitable.

Nonetheless, Gyandoot inspired other, NGO-, or corporate-led initiatives with similar goals. One is as TARAhaat ("star marketplace") in Madhya Pradesh and Uttar Pradesh, and later in Punjab, which began in 2000 and was implemented by an NGO, Development Alternatives. TARAhaat offers a cornucopia of services in 22 centers "like TARAbazaar (e-bazaar), TARAvan (mobile kiosks), TARAguru (e-education), TARAdhabi (cybercafé), TARAreporter (news), TARAdak (email), TARAvendor (e-commerce), and TARAcard (greetings)" (Harris and Rajora, 2006, p. 7). It also provides weather forecasts, computer training, and career counseling. In south India, Kerala is India's most literate and educated state. Its educational wing formed the IT@ School project to bring the internet into 12,000 schools, and is now used by 200,000 teachers and 5 million students. In 1999, Kerala launched the Information Kerala Mission (IKM), an agency whose purpose is to decentralize and democratize regional planning through the use of IT among 1209 local public institutions, enhancing the public's trust (Unnikrishnan, 2006). It is one of the most ambitious e-government programs in the country. Following several pilot programs, IKM placed numerous kiosks (*janasevanakendrams*) in hospitals and public offices throughout the state, using elected village councils (*panchayats*), which allow birth and death registrations, issuances of licenses and permits, payments of pensions, and collection of taxes. The time needed for the issuance of permits dropped from 5 days to 5 hours. It also created an integrated database of users and allowed for citizen input, including grievances and calls for emergencies. However, it was plagued by shortages of skilled staff and webpages that were not updated regularly.

One of India's best known and most successful efforts to confront its digital divide is Kerala's Akshaya ("perpetuating prosperity") initiative that began in 2002 (Radhakumari, 2006). Akshaya provides wireless, broadband internet access to over 3.3 million people through privately operated 2760 e-learning centers (the eventual goal is 5000, and to have one member of each of the state's 650,000 families become IT literate). It includes an explicit e-literacy campaign aimed at making Kerala one of India's most computer literate states, a program that unfolded in cooperation with women's groups, childcare centers, and political parties (Prasad, 2012). It too was formed as a series of public–private partnerships, and began as a pilot project in Malappuram. Guha and Chakrabarti (2014, p. 333) note, "The project was born out of a proposal submitted by the Malappuram Panchayat, the local self government." The kiosks provided several services in Malayalam, including email, digital albums, the issuance of birth and death certificates, e-payments of government salaries, a telemedicine initiative called Cancernet, an e-library, and training in English and Arabic; the e-cop program allows citizens to network with the police. Many families used it to stay in touch with relatives working abroad, notably in the Persian Gulf, and unlike most rural IT projects, many users were women. The cost-free e-Krishi application allows agriculturalists to stay in contact with one another and with interested stakeholders, allowing them to share data on crops, yields, prices, and land holdings. Akshaya also began to shift into m-government, with 20 services available through mobile phones (Prasad, 2012). Administrators and entrepreneurs explicitly recruited as many women as possible to participate in the project, greatly enlarging the pool of users, in keeping with Kerala's long egalitarian tradition.

Kerala has been innovative in other ways. It built a "TechnoPark" at Trivandrum, India's first such institution, hosting dozens of IT professionals. It passed initiatives such as Package for Effective Administration of Registration, a digital land registration system, and Fast Reliable Instant Efficient Network for Disbursement of Services (FRIENDS) that enables citizens to access several public services electronically. FRIENDS began in 2000 in Thiruvananthpuram, and offers 14 one-stop kiosks for the payment of electricity, water, and telephone bills; fees for Kerala University; applications for ration cards, food, and trade licenses; and payments of motor vehicle taxes and registration fees. All payments are made in cash. On any given day, roughly 500 people use a kiosk (Harris and Rajora, 2006). Also in Kerala, Kudumbashree ("prosperity of the family"), a poverty-fighting scheme aimed at women launched in 1999, involves 1200 units that deploy IT to hire women as data entry workers (in English, Malayalam, and Tamil), offer IT educational services, extend microloans, and cultivate entrepreneurs.

One of India's most successful ventures was e-Choupal ("village meeting place"), kiosks that allow soybean farmers to check on crop prices and bypass predatory middlemen (Kumar, 2004; Gorla, 2008; Walsham, 2010). Started in 2000, it was the brainchild of the India Tobacco Company in Madhya Pradesh. It started in 42 villages in Ujjain district and eventually involved 6500 centers serving 40,000 villages in 10 Indian states, catering to more than 4 million farmers. Run by *sanchalaks*, or trained, entrepreneurial farmers, in whose homes the kiosks are located, they provide information, in the vernacular, to farmers about prices, weather, best practices, and allow them to apply for soil, water, and virus testing services. Technical problems were confronted by upgrading the IT connections to satellite broadband and using solar-powered generators. e-Choupal was first implemented for soybean farmers, and was subsequently adopted by coffee, wheat, rice, pulse, and shrimp producers. Farmers report easier access to seeds and fertilizer, lower transactions costs, higher quality output at higher prices, and by cutting out intermediaries, higher profit margins. It succeeded in part because rather than replacing intermediaries (*mandis*), it reallocated them to managing the shorter supply chains, from which they earned a commission; it also leveraged the knowledge of grain merchants or *sanjoyaks*. The fact that its services were offered in five languages (English, Hindi, Marathi, Kannada, and Telugu) helped immensely. It is one of the few initiatives that uses e-commerce to alleviate poverty and offers an excellent example of sustainable development and corporate responsibility.

In Gujarat, Akashganga ("milky way"), founded in 1996, is a program to use IT to assist rural dairy farmers (Keniston and Kumar 2004). A pilot study in Gujarat led to a system whereby farmers delivering milk (mostly women) had it weighed and all accounting information was then handled online. The Centre for Electronic Governance at the Indian Institute of Management, in Ahmedabad, developed a Dairy Information System, used by 50,000 dairy farmers, to share data about cattle and milk prices, allowing them to act cooperatively in the market. Akashganga involves automated solar-operated milk collection systems, hand-held sampling devices, digital data transfer from farmers to chilling plants, and smart cards for automatic payments. In essence, it united disparate farmers into a milk producers' collective.

Pondicherry created iVillages (a.k.a. Village Knowledge Centers), in 2000, a hub-and-spoke model of kiosks designed to carry e-government services to remote villages. "Typically, each center provides locale specific information of weather and local weather forecasts, prices of agricultural inputs and outputs, potential for export, entitlement of government and other benefits, health care, cattle diseases, transport, wave heights, areas of abundant fish catch, etc." (Rao, 2007, p. 504). When the December 2004 tsunami struck southern India, iVillages reported rising wave heights to villagers, allowing them to move to safety.

Rajasthan also has developed several initiatives. Haque (2002, p. 236) notes that "The Department of Information Technology in Rajasthan has developed such programs as RajSWIFT to facilitate the use of online data and email communication among officials; and RajNIDHI to provide services to citizens in a transparent and responsive manner." However, the RajSWIFT project never completely materialized, in part due to its overly top-down nature, insensitivity to local conditions, insufficient infrastructure, and lack of public enthusiasm. In 2002, the state also created Janmitra, an integrated e-platform for rural areas through public–private partnerships, which offers a series of one-stop kiosks. Started on a pilot basis in Jhalawar, it provides the standard range of services, including filing of grievance e-education and e-health services. However, little of the content was offered in the local language. Rajasthan's TechMODE (**Tech**nology **M**ediated **O**pen and **D**istance **E**ducation) project created Gramdoot ("messenger for the villages") in 2004, an initiative in the Jaipur district. It provides broadband services to 200 *pachayats*, and allows filing of grievances, offers information on crop prices, online sales of products, matchmaking services, and printing of land records. It suffered cuts to its fiber cables by thieves, which periodically disrupted service (Harris and Rajora, 2006). Moreover, the usage fell below expectations and its long-term financial viability was questionable.

Tamil Nadu, in southern India, which has not participated significantly in India's economic growth, imitated the CARD system that arose in Andhra Pradesh, developed Registration Department Encumbrance Certificate Network, a website that identifies the value of every property in the state, and unlike CARD, which was available on in English, offers information in Tamil. In Thirupillachalli, a public trust, Activists for Social Alternatives, which works to empower rural women, set up 200 kiosks, or Community Technology Centres, which provide matrimonial and educational services, grievance redressals, and discounts to local hospitals (Harris and Rajora, 2006).

In Goa, the Dharani Project, which started in 2001, computerized land records and crops through a series of state-issued Netbook personal computers in all 11 *talukas* (districts). A web-enabled touch screen interface is available that deploys biometric authentication. Each Netbook is provided with land use data, cadastral maps, and a means for recording cultivators.

Other local examples abound. Ahmedabad implemented 16 civic centers to deliver three services online: annual collection of property taxes, birth and death certificates, and shop licenses (Bhatia et al., 2009); about 1.25 million transactions are processed through them annually. In Maharashtra, the Warana Wired Village Project created networked "facilitation booths" staffed by local youths to provide internet access and 12 public services to 25 local cooperative societies, particularly 22,000 sugarcane and dairy producers distributed around 70 villages (Saji, 2006). However, lack of investment in human capital led the project to fail. The LokMitra project, in Himachal Pradesh, set up a rural intranet to allow rural villagers to express grievances to officials. In 2014, Aadhar created Jeevan Pramaan, which obviates pensioners from physically submitting Life Certificates to ensure continuity in their pension payments. The city of Aurangabad, in Maharashtra, erected Setu ("bridge"), a so-called Citizen Facilitation Centre that functions as a one-stop kiosk.

Finally, Indian states have adopted a whole raft of other programs aimed at improving the quality of life in various respects (Yadav and Singh, 2012). Andhra Pradesh started Prajavani for online monitoring of grievances against the government. Himachal Pradesh implemented Samadhan in the same vein. Kerala developed an e-health initiative. Several states allow online vaccination appointments and disease-monitoring system. Changidar created a centralized system to coordinate hospital appointments. Chhattisgarh, a new state created in 2000, formed a series of e-government initiatives, including: Bhuiyan, to computerize land records; E-Sangwari, to provide online access to birth, death, and caste certificates; E-Panchayat, to inform rural people about welfare programs (Subramanian and Saxena, 2006); and an online leprosy eradication program.

5.1.3   E-government and the digital divide in India

In a nation as vast and diverse as India, the digital divide looms large, particularly between urban and rural areas. Urban incomes are much higher than rural ones, and urbanites tend to be better educated. Throughout India, as in many countries, internet users – and thus those who benefit from e-government – tend to be younger and male. As everywhere, social differentials in access to the internet and thus e-government are matched by geographic ones (Sethi, 2006, p. 326).

This digital divide exists at all the levels of society, for example, the tribal minorities in India vs. the majority population; the rural illiterate in India vs. the urban educated; the least connected North Eastern states vs. India's "most wired city," Hyderabad; the most corrupt state in India, Bihar, vs. the least corrupt state of Kerala.

India has taken several steps to address its considerable digital divide. One of these is the promotion of the "Simputer," a low-cost, internet-capable pocket PC able to send handwritten or voice emails on a touch-sensitive screen, access smartcards, with capabilities in two Indian languages, using the Linux operating system. The Simputer's ability to send handwritten messages is crucial because of the lack of available fonts for many Indian and other languages. In addition, private ISPs such as n-Logue have focused heavily on rural areas.

There is an enormous literature on telecenters in rural India (e.g., Rao, 2005; Bhatnagar, 2006; Best and Kumar 2008; Bhatnagar and Singh, 2010; Hirwade, 2010; Venkatesh et al., 2014). By some estimates there are roughly 150 rural telekiosk projects across the country with roughly 100,000 so-called Common Service Centers. These are intended to replace traditional forms of government–citizen interactions, obviating the need for time-consuming trips to offices. For hundreds of millions of people, these form their first segueway into cyberspace and first opportunity to use e-government services. Some are privately owned and operated, others run by NGOs, and yet others by the national or state government. Public–private partnerships are a popular business model, and seem necessary to ensure financial stability (Kuriyan and Ray, 2009). Telecenters or kiosks can empower rural residents by providing them with information (e.g., about crop prices or health care), enabling them to inquire about bank loans, allowing them to file grievances, and access land records. These also form a potent symbol that the government takes rural poverty seriously and helps to curry favor with the rural electorate. As Kuriyan and Ray (2009, p. 1669) put it, "The state is, in effect, using entrepreneur-run telecenters to renegotiate its legacy of inefficiency." Inevitably, the process of inserting advanced digital technologies into semifeudal societies will be accompanied by mistakes, suspicion, and resistance. A series of illustrative examples follows.

Kerala, with a long history of education and egalitarianism, launched a project in 2001 called A PC for Every Home through the Kerala Electronics Development

Corporation. The state also initiated the Information Kerala Project that provides guidance to local *panchayats* on networked databases concerning land holdings, tax payments, and public health. It also created free FRIENDS centers, a series of one-stop centers that later changed to for-profit Keltron Information Kiosks. They operate 7 days/week.

Some of India's most successful efforts confronting the digital divide have focused on rural areas, including satellite internet access. The Vijayawada Municipal Corporation created the Vijayawada Online Information Center in 1999, which includes five free internet kiosks in the town. Through them, "Citizens could get most of the services as well as information online, including building approvals, payment of taxes, public health, and engineering, municipal budget allocations, tax payment, grievance registration and monitoring, birth and death certificates" (Patak and Prasad, 2005, p. 446). The Rural Access to Services through Internet program supplies 100 kiosks in villages to provide educational information as well as that pertaining to health and animal husbandry.

Tamil Nadu initiated the collaborative venture Sustainable Access in Rural India (SARI) project in 2001, which included Indian and American universities. SARI erected 80 internet kiosks in which even impoverished farmers could use email, webcams, access birth and death records, health information, caste certification (for the poor to obtain government services), apply for pensions, lodge complaints, and get health and veterinary information (Kumar and Best, 2006; Best and Kumar 2008). Young adults from the area who went overseas could email their families, generating cost savings. Technical support was provided by the company n-Log, which was also involved in Gyan Ganga. The number of users indicated that roughly 3–14% of the surrounding village population and 11–26% of the village households were using the system. Some of the kiosks were privately operated, while others were maintained by an NGO, the Dhan Foundation. Best and Maier (2007) explored the role of gender on ICT access in five rural villages in the region that participated in SARI, and concluded that their needs and uses were different from men's: more women than men were ignorant of the internet, for those women who did use the kiosks, usage revolved around chores and childcare. Three years after it began, in 2004, most of the privately operated kiosks had closed, while those run by the NGO stayed open. Factors that contributed to the closures of private kiosks included insufficient training of kiosk operators, lack of voice telephony, insufficient number of customers, and poor internet connectivity.

In 2006, this effort was replicated by the sugar manufacturer EID Parry, which in partnership with n-Logue, established 38 kiosks ("Parry's corners" or MinArsu) that offered information in Tamil. They provided email, news, updates on weather and prices, IT training, and telemedicine consultations. However, this project also encountered similar problems of lack of trained personnel and insufficient revenues for operators (Walsham, 2010). Similarly, Hindustan Lever created an e-Shakti online store for rural producers.

Other states developed their own telecenter projects. Himachal Pradesh has centers that offer price information, allow filing of grievances and registrations. In the remote and impoverished northeast as well as Sikkim, India established 487 community information centers in 2002 that provide basic email; birth, death, and marriage certificates; applications for pensions and employment cards; agricultural prices; information on job opportunities; and citizen-centric services such as E-Suvidha, which enables citizens to submit requests for services; they are also used to announce the results of elections and examinations (Chaudhri and Dash, 2006). It won the e-ASIA Award in 2004.

5.1.4   Obstacles to Indian e-government

India faces formidable barriers to adopting the Internet for public purposes (Faisal and Rahman, 2008). Many public servants are accustomed to conducting business manually and are ignorant or distrustful of digital technology, and resent the limitations it may place on them for lining their own pockets.

Restrictive gender norms for women deprive them of access to many information technologies (Best and Maier, 2007). Subramanian and Saxena (2006) detail the formidable obstacles to women's use of e-government in the state of Chhattisgarh: men are entitled to first right to use everything; women's domestic chores keep them too busy; women have lower incomes and literacy rates and are less technologically savvy; IT courses are aimed at men; cybercafes are dominated by men; and technology in general is seen as a male domain hostile to women. For many women, simply getting by or surviving household violence is all they can do, and e-government is a distant and irrelevant luxury. Women who do visit kiosks strongly prefer those staffed by women and often refuse to visit them if staffed by men.

Similarly, caste plays a role in excluding low-caste people, including illiteracy. Farmers are frequently suspicious of computers: many people in rural areas "have 'computer fear' as they have not been exposed to computers previously" (Venkatesh et al., 2014, p. 254). Financing for many e-government projects is inadequate, and equipment can quickly become outdated. Electricity shortages in most villages make kiosks inoperable, a factor that helped to doom the Gyandoot project, and dial-up internet connections can be too slow or unreliable (Lucknow Lab and Media Lab Asia developed a human-powered pedal generator to charge batteries.)

India's linguistic diversity, including 22 official languages, poses a problem for some of the country's netizens, and hence access to e-government. Often software requires a knowledge of English, which many rural inhabitants do not speak or read; content in local languages is usually quite limited. Some agencies have responded by creating content in the vernacular. For example, for those who do not speak English, Tamil Nadu established a Tamil Internet Research Centre to promote the use of Tamil on the internet.

5.1.5   Indian Internet censorship

India, despite its generally democratic practice of governance, has nonetheless also engaged in moderate internet censorship. In 2000, the Indian Parliament approved the ITA to crack down on cybercrime, allowing cybercafes and internet users' homes to be searched without warrants as part of criminal investigations. The powers granted under the ITA were expanded following the 2008 terrorist attacks on Mumbai. The state also allowed the government to block access to sites considered pornographic or that "endanger public order, the integrity and security of the nation and relations with other countries." Those setting up "anti-Indian" websites can be jailed for up to 5 years. In 2002, India enacted the Prevention of Terrorism Ordinance Act authorizing the government to monitor electronic communications, including personal email. The Indian cybercafé association, the Association of Public Internet Access Providers, strenuously protested against the measures, which it said would lead to the closure of most of the country's 3000 or so cybercafés. In 2003, Yahoo links to separatist websites were blocked. The state consistently bans websites for pornography and escort services. The government adopted new rules in 2011 to modify the 2000 IT Act, but continues to block websites it deems "defamatory," "hateful," "harmful to minors," or "infringes copyright." Cybercafes must photograph their customers, and the state has asked social media companies such as Google, Yahoo, and Facebook to prescreen user content. All Indian internet service providers are obliged by law to sign an agreement that allows government authorities to access user data, and must have designated employees who handle government blocking requests.

5.1.6   Indian e-government in perspective

India has enjoyed modest success in e-government and has unleashed a vast array of projects, largely at the state and local levels (Table 5.2). In many cases, this process has reduced trips to government offices, waiting times, and opportunities for bribery, and has often empowered the rural poor. Outstanding examples include Project Bhoomi in Karnataka, Akshaya in Kerala, and multiple programs in Andhra Pradesh. In other cases, however, the gap between promises and expectations on the one hand and the delivered reality on the other hand remains large. In Haque's (2002, p. 244) rather dour assessment,

> In the case of India, beyond the issue of public access and participation,
> egovernance has not shown any promising results even in terms of service delivery.
> … Examples of total or partial failure include such cases as the creation of district-
> level information centres by the National Informatics Centre; the computerization of
> the Income Tax Department's tax system; the use of the executive information system
> in the management of adult literacy programmes; the adoption of a computerized
> decision support system in the Narmada Irrigation Project Authority; and the
> implementation of the Rural Information Systems Project.

Similarly, telecenters often fail due to "a range of reasons for the failure including lack of trained staff, movement of key officials and, at a deeper level, opposition from government officials at the local level who perceived a threat from the kiosks to their role, authority and influence in the community and, more darkly, to their opportunities for corruption" (Walsham, 2010, p. 6). Despite setbacks, India is a model of how to confront the digital divide in developing countries.

This view is somewhat hard to sustain given India's successes noted above. Indeed, for all of their problems, e-government programs appear to have reduced corruption

Table 5.2 **Major state e-government projects in India**

Project	State(s)	Description
ITPolice	Karnataka	Allows emails to police departments
Khajane	Karnataka	Connects treasuries by satellite
KAVERI	Karnataka	Online land registration
Bhoomi	Karnataka	Online land registration
PROOF	Karnataka	Online disclosure of state budget
Gyan Ganga	Gujarat	Telecenters
Mahitishakti	Gujarat	Telecenters
SmartGov	Andhra Pradesh	Online land registration
E-Seva	Andhra Pradesh	Telecenters
eCOPS	Andhra Pradesh	Enhance transparency of police departments
Samaikya Agritech	Andhra Pradesh	Telecenters
CARD	Andhra Pradesh	Online land registration
Saukaryam	Andhra Pradesh	Telecenters
Drishtee	Six states	Telecenters
Sampark	Punjab and Haryana	Telecenters
Gyandoot	Madhya Pradesh	Telecenters
TARAhaat	Madhya Pradesh	Telecenters
Uttar Pradesh and Punjab		
IT@School	Kerala	Distance education
Information Kerala Mission	Kerala	Telecenters
Akshaya	Kerala	Telecenters
FRIENDS	Kerala	Telecenters
Kudumbashree	Kerala	Telecenters for women
e-Choupal	Madhya Pradesh	Telecenters for farmers
Akashganga	Gujarat	IT for dairy farmers
iVillages	Pondicherry	Telecenters
RajSWIFT	Rajasthan	Enhance intergovernment communications
Janmitra	Rajasthan	Telecenters
REGiNET	Tamil Nadu	Telecenters
Dharani	Goa	Online land registration
Warana wired village	Maharashtra	Telecenters
SARI	Tamil Nadu	Telecenters
E-Suvidha	Sikkim, northeast	Telecenters

across the board. Projects that succeed have determined leadership, sufficiently skilled staff, include women, are tailored to communities' local needs, and provide a wide array of services. However, e-government is highly uneven across the Indian landscape, being highly developed in states such as Karnataka and Andhra Pradesh and much less evident in, say, West Bengal. In sum, e-government is no panacea, for the country's vast diversity and inequalities are mirrored in the successes and failures of its e-government.

5.2   Pakistan: unrealized potential

A predominantly rural country of 190 million people, Pakistan is the world's only nuclear-armed Muslim power. Forged out of British colonialism as the Islamic twin to India, it has long endured military dictatorships, military coups, instability, deep poverty, and severe, entrenched corruption. Instability, terrorism, and the wars in Afghanistan have left parts of the country ungovernable. Literacy stands at only 58%. The economy is largely agricultural, with some exports of rugs and soccer balls.

Given these circumstances, it is unsurprising that the country's preparedness for e-government is not encouraging. In 2015 Pakistan's e-government score was 0.2823 (lower than Cambodia's), e-participation was 0.1316, and Internet penetration was only 17.8%, a population consisting mostly of young, relatively well-educated men. About three-quarters of Pakistanis have a mobile phone. The telecommunications infrastructure is rudimentary, broadband usage is low, and dial-up services are still the norm. The telecom network in rural areas is particularly lacking.

Although belatedly, Pakistan did take steps toward implementing e-government. In 1996 it passed the Pakistan Telecommunications Act, and established the Pakistan IT Commission in 2000. The year 2002 was a milestone, with the government's most important effort, the creation of the Electronic Government Directorate in 2002 within the Ministry of Science and Technology (Shah et al., 2011), and the Promulgation of Electronics Transactions Ordinance, designed to facilitate e-commerce, which legalized electronic signatures and listed computer crimes. Pakistan deregulated telecommunications in 2003 by abolishing the monopoly held by the Pakistan Telecommunication Company. In 2005, the National E-Government Council unveiled a 5-year plan to initiate the construction of an e-government infrastructure and attempt to deliver services to citizens online. Little progress has been made since then (Ahmad et al., 2013). It has toyed with creating software technology parks in Lahore, Karachi, and Islamabad, and training programs exist in the National University for Science and Technology and the COMSATS Institute of Information Technology. Although the government announces lofty goals, such as Pakistan 2030 and e-Pakistan vision, the rhetoric is rarely accompanied by deeds. Most programs are designed and adminis-tered in a haphazard and *ad hoc* manner. Indeed, senior management is often reluctant to release funds for e-government programs (Qaiser and Khan, 2010).

As elsewhere, the first step in understanding the country's e-government is its web portals. One of the prime duties of the Electronic Government Directorate is the cre-ation and maintenance of the state's primary portal (www.pakistan.gov.pk) that allows roughly 500 forms to be downloaded in English and Urdu (see also www.e-gov.pk). Other efforts include digital disbursement of public employee salaries, training pro-grams, technical support, and the collection of *zakat* (Islamic taxes). Other ministerial websites fared less well, and were criticized on the basis of legibility and aesthetics (Saeed et al., 2013). The Pakistan Development Gateway includes "searchable infor-mation about Pakistan from more than 2,000 websites" (Shafique and Mahmood, 2008, p. 73). The first portal to offer agricultural advice, Pakissan, offers information in English and Urdu on crops, fishing, horticulture, and forestry, as well as government policies, weather, and prices.

Beyond simple webpages, perhaps the branch of government most affected by e-government is revenue collections. The Central Board of Revenue began allowing e-filing of taxes in 2005. As Andersen (2009, p. 202) points out, "In Pakistan, the entire tax department is undergoing restructuring; information and communication technology (ICT) systems are being introduced with the stated purpose of reducing contact between tax collectors and tax payers."

E-commerce in Pakistan is in its infancy, but the state has taken steps to encourage it. The State Bank of Pakistan opened the Internet Merchants Account. The Small and Medium Sized Enterprise Development Authority created SMEDA, an online forum to provide advice and business leads. The Pakistan Trade Office, operated by the Ministry of Commerce, provides free information about investment opportunities via Pak Trade (www.paktrade.org; Shafique and Mahmood, 2008). Chambers of Commerce in Lahore and Islamabad facilitate trade through those cities with online portals. The Export Processing Zones Authority Pakistan (www.epza.com.pk) provides economic and legal information to potential investors.

Two bright spots in the Pakistani e-government landscape are health care and education. For example, TelMedPak (www.telmedpak.com), a repository for health information established by an NGO, is the country's first health portal and offers advice to doctors and patients alike. A pilot telemedicine project was established in a hospital in Taxila, near Islamabad, which allows patient reports to be emailed to experts nationwide. When Punjab was confronted with a dengue fever epidemic in 2011, it created a smartphone application for workers and officials to track it. Other health websites of some importance include Doctor.org.pk, Medisure, and the Pakistan Reproductive Health Network, a platform aimed at women to provide information on gender and sexuality. Teledoctor, started by Telenor Communications in 2008, allows clients to obtain health information over their phones in eight local languages. Some educational institutions have experimented with distance learning courses, particularly the Allama Iqbal Open University, which serves 1 million Pakistanis as well as students in other countries. The Ministry of Science and Technology erected a virtual university in 2002, with free satellite and internet broadcasts, and the Higher Education Commission established a National Digital Library (Shafique and Mahmood, 2008). The government also offers online tracking of *hajj* participants.

However, many Pakistanis do not seem well prepared to adopt e-government services. Given the low rate of internet penetration, most simply are not aware of its existence. A study by Rehman and Esichaikul (2012) of citizen perceptions of government websites indicated that many had concerns about their trustworthiness and the safety of private data (see Ahmad et al., 2013), a problem compounded by the poor quality of many public webpages. Many are not updated regularly (e.g., that of the Ministry of Railways), have broken links (e.g., the Revenue Department), or are not user friendly.

The obstacles to e-government in Pakistan are many, obvious, and daunting (Kayani et al., 2011; Kamal et al., 2013). Inept governance, low literacy rates, insufficient supplies of electricity, low Internet penetration and computer access, computer anxiety, and serious constraints to women's participation are some. Widespread distrust and cynicism about the government also play a role. The vast bulk of rural Pakistanis do not speak English, and content in Urdu, Punjabi, or Balochi is sparse.

Confronting the digital divide in Pakistan, the government formulated the Digital Opportunity Initiative, although it has yielded few substantial results. The Pakistan Telecommunication Authority initiated a multibillion rupee project, the Universal Service Fund, to subsidize operators in rural areas, and proposed a telecenter project called Rabta Ghar that would establish 400 centers throughout the country. Post offices in most large cities have been networked, but do not provide public internet services. Public libraries are also ill equipped for the task (Khan and Bawden, 2005).

The contrast with India is striking. Whereas India has numerous programs to develop rural e-government kiosks (e.g., Bhoomi, Gyan Ganga, E-Sewa, Gyandoot, Akshaya), Pakistan has almost none. Tentative steps include cybercommunity centers established in 2001 in Gwadar in Balochistan, Mithi in Sindh, and Usterzai Payan in the Northwest Frontier Province, now Khyber Pakhtunkhwa (Mahmood, 2005); each has only one assistant, have tenuous internet connections, and the latter is restricted to local students and not open to the public. In the far north, the NGO-funded Gilgit Internet Service started connecting a few isolated villages through an e-facility center in 2012.

Pakistan's government has engaged in moderately severe internet censorship. The Pakistan Telecommunications Authority (PTA) repeatedly filters Internet content deemed to be irreligious, antimilitary, or secessionist. All international traffic to and from the country is routed through three sites owned by Pakistan Internet Exchange, with locations in Islamabad, Lahore, and Karachi. The 2006 Net Café Regulation bill requires Internet cafes to monitor patrons, although its enforcement has been dubious (Reporters Without Borders, 2004). The PTA has banned dozens of URLs that published Danish cartoons ridiculing the Prophet Mohammed; indeed, the Pakistani police attempt to register all websites containing "blasmephous material" (Ahmed, 2002). Balochi nationalist and human rights sites are also blacklisted. The Pakistani cybercommunity responded to these initiatives with a "Don't Block the Blog" campaign (http://dbtb.org/), which, among other things, has exposed the military's numerous civil rights violations. The OpenNet Initiative (2012) notes that "In 2010, Pakistan made global headlines for blocking Facebook and other Web sites in response to a contest popularized on the social networking site to draw images of the Prophet Mohammad." In 2012, amid growing concern about greater restrictions on internet access in the country, the Human Rights Commission of Pakistan, an independent body, said that roughly 13,000 websites were inaccessible. In May 2014, Pakistan's parliament voted unanimously to lift a ban on YouTube, which had been blocked in the country since 2012.

5.3 Bangladesh: "limping into the information age"

With 160 million people, Bangladesh is more populous than Russia. Threatened by rising sea levels, densely populated, and impoverished, the country faces formidable development obstacles. The literacy rate in 2015 was only 61%. Widespread corruption and an inefficient bureaucracy have retarded economic growth. An overwhelming agricultural economy, nonetheless it has become an important exporter of garments and textiles, which form the vast bulk of its exports.

The Bangladeshi telecommunications infrastructure shows classic symptoms of underinvestment. Broadband access is limited and unaffordable for most people. Only 33% of the population had internet access in 2016. Its 2015 e-government readiness score was 0.2991 and e-participation was rated 0.0789, indicating a society poorly prepared to utilize IT. Mobile phone usage stood at 80%. Broadband is available in major cities but not in rural areas. Under conditions like these, one might expect e-government to be entirely absent. Yet even in such a poor and undeveloped place, it has taken root (Hasan, 2003). Control of rampant corruption is a major incentive for e-government adoption in the country (Rajon and Zama, 2008; Mahmood, 2010; Bhuiyan, 2011). Many of its initiatives were instigated at the behest of NGOs or the World Bank.

The legislative history of e-government is mixed. The Bangladeshi government established the Bangladesh Computer Council in 1990 to encourage the growth of IT activities. Telecommunications were liberalized in 1998. In 2000, the Public Administration Reform Commission initiated the initial steps toward e-government (Faroqi and Siddiquee, 2011). The Bangladesh Telecommunication Act 2001 recognized the internet as a telecommunication service. The country created a national IT policy in 2002 (and another in 2009) and subsequently passed the ICT Act of 2006. The Official Internet Connection and Usage Policy in 2004 instigated the use of the Internet in government offices. In 2009, it passed a Right to Information Act. The same year the Bangladesh Awami League announced Digital Bangladesh as part of its Vision 2021, with the goal of spreading IT in a democratic manner, and began to implement it following the party's victory in the election (Islam and Khair, 2012), although the concept was criticized as overly utopian in light of basic problems such as electricity shortages. As in many countries, achievements fell short of expectations, and Bangladesh's legal context for e-government is poorly developed. For example, the Official Secrets Act of 1923 remains operative (Bhuiyan, 2011). While it passed the Software Copyright Act in 2000, in practice intellectual property laws are vague and rarely enforced. Lack of guarantees for privacy and security inhibit some users from participating in e-government programs. The country has yet to enact a cyber-crimes law, and issues such as identity theft and electronic signatures are in legal limbo. There is no central body to coordinate e-government implementation.

Most e-government in the country is confined to a few public webpages that provide simple information. Few e-government services involve two-way interactions utilizing web 2.0 interfaces, and thus are reduced largely to the role of simply providing information. The national web portal (www.bangladesh.gov.bd) was launched, which provides information on issues such as education, disaster management, university admission, and corporate opportunities, as well as downloadable forms for passports and taxpayer identification numbers. Bhuiyan (2011, p. 58) notes that of the 50 ministries of the national government, "42, including the offices of the President (www.bangabhaban.gov.bd) and the Prime Minister (www.pmo.gov.bd), the Parliament (www.parliament.gov.bd), and the Election Commission (www.ecs.gov.bd) have their own websites and provide important information and e-services to citizens and businesses." Aside from the national portal, the Bangladesh Government Digitized Forms website allows 65 forms to be downloaded. The Citizens Service Application (www.forms.gov.bd) portal allows numerous forms to be downloaded. The Ministry of Education publishes the results of public examinations online (Bhuiyan, 2006).

The Ministry of Religious Affairs introduced a *hajj* website in 2002 to service thousands of Bangladeshi pilgrims who go to Mecca annually. By using passport information, users can ascertain the actions of any registered hajj pilgrim, communicate with them via email, and receive news about health alerts, weather conditions, or flight delays (Faroqi and Siddiquee, 2011).

Beyond simple webpages, the Bangladeshi government has instigated several e-government initiatives. It took hesitant steps toward m-government, such as disseminating disaster warnings via SMS and allowing citizens under duress to request aid. Steps to introduce IT in the schools and promote distance education have largely failed due to severe shortages of equipment and technical knowledge among teachers, who are underpaid and overworked (Khan et al., 2012). The state has also taken to publishing parts of the budget online, particularly national funds distributed to local municipalities known as Union Porishods (Sein, 2011). The Chittagong customhouse, the largest single source of government revenues, automated its operations in 2008 using a public–private partnership to allow online data and document management, customs declarations, and tax calculations. The National Board of Revenue followed suit. In 2008, the government also introduced smartcards that allow 18 services to be conducted online as a precursor to national identity cards. Online payment of taxes began in 2009. As Faroqi and Siddiquee (2011, p. 45) write,

> *Service providers such as the Power Development Board (PDB), Dhaka Electricity*
> *Supply Authority (DESA), Water and Sewerage Authority (WASA), Titas Gas,*
> *and Bangladesh Telegraph and Telephone Board (BTTB) have all made several*
> *contracts with different banks and mobile operators for their bills to be paid*
> *electronically using Internet banking, ATMs, Ready Cash card, Q-Cash card, POS,*
> *SMS and other channels.*

The government also edged toward online procurement through e-tendering in 2010 (Bhuiyan, 2011). This process was instigated in large part due to pressure from the World Bank to curb corruption in that area: as Mahmood (2010, p. 107) notes, "In Bangladesh civil society leaders called for introducing e-procurement system in public tenders to eliminate corruption and collusive bidding practices to ensure transparency." Such a move increased the number of bids for contracts and reduced the time to process tenders.

Rural development and agriculture are major foci of the country's e-government. It created the Agricultural Market Information Improvement (or AgriNet Bangladesh) system to provide an online guide for farmers about commodity prices. Preliminary evidence indicates that the process has helped to reduce the country's notoriously corrupt government agencies, for example by eliminating black-marketers in railroad ticket sales (Knox, 2009). In 2006 the Ministry of Agriculture gave birth to e-Governance Application and Online Daily Market Price, run by local offices throughout the country, which unlike AgriNet, is interactive (Islam and Grönlund, 2007). Its web portal (www.dam.gov.bd) offers dynamic information on hundreds of commodities in wholesale markets. However, it is confined to English and does not provide information in Bengali, a major limitation to the rural poor. The Ministry also created the Northwest Crop Diversification Project to divulge price information via mobile phones (Islam and Grönlund, 2010), an innovative step toward m-government.

In addition, the famous Grameen Bank, winner of the Nobel Peace Prize, provides loans to more than 360,000 borrowers (almost all women) to purchase solar-powered cell phones, who then earned a living charging local residents for calls. The Grameen Phone Community Information Center initiative, which began in 2006, created kiosks operated by private operators who charge modest fees for email or Skype services, as well as assistance with government forms and job searches (Sein, 2011).

Bangladesh has taken steps toward telemedicine as well. Its first functional link was established in 1999 by an NGO, Swifne Charitable, which linked hospitals in Dhaka and Britain. The Ministry of Health and Family Welfare worked with a private firm, Telemedicine Reference Center Ltd., to develop rural telemedicine facilities. With support from the EU, Bangladesh University of Engineering and Technology began a program of telediagnoses. In 2005, Grameen Telecom and the Diabetic Association of Bangladesh launched a service to give patients in the district of Faridpur access to specialists in Dhaka. A collaborative project helped to improve the performance of rural health workers in the district of Magura. The state has also experimented with telepsychiatry programs.

Below the national state, there are a number of successful e-government initiatives. Arguably the best local example of e-government in Bangladesh is the birth registration project of Rajshahi City Corporation introduced in 2001, which was supported by United Nations Children's Fund (Haldenwang, 2004). In computerizing records, it gave the local health department information with which to immunize children, and enabled the educational system to issue identification cards allowing them to enroll. All six of the country's municipal corporations – Dhaka, Chittagong, Rajshahi, Khulna, Sylhet, and Barisal – have their own websites and provide information pertaining trade, licenses, housing, health, education, and birth registration. The Dhaka Metropolitan Police Department offers an online service called Citizens Help Request. Some educational institutions allow for SMS delivery of admissions and registration information.

Confronting the digital divide, Bangladesh established a series of Union Information Service Centers, a series of one-stop service counters. They began operations in 2009 in 30 Union Parishads and subsequently were expanded in 2010 so that there is one each located in the Deputy Commissioner's office in each of the country's 64 districts. Each is run by two entrepreneurs, one male and one female. The primary function concerns land records, although users may also use email, learn English, access banking and legal services, apply for licenses and permits, and inquire about pensions, public examinations, and educational opportunities. Applicants receive confirmations and updates through SMS messages. The state has also implemented cyberkiosks in some post offices (Siddiquee and Faroqi, 2013).

It goes without saying that Bangladesh confronts insuperable obstacles to e-government implementation. Shortages of funding, hardware, and human capital loom chief among these. Often junior officials are better informed than senior ones due to their more recent educations (Gregor et al., 2014). Low literacy rates and extreme poverty contribute to low internet penetration. Corruption persists, and many officials resist changes that threaten a profitable status quo. Lack of fluency in English excludes many rural people. Finally, Bangladeshi women face highly restrictive gender roles.

To its credit, Bangladesh's censorship of the internet has been fairly light. On occasion the Telecommunication Regulatory Commission attempts to block access to Facebook or WhatsApp, citing "national security" such as when faced with threats from Muslim extremists. In 2008, it blocked access to the blogging platform Sachalayatan. The state also announces a panel of Internet censors to trace supposed blasphemy on social networks. When atheist bloggers criticized leading Muslim clerics, the government blocked about a dozen websites and blogs to stem the violence, and stepped up security for the bloggers, some of whom were threatened by the activists of a leading Islamic party.

Notwithstanding the argument that e-government can form a "sweet spot" that unleashes rounds of catalytic change (Gregor et al., 2014), Bangladesh has far to go in this regard. While recognition of the importance and potential of IT for the government is increasing, leadership on the issue has been haphazard and uncoordinated. Hoque (2006) notes that the lack of a coherent policy has led to conflicting policies implemented by different agencies. It is little wonder that Faroqi and Siddiquee (2011) argue the country is "limping into the information age."

5.4   Nepal: what does Himalayan e-government look like?

The landlocked, mountainous Himalayan kingdom of Nepal, one of the world's poorest countries, has a population of 28 million, who live primarily in small rural villages. One-third of the population lives on one dollar a day or less. The literacy rate is 64% and the state has been marred by instability, corruption, and nepotism, including an on-and-off Maoist rebellion.

Such conditions do not lend themselves well to e-government. Nepal's e-government readiness score was 0.2664, e-participation stood at 0.0263, and in 2016 internet penetration was only 19.9%. However, 81% of Nepalis have a mobile phone. The state-owned telecommunications provider, Nepal Telecom Company, provides most services, although the liberalization of the sector that started in 1992 opened the door for private providers. Although it never developed a significant landline network, Nepal has worked on wireless connections, some of which allow internet connectivity. One example is the Nepal Wireless Network Project, which started in 2003 and provides email, VOIP, and bulletin boards.

As Sharma et al. (2014, p. 85) note, "Nepal's government is facing numerous challenges in introducing and implementing e-governance. These include political issues, inadequate human resources, the lack of a legal framework, little public awareness about ICT and poor ICT infrastructure across the nation." Despite these obstacles, the state has taken hesitant steps. In 1996, it created the Ministry of Science and Technology for the development and implementation of ICT activities, and in 2001 the National Information Technology Center. The High Level Commission for

Information Technology created the National Information Technology Center initiative in 2002. The year 2004 saw the passage of the Electronic Transaction and Digital Signature Act, which regulates e-commerce and specifies penalties for cybercrimes. In 2006, the state passed an e-government master plan with the support of the Korea IT Industry Promotion Agency. Some examples of Nepalese e-government include: online registration by the Inland Revenue Department; an online tender system for the Department of Roads; online passes issued by the National Information Technology Center; web-based land records in the Ministry of Land Reform Management; and online vehicle registration. Several hospitals, such as Kathmandu Medical College, offer health information and guidance through telemedicine programs. Some agencies have experimented with social media. E-procurement is widely seen as a means of curbing corruption (Neupane et al., 2014).

Although it is a small country, Nepal faces a digital divide. In Kathmandu, the only metropolitan government in the country that has a website (http://www.kathmandu.gov.np) allows a few forms to be downloaded, but it is not updated regularly. The Ministry of Information and Communication has attempted to create a wireless broadband connectivity program for rural areas. Nepal's first rural telecentre was established by E-Network Research and Development in 2002, at Himanchal Higher Secondary School of Myagdi District. Starting in 2004, several ministries and the Postal Service, as well as NGOs, established 80 telecenters in selected villages (Amatya, 2009; Lee and Sparks, 2014), which eventually grew to more than 420. Some disperse price information about crops via SMS text messages. However, most telecenters struggle to be sustainable. Users are primarily young people and the public's usage of e-government services is low.

Nepal is not above light internet censorship. In 2005, King Gyanendra shut temporarily down the internet and telephone lines upon taking power from the parliament and prime minister. Nepali bloggers became an important voice of political opposition.

5.5   Bhutan: first steps in the Land of the Thunder Dragon

Tiny, remote, and impoverished, it is a wonder that Bhutan has any e-government at all. Its economy relies on agriculture and tourism. Bhutan's e-government readiness score was 0.2942, e-participation was rated 0.0263, and in 2016 internet penetration was 38.6%, but is growing rapidly; Internet service started only in 1999. Roughly 82% of the Bhutanese population has a mobile phone. A rudimentary fiber system strung along the Bhutan Power Commission network and occasional broadband access is complemented by satellite internet channels.

Good governance is one of the pillars of the Bhutanese government's famous, unique philosophy of Gross National Happiness. Like most countries, Bhutan created an E-Government Masterplan to guide it into the golden age of the information economy, and like most countries it was met with more hyperbole than deeds. However, the state still lacks an appropriate legal framework for electronic documents and signatures. The Department of Information and Telecommunications has promoted online service delivery, although it is still rudimentary. Mobile e-government applications are nonexistent.

The national government portal (www.bhutan.go.bp) links to the websites of various ministries as well as an intranet and security clearance systems. In 2010, the state initiated a G2C program aimed at improving accessibility and fostering e-governance programs. However, by 2012 only 22 services were available online. In what is essentially the only published study to date of e-government in Bhutan, Miyata (2011) notes that starting in 2004 the Bhutanese Road Safety and Transport Authority allows for online registration of vehicles and driver's licenses. The Education Department budgeted funds to introduce the internet in schools, a process still unfolding. Since 2004, the National Institute of Education in Samse has been using IT for teacher education (Jamtsho, and Bullen, 2007). Few Bhutanese speak English, but Internet content in the vernacular is rare. Among government websites, only those of the Bhutan Broadcasting Service and the Dzongkha Development Commission include material in Bhutanese.

5.6   Sri Lanka: e-government in Serendip

Just off the southeast coast of India lies the largely rural island state of Sri Lanka with 21 million people. Its economy is primarily based on agriculture, notably tea, tourism, and apparel production. It suffered an intense civil conflict between the Sinhalese majority and a Tamil minority in the north that left tens of thousands dead.

Sri Lanka's 2015 e-government readiness score was 0.4357, e-participation was rated 0.0789, and in 2016 Internet penetration stood at 27%; users are concentrated in urban areas, notably Colombo. Broadband is available but not common, notably through the satellite carrier Etisalat, and recently has grown rapidly. Sri Lanka is well endowed with mobile phones as the penetration rate in 2015 exceeded 103%. Like many poor countries Sri Lanka has faced numerous obstacles to e-readiness (Davidrajuh, 2007). For a small country, its e-government initiatives have received considerable attention (e.g., Weerakkody et al., 2009; Waththage et al., 2012).

The country took steps toward the implementation of IT remarkably early, including establishing the National Computer Policy of 1983, the Council for Information Technology in 1984, and the Telecommunications Regulatory Commission of Sri Lanka in 1996. The deregulation of Sri Lanka Telecom paved the way for competition and lower prices. It created a Ministry of Information Technology in 2000, and an e-government policy in 2009. The national web portal (www.srilanka.lk) was installed in 2002 and offers 20 e-services such as license issuance and payment of water bills. The government's websites in general are not celebrated for their clarity, interactive capacities, or user-friendliness (Rajapaksha and Fernando, 2016), and most do not offer input from citizens. However, this status began to improve after the 2004 tsunami (Dissanayake and Dissanayake, 2013).

Some of the country's first steps occurred within the domain of education. Starting in the 1980s the state began to weave IT into various agencies (see Hanna, 2008 for a detailed history). In the 1990s, universities formed the Lanka Education and Academic Research network. The Sri Lanka Development Administration began a distance learning program aimed at public servants. In 2001, the European Council of Information Systems Development initiated the initial efforts toward e-government with the aim of linking the country's schools and universities to the internet. The Open University of Sri Lanka, established in 1980, adopted the plans with enthusiasm and began offering internet-based courses to thousands of students. The main campus lies in Colombo, with branches in Kandy, Jaffna, and Matara. The Department of Examinations began releasing the results of national exams on the internet in 2003. However, distance learning opportunities are minimal.

The country's most ambitious step toward e-government was the e-Sri Lanka Development Project, launched in 2002 under a partnership with the World Bank, a road map to acquire e-government within 5 years (Davidrajuh, 2004; 2007). It involved numerous components, including cultivating IT leadership training, fomenting regional networks, plans for telecenters, reengineering government, and broader goals of creating an e-society. It was inspired in many respects by the successes in Andhra Pradesh (Hanna, 2008). The plan created the Information and Communication Technology Agency (ICTA) in 2003, which was empowered to carry it out and was free of many of the constraints of most public agencies. The program received funding from the World Bank (a $53 million loan) and development agencies in Sweden, Canada, and South Korea. However, it has made only gradual progress (Karunasena et al., 2011). In part its lack of progress reflects the absence of a unified, coherent implementation strategy, despite the mandate of the ICTA. However, Wanasundera (2012, p. 406) notes "In 2004, Sri Lanka initiated its national program to expand digital technology applications through institutional reforms, regulatory changes, infrastructure development, and streamlined government processes."

Successes in the country's adoption of e-government include an online national population registry and motor vehicle registration system (Weerakkody et al., 2009; Karunasena and Deng, 2012). The e-pension program moved the application for social benefits online. It also created the Integrated Financial Management Information System to coordinate the management of funds across government bodies, although it became the focus of intense interagency squabbles with varying visions of e-government (Heeks and Stanforth, 2011). Preliminary evidence indicates that online accounting has improved transparency and efficiency (Yapa and Guah, 2012).

The country has also taken steps to address its digital divide (Gamage and Halpin, 2007). In 2004, it launched the Global Knowledge Centres program, a series of kiosks (*nenasalas*) in small rural communities in the country's south and northeast; 765 have been built to date (Windsor and Royal, 2014) and plans called for a total of 1000. These are aimed at the rural poor, and offer email services; IT training classes in Sinhalese, Tamil and English; and e-libraries. Most users are youths and young adults. The use of UNICODE fonts allows local languages to be used and include a Firefox plug-in in Sinhala and Tamil. Following the devastating 2004 tsunami, the government installed kiosks in camps housing displaced people. In addition to government projects, a for-profit initiative called EasySeva ("easy service") seeks to bring wireless broadband to rural areas, essentially by establishing kiosks as franchises; its primary application is VOIP service, particularly to the large expatriate community (Hosman and Fife, 2008). In the central part of the country, the United Nations Educational, Scientific, and Cultural Organization-funded Kothmale Community Internet Radio project involves volunteers who translate news and deliver it to villages over the web. Finally, USAID has a Sri Lanka Last Mile Initiative in which it partners with private firms to enhance rural connectivity.

Despite its successes, Sri Lanka faces several constraints to furthering e-government. Programs are generally underfunded. Most e-government content is in English, which is spoken by communities in Colombo but not in outlying areas. It has a bloated civil service hampered by widespread patronage and a poor record of reform. Additionally, although Sri Lanka has a high rate of literacy (93%), e-literacy still remains low. It relies heavily on foreign donors to advance e-development initiatives. Thus, although the country has been spared the devastating illiteracy and corruption that plague, say, Pakistan, the political impediments are still formidable.

Finally, although the Sri Lankan government is not known as an internet censor, at times it has curtailed access to and content on the web. In 2007, it restricted access to the internet and mobile phones in the northern and eastern parts on national security grounds. In 2011, the Ministry of Mass Media and Information started to require news sites to "register" with it. At times the state has blocked access to the Colombo Telegraph, the country's most iconoclastic investigative news website. The Tamil insurrection in the north has inspired the state to curtail access to websites sympathetic to that cause, such as Tamilnet.

5.7   Maldives: e-government in an archipelago of atolls

A tiny archipelago of 26 low-lying atolls consisting of 1190 islands, 200 of which are inhabited, the Maldives lies off of the southwest coast of India, with a population of roughly 400,000 people. Its economy revolves largely around tourism and fishing.

In 2015, the Maldives' e-government readiness score was a surprisingly high 0.4994 (the highest in South Asia), e-participation was rated 0.0263, and in 2016 internet penetration was 68.7%, by far the highest in the South Asian region. The state initiated the Maldives IT Project in 2001 that connected 20 atolls, and the first international fiber optic cable connected the country in 2006. There are almost twice as many mobile phones as there are Maldivians. Internet connections are relatively good, especially in the capital, Male, in which one-third of the population lives. Shareef et al. (2008, p. 409) note, "Strategic e-government planning for the Maldives requires taking into account local (Atoll) governments and international development partners, in addition to the central government." Multiple stakeholders are involved, including the state, citizens, and NGOs.

In 2003, the government established the National Center for Information Technology to coordinate the development of e-government in the country. Its goals included putting "citizens online, not in line." However, the legal framework remains murky: e-procurement legislation does not exist, and many government websites lack even elementary privacy policies. The results of these efforts included an e-government platform and internet kiosks in Male.

Maldivian e-government successes include e-policing; the security services have their own fiber optic network, the Police Information Management System, which connects all 39 police stations with security cameras positioned at traffic lights. The Ministry of Education has systematically introduced the Internet into Maldivian schools, although it is questionable to what extent it is incorporated into teaching (Hoque et al., 2012). The Maldives's leading telecom service provider, Wataniya, launched a mobile learning service that offered instruction to students in remote areas with a laptop computer and internet connection.

With World Health Organization and World Bank funding, the government established a telemedicine project in 2002, although it was unsuccessful due to limitations of the infrastructure, human capital shortages, lack of political commitment, and public mistrust (Kodukula and Nazvia, 2011). In Madurai, Aravind, the largest eye health service in the world, runs a teleophthalmology service, including three telecenter vision centers. SkyHealth, a franchise, operates teleprograms in family planning and female health around New Delhi.

Small though it may be, the Maldives nonetheless has a digital divide that it has confronted as best it can, particularly between Male and the rest of the nation (Shareef et al., 2010). Plans for kiosks in outlying islands have yet to materialize, but the high rate of mobile phone penetration implies some opportunity to address the issue.

5.8 Conclusion

Vast and sprawling, with enormous populations living in poverty, South Asia has nonetheless made gradual progress toward effective e-government. Internet penetration rates have grown, and most governments have striven to put at least documents, forms, and information online, if not deliver services through two-way interactions. India and Sri Lanka are notable for their attempts to confront the digital divide through multiple series of telecenters, which offer badly needed services to the rural poor. Land registration and the filing of grievances appear to be top priorities in many cases. Such steps are necessary if e-government is not to benefit only the well-educated urban professionals. By all accounts, corruption and waiting times for licenses and permits have declined. However, e-literacy remains low compared to East Asia, and many e-government initiatives are hampered by lack of funds, resistant bureaucrats, unreliable electricity supplies, and restrictions on women's participation. All of the region's governments practice censorship to one degree or another, although it is mild compared to, say, China, North Korea, or Central Asia.

Central Asia

6

Central Asia encompasses seven countries in the vast interior of the Eurasian continent. All are poor and landlocked. All except Mongolia are predominantly Muslim. All, to one extent or another, were once part of the Soviet empire, either as republics within the USSR (Kazakhstan, Uzbekistan, Turkmenistan, Tajikistan, and Kyrgyzstan, which broke away in 1991), as a client state (Mongolia), or the victim of invasion (Afghanistan). The region has some of the most blatantly and severely corrupt governments—frequently unrepentant dictatorships—in the world.

Still hampered by the crippling legacy of Soviet rule, Central Asia has been relatively slow to be enfolded into the world's telecommunications networks. In Central Asia, the principal fiber optic line is the 27,000 km-long Trans-Asia-Europe Fibre Optical Cable System (TAEFOS)—the world's longest overland route, which began operations in 1998. It begins in Frankfurt, extends to Turkey, crosses Iran, has trunk lines northward to Georgia, Armenia, and Ukraine, and follows the ancient Silk Road route into western China and hence to Shanghai. (In 2003, NATO sponsored a virtual Silk Road that links the region's universities.) Satellite Internet provides another opportunity for providing access where terrestrial connections are not viable or are prohibitively expensive, and many Central Asian ISPs rely on satellite services. International satellite services such as Intelsat, Eutelsat, and AsiaSat offer services to Central Asian ISPs. Some governments in the region have taken steps in this direction. In Kazakhstan and Mongolia, wireless technologies now allow for the rise of yurt-based Internet access (Davison et al., 2003). However, most Central Asian states practice censorship, often severe, shrinking the space for independent media (Allison, 2006).

Of Asia's vast and diverse set of countries, Central Asian ones have exhibited relatively modest efforts to implement e-government, largely because the region is ruled by authoritarian regimes and suffers from high levels of corruption. As Johnson and Kolko (2010, p. 16) note, "In the authoritarian states of Central Asia, citizen demand for government services via the Internet is very low." This observation implies that e-government implementation in such states differs from that in democratic societies, testimony to the context-dependent nature of its adoption (Table 6.1).

6.1 Kazakhstan: e-government on the Asian steppes

Although it is the ninth largest country in the world in terms of land area, Kazakhstan has only 15 million people, making it one of the least densely populated. Its economy relies heavily on the extraction of natural wealth, notably petroleum and natural gas. However, it has fared reasonably well, poverty has declined, literacy is high, and computer penetration increased markedly. Its democratic credentials are suspect: former autocratic President Nazarbayev won a third term in 2005 with more than 90% of the

e-Government in Asia: Origins, Politics, Impacts, Geographies. http://dx.doi.org/10.1016/B978-0-08-100873-7.00006-4

Table 6.1 **Internet and e-government statistics for Central Asia, 2015**

Country	2016 Internet penetration	2015 E-government readiness	E-participation	Mobile phone penetration
Afghanistan	12.3	0.1701	1316	74.9
Kazakhstan	54.3	0.6844	0.5932	172.2
Kyrgyzstan	36.2	0.4879	0.2895	134.5
Mongolia	49.5	0.5443	0.6053	105.1
Tajikistan	19.5	0.4069	n.a.	95.1
Turkmenistan	14.9	0.3813	n.a.	135.8
Uzbekistan	52.4	0.5217	0.3268	78.4

vote, and the country has been criticized for its numerous and severe human rights abuses and deeply entrenched, widespread, very severe corruption.

Like most developing countries, its telecommunications infrastructure is in its infancy. However, 54% of the population has Internet access, the highest rate in Central Asia. Half of the netizens access the Web from their homes and are overwhelmingly concentrated in cities such as the capitol, Astana and Almaty. Almost all schools are web connected. The country's e-government score in 2015 was 0.6844, the highest in Central Asia, and its e-participation rating was a respectable 0.5932. Kazakhs love mobile phones: there are 172 of them for every 100 residents. Broadband is still uncommon and three-quarters of users rely on dial-up connections. In 2006, Kazakhstan launched its own satellite, KazSat, followed by a second in 2009, which lowered the costs of satellite telecommunication services, and satellite Internet is popular. The cost of gaining entry to the Internet is high, prohibitively so for low-income people. Kapitsa (2008, p. 45) notes that

> in Kazakhstan, the unlimited dial-up Internet connection package offered by Kazakhtelecom cost about €86 per month, the unlimited ADSL connection – from €102.45 (at 64 Kbps) to €3278.57 (at 2048 Kbps) per month, and the unlimited cable Internet connection – from €9,163.09 (at 3 Mbps) to €24,432 (at 10 Mbps) per month. Taking into consideration that the average monthly salary in Kazakhstan was 292 euros (as of January 2007), it is not surprising that most of Internet users have been accessing the Internet at their workplaces.

This situation improved with the partial liberalization of the telecom sector (Kazakh Telecom retains a near-monopoly position). However, the government studiously resists attempts by foreign firms to enter its market. Kazakh Telecom introduced the Megaline Wi-Fi service to Astana and Almaty.

Although its efforts have been tentative, Kazakhstan has by far the best-developed e-government system in Central Asia; it initiated Internet-based governance as part of a broader set of modernizing reforms of the public sector (Knox, 2008; Bhuiyan, 2010; Bhuiyan and Amagoh, 2011). In 2003, it passed several laws pertaining to property rights in cyberspace, including digital signatures. It also created a national database on "legal persons," entities defined by law with business identification numbers. The state floated the first formal conception for e-government in 2001, Programme on Formation and Development of National Information Infrastructure for 2001–03, which led to two e-government programs for 2005–07 and 2008–10. The Ministry of Transport and Communications created the Agency for Informatization and Communications to oversee the implementation of e-government initiatives. The state has labored to create cross-agency intranets and a national identification card.

In 2006, the Kazakh government launched a web portal (www.e.gov.kz) that offers 900 services digitally in Kazakh, Russian, and English, including a broad array of applications for permits, licenses (e.g., for businesses), and pensions; certificates (e.g., birth, marriage, divorce, unemployment, disability, military service, and occupational specialization); fee, utility, and penalty payments; credit histories; educational enrollment documents; job matching; real estate services; and telemedicine consultation opportunities. Of services available, 17 could be accessed by smartphones and 2 by SMS. By the end of 2014, it had 2.6 million registered users, roughly one-quarter of the adult population. The Kazakh Parliament maintains a website (www.parlam.kz) that publishes information on legislation and its activities. Electronic workflows and digital signatures have been implemented in 39 state agencies. Most state websites offer little to no interactivity (Johnson and Kolko, 2010). Numerous Russian language websites and search engines exist, sometimes comprising the vast majority, which gives a significant advantage to the Russian minority and limits Internet access for non-Russian speakers. Freedom House (2011), for example, found that 94% of Kazakh websites were in Russian. Because local language websites are underdeveloped, many users see the Internet as a means of accessing foreign material but of limited use in obtaining information about local events.

Most Kazakh e-government consists of little more than webpages and downloadable forms. Electronic payment of taxes and e-licensing has proved popular with the business community, and over 80% of firms do so electronically (Beklemishev, 2008). It also introduced a touch-screen e-voting system called Sailau ("automated information system"), which uses the national identification smart cards, and was used in parliamentary elections in 2005 and 2007 and in presidential elections in 2005. Sailau does not leave a paper trail, and given the Kazakh government's corruption and highly authoritarian nature, abuse of e-voting is quite possible if not likely. In 2008, Seoul and Astana signed a memorandum of understanding for exchanging experiences and strengthening cooperation related to e-government, which allows Kazakhstan to import Korean consulting services in building the government intranet. With assistance from South Korea, the postal system, KazPost, is modernizing its logistics using information technology.

E-commerce in Kazakhstan is in its infancy, but the government has studiously encouraged it. It began electronic licensing of firms in 2013. The state also initiated an electronic procurement website, http://goszakup.gov.kz and an e-license portal, http://elicense.kz, which by 2015 had issued 30,000 corporate licenses. One result was that the time needed to obtain a permit to start a construction business fell from 30 days to 15 minutes.

Optimists hold that e-government has the potential to reduce the country's endemic corruption by increasing transparency in procurement and licensing (Sheryazdanova et al., 2016). Thus, Bhuiyan (2010, p. 31) concludes the "Kazakh government has moved toward e-government paradigm to ascertain a people-centered, accountable and transparent government." However, such assertions fail to acknowledge how deeply entrenched the obstacles to reform are, including patronage and overstaffed, bloated bureaucracies fearful of change.

Education is a Kazakh success story in e-government. The state has taken tentative steps toward adopting distance learning in the schools (Nurgaliyeva and Artykbayeva, 2011) and a national electronic library (http://www.kazneb.kz). Roughly, 34 universities offer classes online, and they formed a research network called KazRENA in 2003. With UNESCO funds, the National Center of Information created distance education modules for secondary schools in remote areas, although most schools do not have broadband access.

At the local level, almost all *akimats* (city governments) have created virtual reception rooms—by state mandate—that allow visitors to search for various officials. Most of the largest cities started online vehicle registrations and payments of fines and fees.

To ameliorate the digital divide, the government undertook several steps, including the bluntly named Programme for Bridging Digital Divide in 2007–09. The government subsidizes computers for low-income families. A program launched in 2007 called Integrated System for Citizen Service Centers created 460 one stop shops available in 16 cities (Beklemishev, 2012; Janenova and Kim, 2016). It also created 270 mobile service centers in rural areas (Ulman et al., 2016). These allow applications for social services, approvals for international trade in pharmaceuticals, and legal letters of property ownership; the time required for the latter dropped from 3 days to 30min.

The obstacles to Kazakh e-government are many, obvious, and varied (Tleuberdinova and Britskaya, 2013). Many residents are too poor to own a personal computer and must turn to cybercafes and telecenters. Electricity supplies are unreliable. Rampant government corruption is widespread and funds are not often spent efficiently. Restrictive roles for women in deeply Muslim states curtail their participation.

The Kazakh government routinely engages in Internet censorship. The state mandates that all websites with the.kz domain name must be physically located in the country. In 2001, it enacted Draconian legislation that deemed all Internet communications to be "mass media," all bloggers were to be considered journalists, and negative information about the government or that which promoted ethnic conflict was banned (Lambroschini, 2011). ISPs must retain electronic records of the Internet activities of clients and are prohibited from posting material deemed pornographic or amenable to terrorism as well as information about the president's private life, health, and financial affairs. A journalist from the news website kub.kz, Kazis Toguzbayev, was given a 2-year prison sentence in 2008 for posting an article accusing the regime of protecting the killers of opposition leader Altynbek Sarsenbayev. In 2003, it created a new agency to police the Internet, the Kazakh Agency for Information Technology and Communications. The state regularly bars media coverage of political upheaval in neighboring states. It encouraged government officials to create their own personal blogs but has not been above arresting Internet activists such as Zhanna Baytelova and Irina Mednikova, who protested Kazakh Telecom's blocking of the opposition websites LiveJournal and Respublika (Freedom House, 2011). Finally, the Ministry of Internal Affairs created "Department K" to prosecute cybercrimes and cyberattacks. Websites of opposition groups are routinely blocked.

6.2 Uzbekistan: e-government in the Land of White Gold

About 32 million people inhabit Uzbekistan, where many of the classical cities of the Silk Road are to be found (Tashkent, Samarkand, Bukhara). With an economy centered largely on agriculture—it is one of the world's largest producers of cotton ("white gold"); it is also rich in mineral wealth. The country enjoys an extremely high rate of literacy, essentially universal. Since throwing off the Soviet yoke, the country has gradually liberalized several sectors.

The country's telecommunications infrastructure largely dates to the Soviet era. In the 1990s, foreign donors such as USAID and the Open Society Institute began providing the country with IT equipment. UzbekTelecom retains a legal monopoly status even after it was privatized. Since 2002, this situation has gradually improved as the government devotes resources to encouraging its growth, with capacity rising and prices falling. In 2005 the Asian Development Bank extended a $30 million loan to integrate the Internet into the school system. The government's Program for Computerisation and Informatisation is gradually replacing copper wire lines with fiber optic cables, using grants from the Japanese and Chinese governments (Zaynuddin, 2008). More than 52% of the population uses the Uzbek Internet, or "Uznet"; 73% of Uznetizens are concentrated in Tashkent. However, a significant gender gap remains: in Uzbekistan, two-thirds of Uznetizens are male (Wei and Kolko, 2005). Its 2015 e-government readiness score was a respectable 0.5217 and e-participation stood at 0.2368. Like most Central Asian countries, mobile phones are popular with Uzbekis, as more than three-quarters of the population owns one.

Uzbekistan has taken several steps toward a legislative framework for e-government, although it could be improved, such as copyright protection and freedom of information laws. It adopted an electronic signature law in 2003, and opened three Digital Registration Centers, an electronic commerce law in 2004, and an electronic payments law in 2005, which led to its first online purchasing system in 2007. The State Committee for Communications and Information and Telecommunication Technologies is responsible for implementing IT policies. Since 2012 the government announced several initiatives, including ICT Infrastructure Development Program 2015–2019 (nine projects) and the E-Government Development Program 2013–2020 overseen by the Ministry for Development of Information Technologies and Communications.

In 2015, Uzbekistan launched an Open Data Portal, gov.uz, where the government uploaded 709 data sets on 15 subject areas. It allows for the standard suite of popular services, including birth, marriage, and death certificates; applications for welfare services, passports, and drivers' licenses; job searches; and applications to enter universities. In the domain of government-to-business relations, it offers online applications for permits and documents, payments of income and VAT taxes, and some types of procurements. A mobile version (m.gov.uz) offers contact information for government officials and payments of vehicle traffic violation fines.

The number of government services offered online has increased steadily from 49 in 2007 to roughly 600 in 2015. In the domain of education, the portal eduportal. uz promotes best practices in Uzbek and Russian. The portal ZiyoNET accesses a national online library. The state automated its national property register to allow online use of cadastral systems (Samborsky and Popiv, 2015). To promote health care in rural areas, the state established three telemedicine projects and two e-referral projects, one led by the Swinfen Charitable Trust and the other by NATO (Doarn et al., 2005). The government also set up a social networking site through which it can monitor users and draw them away from Facebook.

Uzbeki e-government faces severe obstacles. Entrenched bureaucracies view it with great distrust, in part because it may challenge endemic corruption there (Rakhmanov, 2009). The digital divide remains severe, and rural areas are hardly ever web connected. Leadership on the issue has been fragmented and haphazard, and financing inconsistent.

The Uzbek government's controls over the Internet have become increasingly severe (Kozhamberdiyeva, 2008; Kendzior, 2010). Despite the government's alleged adherence to democratic ideals, control of the digital press is prevalent. ISP providers must operate under the government's web filter, Uzpak, which monitors all Internet traffic in the country. Cybercafe owners are obligated to check their customers' web-browsing habits and report on disagreeable searches. The state often shuts down uzbekistanerk.org and birlik.net, the websites belonging to the largest opposition parties. It has also moved against Islamicist websites protesting the treatment of Muslims in the country. In 2007 the government required all blogs and websites to register with the authorities. Invoking an older Soviet tradition, Uzbek Internet journalists who publish criticisms of the government are occasionally forced into psychiatric hospitals. The Uzbek "For a Free Internet!" campaign, for example, has monitored bills in the lower house of parliament, the Mazhlis, which attempt to extend the government's censorship. In 2007, Alisher Saipov, a vocal critic of Uzbek Internet censorship, aged 26, was gunned down, a political assassination that followed weeks of scathing online attacks on his character by the Karimov administration (Kendzior, 2010). However, the regime appears to have gradually liberalized its restrictions on the use of ICT in the hopes of obtaining more foreign aid. An outspoken diaspora of exiled Uzbek dissidents has constructed dozens of websites commenting on the country's political affairs, such as ferghana.ru. Many Uzbeks access these through proxy servers. Such events highlight the Internet's role as a contested political space through which political discourse is mobilized to serve competing ends.

6.3 Tajikistan: how not to do e-government

With 8.5 million people, Tajikistan is an impoverished, mountainous country run by a despotic regime. It was the least developed of the former Soviet republics. Its economy relies heavily on cotton and aluminum production, and remittances from its diasporic population. However, it enjoys essentially universal literacy. The Tajik majority lives alongside an Uzbek minority. It suffered a 5-year long civil war during 1992–97.

The country's telecommunications infrastructure is very poorly developed. The country is not connected to the Trans-Asia-Europe Fibre Optical Cable System. Most Internet connections use very small aperture terminal (VSAT) technology (Ibodova and Atoev, 2008). The country's e-government score was a surprisingly high 0.4069, but its e-participation data were so low they could not be measured. Internet penetration was a lowly 19%.

The government announced its National Program of Communications Development in the mid-1990s. Gradual improvements followed in the wake of the liberalization of the state monopoly, Tajiktelecom in 2004. Most of the telecommunications infrastructure has been funded by foreign donors, including the World Bank and the Asian Development Bank. Plans call to install a fiber link along the gas pipeline to China. The privatization of the Tajik operator Tochiktelecom began in 2003 but has not advanced much since then. Internet penetration in 2016 was an abysmal 19.5%, with almost all users concentrated in the capital, Dushanbe. A network of 400 Internet cafes forms the dominant points of entry into cyberspace; the average café costs $US0.73 per hour, compared to the national minimum salary of $US7.00 per month. Its e-government score was 0.4069. Nonetheless, mobile phone usage is almost universal in the country (95%). Fixed broadband essentially does not exist, although some providers offer 3G mobile broadband.

E-government programs are almost nonexistent with formal consideration beginning only in 2011. As Ibodova and Atoev (2008, p. 185) note, "State authority bodies, ignorant of ICTs, make employees use outdated technologies or use a computer simply as a typewriter. Tajik officials visited Kazakhstan to learn about its successes." A state intranet links the civil service and the president's office. Most state agencies have their own webpages. The government first used video conferencing services in 2011. The Customs Department has begun to move toward online registration of imports and exports. In 2016, it signed an agreement with the World Bank to fund a financial management modernization project.

The country's digital divide is manifested in a sharp division between low lying and mountainous areas. Like many IT initiatives in Central Asia, Tajikistan relies heavily on foreign donors to bridge its digital divide. The U.S. State Department initiated Global Connections program there in 2003 to bring 26 Internet Learning Centers, each with roughly 10 computers, to high schools in remote mountainous areas. These encountered formidable obstacles such as insufficient supplies of electricity.

Like all dictatorships, the Tajik government heavily censors the Internet (Shafiev and Miles, 2015). It has blocked access to Facebook and YouTube numerous times. The Tajik government's attempts to criminalize some forms of cyberspeech as libel against the state were met with heated opposition led by Nuriddin Qarshiboev, Head of the National Association for Independent Media in Tajikistan. Moreover, Tajik cyberjournalists petitioned the government to abolish the requirement that the president be called "worthy" and "reliable" everytime he was mentioned. More recently, those seeking to avoid government censorship can download software designed to help them do so, such as the Canadian "censorship circumvention" program Psiphon.

6.4   Turkmenistan: "the Internet is about as familiar as a flying saucer"

With 5.5 million people, Turkmenistan is another destitute, landlocked country, a closed, corrupt, police state. Largely a desert nation, it relies heavily on natural gas, oil, and cotton production. About half the population lives in rural areas. However, the country enjoys universal literacy.

Turkmenistan had an Internet penetration rate in 2016 of only 14.9%, the lowest in Central Asia (almost as low as war-torn Afghanistan); its e-government score was 0.3813, but like Tajikistan, its e-participation was unmeasurable; oddly, it has the highest rate of mobile phone usage, 135%. As the International Crisis Group put it, "to most people in Turkmenistan, the internet is about as familiar as a flying saucer" (quoted in Ó Beacháin, 2010, p. 232). Almost all (95%) netizens are concentrated in the capital city, Ashgabat (OpenNet Initiative, 2010c). Its e-government readiness score was 0.3813, lowest in the region save for Afghanistan. In 2001, following a brief window of privatization that opened with independence in 1991, Turkmenistan granted a monopoly over data services to TurkmenTelecom, driving smaller ISPs out of business. TurkmenTelecom operates 15 cafes in the country (OpenNet Initiative, 2010c). Sartor (2010, pp. 33–34) writes

> *Less than ten Internet cafes exist in Ashgabat, Turkmenistan's capital city; they are small, dimly lit, cramped spaces, with few workstations. Only the US Embassy offers Internet access free of charge via the Information Resource Center (IRC) in its Public Affairs Office.*

Prices in these cafes in 2012 averaged $US4 per hour (compared to an average income of $US100 per month), although after President Berdymukhamedov reprimanded the minister of communications for such high charges they dropped to $US2 per hour. These prices are twice those in neighboring Kazakhstan. In 2008, TurkmenTelecom began to offer dial-up home access, but at such high prices it is unaffordable to most residents. In 2012, a Turkmen-language social platform, e-Dostluk ("online friendship") was founded that allowed mobile Internet access; users can send free SMS messages worldwide.

Although Turkmenistan has a national strategy to introduce information technology into government circles, it lacks the political will to move it beyond the planning stages (Orazbayev, 2012). In 2010, it established the commission for ICT Development. However, actual e-government programs essentially do not exist.

Turkmenistan does, however, make the effort to exert extensive control over the Web; indeed, it is one of the world's worst Internet censors. This process accelerated markedly after the forced closure of its only two independent newspapers in 1992. The former dictator, Saparmurat Niyazov, another of Reporters Without Borders's ardent "enemies of the Internet," strove to keep the country hermetically sealed from the outside world via a national intranet. His successor, Gurbanguly Berdymukhammedov, vowed to open it up to the global Internet; this promise was belied, however, by the presence of government soldiers at the doors of Internet cafes (Eurasianet.org, 2009) and government surveillance of all ISPs using deep packet inspection techniques. The government purchased spyware from a British–German company, Gamma International, which installs malware on users computers and mobile phones. Cybercafes in which customers attempt to access banned websites are routinely closed. As Reporters Without Borders (n.d.) notes, "Opposition websites such as XpoHo.tm and Gundogar, and regional news sites covering Central Asia such as ferghana.ru and eurasianet, are blocked." On December 20, 2014, President Berdymukhammedov signed into law the statute "On the Legal Regulation of the Development of the Internet and Internet Services in Turkmenistan," ostensibly on the grounds of protecting the country against "socially dangerous acts."

6.5 Kyrgyzstan: e-government in the Switzerland of Central Asia

With six million people, Kyrgyzstan is a mountainous, largely rural country. Its agricultural economy produces cotton and tobacco and little else. Two-thirds of the population lives in deep poverty. In addition to the Kyrgyz majority, there are minorities of Uzbeks, Kazakhs, and Russians. While not as dictatorial as some of its neighbors, the state is plagued by corruption and nepotism. Literacy, however, is nearly universal.

Kyrgyzstan has entered the information age in fits and starts. Internet penetration in 2016 was 36% but growing rapidly; 77% of Internet users are located in Bishkek. Online gaming is so popular that the government threatened to shut down cybercafes during school hours. Its e-government score was a remarkably high 0.4879, and e-participation was rated 0.2895. Low though its penetration rate may be, the Internet and social media played an instrumental role in the Tulip Revolution of 2005 that led to the ousting of President Askar Akayev.

Much of Kyrgyzstan's information technology infrastructure was funded and/or built by foreign donors, USAID, and nongovernmental organizations such as the Soros Foundation. Internet service is provided by roughly 38 private ISPs and the state-owned monopoly Kyrgyztelecom, although most must lease capacity on state-owned lines from Kyrgyz Telecom. Alternative operators include Saima Telecom and WinLine. The Kyrgyz government has gradually liberalized its telecommunications sector, which improved the affordability of Internet access there. However, as the OpenNet Initiative (2010a) points out, "Kyrgyzstan is an effectively cyberlocked country dependent on purchasing bandwidth from Kazakhstan and Russia."

The country adopted its first IT plan in 1995 and its first telecommunications legislation in 1998. The state issued a series of policy documents and action plans promoting e-government. Implementation is the domain of the Department of Informatization within the Ministry of Transport and Communications, which lacks its own budget. It did create the Information System of Public Administration. Financial assistance was provided by the U.N. Development Program, World Bank, and Asian Development Bank (Baimyrzaeva, 2011). In 1994, it adopted laws on electronic payments and in 2004, one on electronic signatures (Brimkulov and Baryktabasov,

2014). As in many countries where the e-government rhetoric exceeds the reality, Kyrgyzstan has announced ambitious plans, including a program called "Digital Kyrgyzstan 2020–2025." Kyrgyz steps toward e-government include electronic document transfers among government offices, online budgets for the Treasury Department to enhance transparency, online bookkeeping for various ministries, and an automated state registry of the population.

The Kyrgyz government launched a portal for e-services in 2003, www.gov.kg, including municipal services, which primarily only offers information and links to agencies. Services are offered in Kyrgyz and Russian. As Johnston and Kolko (2010, p. 36) note about the government portal, "the content of Kyrgyzstan's national-level site is more oriented toward the international development community than the indigenous population." Subsequently, almost all agencies and ministries developed their own sites. Few offer opportunities for feedback or access to data. Some allow payments of taxes and applications for the widely used personal identification number, and the state procurement website allows electronic tenders. The state also developed a separate website to report corruption (http://www.aks.kg, http://anticorr.gov.kg). However, Ismailova (2015) found frequent errors and security vulnerabilities in its government websites. Brimkulov and Baryktabasov (2014) note that corruption, incompetence, and the resistance of bureaucrats to more effective webpages played a role in hampering development there.

Kyrgyzstan has struggled to combat its digital divide by relying on foreign donors. The first steps included a series of seven e-centers in rural areas funded by the USAID Last Mile initiative in 2006. Each is staffed by three or four people. IREX Kyrgyzstan followed suit by funding 16 free Internet Access and Training Program Centers in 2008. Similarly, UNESCO created 12 Internet Access Centers. The most recent effort is the e-Ayil project, which promotes rural Internet access (Dzhusupova, 2013). Using funds from the Agency for International Development, the government created a small network of 150 subsidized, free access telecenters, including commercial cybercafes (Best et al., 2009; OpenNet Initiative, 2010b; Mambetalieva and Shramko, 2008). However, most are not financially self-sustaining. USAID sponsored a series of 30 for-profit telecenters. A NATO-funded project brought the Internet to some public schools, libraries, and hospitals, using satellites. Finally, the state established a series of 18 access centers in post offices. The majority of users of such centers are young males. Many of these offer training in computer literacy and some offer a unique service called "web cassa," in which users download credit units to their mobile phone. However, such efforts in rural areas often suffer from a lack of reliable electricity supply.

McGlinchey and Johnson (2007) argue that because Kyrgyzstan relies heavily on foreign donors and NGOs, it is less prone to censor the media, including the Internet. But censor it does. During the 2005 parliamentary elections, the government of Kyrgyzstan launched "just-in-time" distributed denial-of-service cyberattacks against opposition party websites, and the government closed Internet connections to neighboring countries (Schwartz, 2005). The Kyrgyz government's botnet used to launch the attacks also affected servers in the United States, whose protests then forced the attacks to cease. Despite its severe control over nondigital media, Kyrgyz cyberspace is relatively deregulated and the government has relatively straightforward rules governing Internet access, which may reflect its reliance on foreign aid organizations (McGlinchey and Johnson, 2007; Srinivasan and Fish, 2009). Kyrgyz bloggers often see themselves as actively creating a new sphere of civil society through online forums such as Diesel and AkiPress (Srinivasan and Fish, 2009).

6.6 Afghanistan: can e-government exist in the Graveyard of Empires?

Can there be any place more sad than Afghanistan? Mired in extreme poverty, it has suffered constant warfare for three decades following the Soviet invasion of 1989, the US invasion of 2003, and an ongoing insurgency from the Taliban and the Islamic State. The population of 33 million is multiethnic, consisting of Pashtuns, Hazaras, Uzbeks, and Tajiks. Its economy, such as it is, is grounded in opium production and foreign aid. Besides poverty and widespread illiteracy, it suffers from crushing, extreme, debilitating corruption. With good reason, few Afghanis trust the state, which impedes the adoption of e-government.

In Afghanistan, Internet usage only began in 2002 following the ouster of the Taliban, which held that the Web allowed foreign and anti-Islamic obscenities to enter the country. Its country domain name.af went live in 2003. The landline telephone system is poorly developed, although three-quarters of the population has access to a mobile phone. There is no national power grid. In 2006, the state awarded ZTE Corporation with the contract to lay down a national fiber optic backbone that connects all 34 provinces. Internet penetration in 2016 was a mere 12%, but growing explosively. The small population of Afghani netizens is concentrated in Kabul, Jalalabad, and Khost. Cybercafés are essentially confined to the airport in Kabul and a few luxury hotels. Its e-government readiness score was an abysmal 0.1701, but e-participation was a surprisingly high 0.1316, higher than Bangladesh, Nepal, or Vietnam. There are six major telecommunications service providers. Many companies and bases with foreign troops have their own VSAT capacities.

Kabul, the capital, is by far the best connected place in the country. As the Intelligent Community Forum (2016) notes, "Using funds from development agencies and the US government, this war-torn capital of Afghanistan has built a telecom-based foundation for government by linking ministries with district offices and military bases throughout the country while expanding mobile service nationwide from 0.01% to 6% in three years." Kabul University has partnered with American colleges for e-learning programs.

Engulfed by violence though it may be, Afghanistan has taken tentative steps toward e-government. The National Information and Communications Technology Council has a mandate to provide advisory services to the government in matters related to information technology. With the support of the World Bank and USAID, the Ministry of Communications and Information Technology (MCIT) developed an e-government directorate, an e-government resource center, and plans for a national data center, a national smart identification card, electronic documents, online vehicle registration, and public kiosks (Khan et al., 2012). Roughly, 120 government ministries have websites. MCIT also developed a road map to put 70% of government services online by 2018 (http://mcit.gov.af/en). Kabul developed video teleconferencing capacities with all provincial governors. As Aziz (2012, p. 98) notes, "The World Bank invested USD 16.8 million to develop the government communications network (GCN) and another USD 3.7 million to rehabilitate the International Satellite Gateway in Kabul." The state established "Management Information for Natural Disasters" centers in Kabul and Kunduz to provide information and guide rescue operations during crises such as earthquakes. Some schools in Jalalabad, Kunar, and Bamiyan provinces have been connected to the Internet. The state also released a mobile phone application that allows farmers to check crop prices.

These projects face serious obstacles. Financial resources for such efforts are inadequate. Highly restrictive Muslim gender roles prohibit many women from taken advantage of information technology. Moreover, the state faces serious problems with cybersecurity, including vulnerability to hacking, viruses, and malware.

Little is known about how Afghanis feel about e-government, largely because so few of them use it. Anwer et al. (2016) suggest that citizen satisfaction with government webpages is shaped by how user-friendly they are and the quality of information provided, but that the social factors that determine the Afghani digital divide play a considerable role.

Even the digital divide in Afghanistan is improving. For example, Cisco created six Cisco centers and 31 ICT training centers across the country. The firm Roshan has developed and offers a General Radio Packet System that allows users to plug their laptops into cell phones, establishing Internet connectivity (Aziz, 2012).

In sum, in an impoverished country with a severe, protracted civil conflict, it is a wonder that Afghanistan has anything at all that could remotely be called e-government. The rhetoric has far surpassed the reality, however, and mostly the country's vision of a wired state suited to the information age remains a distant mirage. Nor is this likely to improve soon: e-government is not a panacea but is deeply embedded in local political contexts. Until there is peace, stability, reliable electricity, and lower rates of corruption in Afghanistan, e-government will not flourish there.

6.7 Mongolia: nomads in yurts adopt e-government in the Land of the Blue Sky

Sandwiched between Russia and China, and long a client state of the former, Mongolia has a rich historical heritage but is a poor country today. A small country of three million people, one-third of whom are nomads, it consists largely of windswept steppes and is the least densely populated nation on earth. The economy largely revolves around agriculture, livestock herding, and mineral wealth. As in most post-Soviet dominated countries, literacy is nearly universal.

However, Mongolia is surprisingly well prepared in terms of information technology. Internet penetration in 2016 was 49%, and the majority of netizens were located in the capital Ulaanbaatar, which also hosts 60 cybercafes. The e-government readiness score was 0.5443, second in Central Asia only to Kazakhstan, and e-participation was 0.6053, the highest in the region. There are more mobile phones in Mongolia than people, with a penetration rate of 105%. Healthy competition in the telecom sector coupled with generous tax breaks has made broadband widely available, even among nomads. Indeed, most people rely on mobile phones for Internet access. Nine ISPs service the country. A fiber network connects the urban centers, and many people and agencies rely on both wireless loop technology and satellite Internet. Various foreign donor organizations, including the United Nations Development Programme, the Soros Foundation, the Asian Development Bank, the World Bank, and the Japanese International Cooperation Agency, have bankrolled other IT projects.

The Mongolian state has edged toward a legal and regulatory framework for e-government in several steps (Ulziikhutag, 2011). In 1995, it sold 40% of Mongol Telecom to Korea Telecom, inviting badly needed foreign investment. In 1997, it initiated work on a Government Information Network LAN to connect 27 agencies, enabling electronic document exchanges. In 2001 the national ITC Council (renamed the Mongolian Information Development Association) established the Mongolian Information Development Application Scheme (MIDAS). The same year it also created the Mongolian Internet Exchange Point to facilitate content transfer among ISPs and passed a telecommunications law that coordinated actions among the state, private organizations, and citizens in the formation of networks. It also passed patent and copyright laws. In 2004, it created a national Information and Communications Agency and in 2005, launched the e-Mongolia program to encourage IT adoption and an e-government master plan. In 2009, the prime minister created and chaired the government's Information and Communications Technology Agency (ICTA), through which several e-government services are now available. Part of the initiative was a commitment to provide free or low-cost Internet access to *gers* (yurt communities) and *soums* (villages). In 2011, the Mongolian parliament passed the Law on Information Transparency and Right to Information, a road map that outlined priorities and strategies. With $20 million in assistance from the World Bank, it adopted a smart government program to enhance the efficiency, accessibility, and transparency of government services. However, the state has not made much progress in other areas, such as a digital signatures law.

E-government initiatives there have taken different forms (Sambuu et al., 2008). The national state website (http://www.pmis.gov.mn) connects to 40 government agencies, which have their own websites. In 2001 the prime minister initiated an "open government" website (http://www.open-government.mn) supported by USAID and the Asia Foundation that allows public comments on proposed legislation and to contact officials. The Joomla project used open source software to facilitate web content management. The Ministry of Education has a system that offers online registration and posts the results of university examinations, which is visited 1500 times daily during the exam period. In 2013, it imported the South Korean e-procurement system. The state created a national smart ID card with biometric facial and fingerprint recognition linked to a secure database accessible to the tax, customs, passport, and military agencies. In 2014, it started a tax e-payment system now used by 520,000 taxpayers.

In coordination with private entities, Mongolia has tried to expand Internet access (Naughton and Ullman, 2012). The center of Ulaanbaatar has a Technology Park, funded in 2003 by the government of South Korea, which offers free Wi-Fi. The Soros Foundation opened a telecenter on the campus of Mongolian National University. In 2005, Khan Bank, one of the largest in the country, established 13 Citizens Information Service Centers (CISC) in Ulaanbaatar as well as remote areas using a public–private partnership model. Six of the 21 *aimags* (provinces) are equipped to allow nomadic rural populations to receive Internet access. The Asian Development Bank provided $1 million in funding to promote Internet service in rural areas. Most schools, post offices, and some of the 357 public libraries provide Internet access. Two free public access centers in the capitol serve visually impaired users. For people in remote areas, mobile access is the only option. Gender does not seem to be an impediment to Mongolian women's Internet participation.

In such a sparsely populated country, it is perhaps unremarkable that Mongolia has turned to the Internet to deliver health services. Telemedicine was introduced to Mongolia in 2007 by a project funded by the government of Luxembourg, which worked with the Ministry of Health to develop an e-health strategy. For example, teledetection of early pregnancies has helped to reduce the neonatal mortality rate in rural areas (Baatar et al., 2012). Parallel systems offer teledermatology and telegynecology services. Similarly, the Health Sciences University in Ulaanbaatar established several distance diagnosis centers using low-bandwidth Internet (Amarsaikhan et al., 2007).

While Mongolia has taken aggressive steps to address its digital divide, severe obstacles remain. Computer literacy is not widespread. With one-third of the population in poverty, many cannot afford Internet access. Content in Mongol is in short supply, although growing. Many donor-funded telecenters are not financially viable once the funding expires.

As a relatively stable, egalitarian democracy, Mongolia does not practice heavy Internet censorship, although it did pass the law entitled General Conditions and Requirements on Digital Content, which restricts pornography, poorly defined, and requires popular websites to make their users' IP addresses publicly visible.

6.8 Conclusion

E-government in Central Asia is the least developed on the continent, with the exception of North Korea. Most are autocratic governments struggling to come to terms with the realities of the digital world, notably the capacity of the Internet to offer access to information outside of state control. The fact that dictatorships can successfully implement e-government raises serious questions about the inherently democratizing impulses of Internet-based governance (Johnson and Kolko, 2016). After all, it is agencies within such states that determine what information is presented, without much concern for conceptual diversity. Mongolia is an exception to this trend, a functioning democracy that has made earnest efforts to utilize information technology to enhance transparency and efficiency.

Conclusions

7

As the Internet winds its way ever more deeply into Asian societies, it is clear that it is having enormous impacts not only on commerce and everyday life but also on how governments interact with their citizens, businesses, and one another. Massive networks of fiber optic cables have been laid across most Asian countries, greatly enhancing Internet access and giving billions the opportunity to use broadband services. More than 1.8 billion Asians used the Internet in 2016, roughly one-half of the world's netizens. Penetration rates vary enormously, from essentially zero in the case of North Korea to more than 92% in South Korea, among the highest in the world. All of the continent's governments have, to one extent or another, attempted to harness the power of this medium.

Touting utopian discourses of the "information society," many states envision an idealized Internet-based future (e.g., e-Japan, e-Bangladesh, e-Sri Lanka, e-Mongolia) in which they become productive members of the global economy. Most governments have toyed with legislation to enable e-government, including the protection of intellectual property and electronic signatures. Often the hyperbole surrounding such ventures exceeds the reality. In poor, largely agricultural societies, the notion of catapulting directly into a globalized, service-based country is laughable. That is not say that e-government does not hold promise for the impoverished masses. Yet one must observe that discourses of e-government may serve to legitimize tyrannical administrations in the eyes of foreign donors or the World Bank, and sometimes have few substantive impacts. It is essential to view this issue with a critical eye.

7.1 Many countries, many models

By now it is obvious that Asia exhibits a wide variety of models of e-government. E-government readiness scores range from a low of 0.17 in Afghanistan to 0.93 in South Korea. Some states, such as in Japan, South Korea, Taiwan, and Singapore, have made life considerably more convenient, safer, and cleaner for their citizens. In China, top-down e-government serves to legitimize the rule of the communist party and promote economic growth. In the Philippines, texting is the basis of the state's electronic interactions with citizens. In India, the primary concern has been combating rural poverty through telecenters. In other states, notably corrupt dictatorships (e.g., North Korea, Tajikistan, Turkmenistan), e-government is in its infancy and unlikely to make much progress until the political context becomes more democratic.

In addition to differences among countries, the sophistication and effectiveness of e-government varies within them. Many Asian nations exhibit a rich array of provincial and metropolitan initiatives, including several "smart cities" (e.g., Yokohama, Seoul, and Chengdu). Many Asian cities have text messaging programs to alert citizens to

e-Government in Asia: Origins, Politics, Impacts, Geographies. http://dx.doi.org/10.1016/B978-0-08-100873-7.00007-6

disasters or epidemics. In Japan, these include tsunami and earthquake warning systems under the guidance of the national state. Seoul, with its SmartSeoul campaign, has perhaps the best municipal e-government system in the world, including digital agoras and ability to file digital complaints; free Wi-Fi; RFID tags to monitor the locations of children and people with Alzheimer's; smart work centers and smart homes; online viewing of public meetings; and smart payment systems and virtual stores. In China, the best municipal e-government is found in globalized city regions that tolerate diverse flows of information. China's leader, Shanghai, for example, developed various types of smart cards; a government data service portal; and online information on air quality (now ubiquitous across China). Similarly, the Digital Beijing program offers access to information about population, traffic, and civil service exams. Other provincial municipal programs include corporate incubators and research and technology parks (e.g., Kerala, Yokosuka, Hsinchu City, Beijing, Hong Kong's cyberport). Malaysia' Multimedia Super Corridor is perhaps the most spectacular example.

E-government should be understood in light of national cultures. For example, Singapore's corporatist, communitarian culture was essential to its success in e-government (Sriramesh and Rivera-Sanchez, 2006), where "any public services that can be delivered online must be digitized" (Ha and Coghill, 2006, p. 107). Malaysia's E-Syariah system caters to clients of the Muslim court system. Bangladesh and Pakistan offer websites that cater to people undertaking the *hajj* to Mecca. In Japan, the culture of *nigate-ishiki* (fear of embarrassment and uncertainty avoidance) hinders Internet adoption.

Clearly, e-government has a geography, one entwined with varying national trajectories of wealth, democracy, literacy, and cultural traits. Such spatial variations invite caution about simplistic "one-size-fits-all" models of e-government that fail to consider different national histories, cultures, and political environments. E-government reflects, even as it transforms, national and local contexts.

7.2   Successes and failures in Asia e-government

E-government succeeds or fails due to a range of factors in different national and local contexts. In countries where e-government succeeds, decisive and determined leadership, including the ability to overcome bureaucratic inertia, is a major factor (e.g., South Korea, Singapore, Hong Kong). The best e-government initiatives involve input from multiple stakeholders rather than top-down mandates and an awareness of local problems, cultures, and institutions. Singapore is perhaps the best example in this regard. Widespread public awareness campaigns are a necessity. South Korea and Brunei are examples of successful programs that informed the public about e-government in advance.

E-government is most likely to succeed in countries where citizens trust their government. Singapore is an excellent example. But in many countries this is difficult to do. In Japan, a culture of mistrust has inhibited initiatives. In China, widespread distrust of the state contributes to suspicion about e-government programs. Similar observations apply to Malaysia, Indonesia, and Afghanistan. Understandably, when corruption is rampant, few people have reasons to think that state programs are initiated with the best intentions in mind.

Factors that inhibit the successful adoption of e-government include low-Internet penetration rates, widespread poverty, illiteracy, insufficient funding, corruption, lack of reliable supplies of electricity, shortages of skilled personnel, low levels of computer literacy, and restrictive gender roles for women (e.g., India). In many Asian countries, most netizens, and thus most beneficiaries of e-government, are males. Lack of clear and consistent leadership is also a hindrance. Bureaucrats who fear e-government, or simply do not want to change their normal way of conducting business, have impeded programs in Japan, China, India, Bangladesh, Kazakhstan, Uzbekistan, and Kyrgyzstan. For some, it fosters fears they may lose their jobs; for others, that opportunities for bribe-taking will decline; and for yet others, a simple fear of change, especially of a technology with which they may be only marginally acquainted.

In many countries, web content in the vernacular is in short supply; the people who need e-government the most may not speak English or even the prevailing national tongue (e.g., Hindi, Urdu, or Bahasa). Obviously the extent and severity of these obstacles vary from country to country. But overcoming these barriers indicates that e-government must be seen as part of a broader strategy of social and economic development.

Overly conservative administrations and political cultures (e.g., Japan, China) often witness reluctance on the part of officials to depart from long-standing ways of doing governance. Turf battles and in-fighting among agencies certainly do not help, as in China and Malaysia. Countries with poor e-leadership generally exhibit unclear priorities and strategies, lack of stakeholder input, duplicated efforts, and high levels of corruption, such as Indonesia, Pakistan, the Philippines, and much of Central Asia.

Foreign donors often play a significant role in instigating e-government programs. The major actors in this regard include the United Nations Development Program, the World Bank, the Asia Development Bank, USAID, and nongovernmental organizations. Such organizations are particularly important in impoverished countries such as Uzbekistan, Tajikistan, and Kyrgyzstan, and may have forced those governments toward being more open and democratic. NGOs played a key role in India's telecenters programs (e.g., Gyandoot, the Sustainable Access in Rural India) and in Pakistan's TelMedPak, Bangladesh's telemedicine initiatives, Nepalese telecenters, and Indonesia's Digital Library Network. Conversely, donors and NGOs are largely absent from wealthy countries and China.

Inevitably, Asian e-government programs include their share of failures. Vietnam's Project 112 is a case in point, undone by corrupt administrators. Bangkok's smart card system did not work out due to poor security and unsystematic implementation. The Warana Wired Village Project, in India's Maharashtra state, collapsed due to lack of human capital, and the Gyandoot telecenters project fatally suffered from unreliable electricity supplies. Other telecenters failed due to a poor business model, lack of demand, and financial insolvency.

Resistance to e-government is not infrequent and not simply among officials with something to lose. In Japan, the Juki-Net program was fought ferociously, and successfully, by citizens and municipalities on grounds that it invaded privacy. In South

Korea, intense resistance to the Informatization Promotion Law of Public Affairs for E-government was also motivated by fears of loss of privacy. Resistance is most likely in well-educated societies concerned about civil liberties with a free media. In tyrannical states like China, Vietnam, and most of Central Asia, it is much more difficult to struggle against programs that residents may feel are overly intrusive. E-government thus does not necessarily foster democracy: on the contrary, it is democracy that enables good e-government.

7.3   The impacts of Asian e-government

What impacts has e-government had on Asian societies? In many cases, public web-pages do little more than offer information or downloadable forms. Many governments aim for one-stop-shop webpages that provide a broad array of services (e.g., India). Frequently, public webpages are not updated with sufficient regularity. Nonetheless, for the information-deprived, even these small measures can empower citizens.

In many cases, e-government allows for unprecedented citizen input. In South Korea, this includes the Blue House's *shinmoongo* system, municipal electronic bulletin boards, and interactive television sets. Seoul's digital "Appeal to City Mayor" program is a perfect example, and Taipei has a similar one. Singaporeans can voice their views anonymously at www.feedback.gov.sg. In some Chinese cities, police departments operate microblogs that allow feedback, although in general the Chinese state cares little about what its citizens think. In India, filing grievances and complaints through telecenters is one of their most popular applications. In such cases, it is likely that e-government is leading national and local governments to be more transparent and responsive to the needs of their citizens. Beyond callous and uncaring states, in countries where Web 2.0 technology has not been widely adopted, e-government remains a one way flow from the state to its citizens.

One significant impact of e-government has been an across-the-board assault on corruption (Andersen, 2009; Bertot et al., 2010; Kim et al., 2009; Neupane et al., 2014). Combatting corruption is frequently listed as an incentive for the state to adopt the Internet (e.g., China, Bangladesh), and e-government has been touted as reducing corruption in South Korea (Cho and Choi, 2005; Iqbal and Seo, 2008), Bangladesh (Knox, 2009; Mahmood, 2010; Rajon and Zaman, 2008), Indonesia (Luckman, 2013), India (Patak and Prasad, 2005), and Kazakhstan (Sheryazdanova et al., 2016). Web 2.0 systems allow citizen input and filing of complaints about police misbehavior and brutality. Not surprisingly, governments that are already the least corruption have been most effective in this regard. South Korea, as it often does, leads the way in this regard. Seoul's Online Procedures ENhancement (OPEN) for civil application is widely heralded as the very model of how e-government can reduce graft and bribery. India's Central Vigilance Commission, which engages in "e-shaming," is another meritorious example. At the local level, projects Bhoomi and Gyandoot, which cut out corrupt middlemen in the land registration process, have also improved governance. Corruption in public procurement and tenders of bids has also witnessed a decline (notably the Korea Online E-procurement

System, which has been exported worldwide). In China, e-government serves as a façade with which the state can pretend to combat corruption but in reality tolerate it to varying degrees, although it has hoped to diminish the role of informal ties, i.e., *guanxi*. In many countries, corruption is so deeply entrenched (e.g., Indonesia, Pakistan) that e-government has little chance of rectifying what is widely considered to be normal business practices, although some attempts are noteworthy, such as Indonesia's Lapor! website. Electronic identity cards, such as the Computer-aided Administration of Registration Department (CARD) system in Andhra Pradesh, can also reign in abuses by officials. Of course, in many countries bureaucrats resist e-government precisely because it reduces the chances for corruption and bribe-taking. Given that some Asian states have bloated public bureaucracies filled through patronage, reductions in staff, and opportunities for bribes are no doubt a good thing.

Across Asia, e-government has significantly reduced waiting times and trips to government offices. In Ningbo, China, the time needed to acquire *houkou* passes has dropped. In India, telecenters such as Bhoomi expedited the granting of land registration. Getting visas and passports has never been easier, notably in Vietnam, Cambodia, Myanmar, Malaysia, Singapore, and the Philippines. E-procurement has greatly reduced the time needed for firms to tender bids, receive contracts, and get paid, notably in South Korea, Hong Kong, Malaysia, the Philippines, Indonesia, Bangladesh, and Mongolia. Malaysia's e-Perolehan e-procurement program has garnered worldwide attention. Digitization of customs clearance expedites the growth of imports and exports. South Korea's Electronic Customs Clearing Service and China's Golden Customs project are cases in point. Online customs houses are also found in Thailand, Malaysia, Singapore, India, and Tajikistan. Reducing waiting times improves efficiency and productivity, accelerates product cycles, and implies that e-government is part of a broader process of time–space compression.

Online payment of taxes is an another positive impact of e-government. Singapore's Electronic Tax Filing is arguably the world's best. Tianjin residents can check their tax records online. Taiwan's model allows taxpayers to use blogs to share best practices. China's Golden Tax program reduced tax fraud and enhanced public revenues but tax evasion remains extremely widespread. Other countries that allow e-filing of taxes include South Korea, Hong Kong, Malaysia, Indonesia, Pakistan, Bangladesh, and Kazakhstan, and in Japan and the Philippines via mobile phones. India allows individuals to file e-taxes but requires firms to do so, and in many states property and vehicle taxes can be filed electronically through telecenters and kiosks.

E-government allows the electronic disbursement of public benefits of various sorts. In China, the government online program allows digital welfare payments. Shanghai allows residents to obtain numerous licenses, permits, and registrations online. Hong Kong delivers a wide variety of services electronically, ranging from marriage registration to drainage inspections. Taiwan's electronic government program offers 1500 services online. In Sri Lanka, e-pensions are disbursed digitally, as they are through some Indian telecenters. Many Asian governments have online job-matching sites.

E-government has made Asian societies safer. Residents in some Chinese cities can report crimes to the police via Twitter, blogs, or text messages, as do South Koreans through the "M-police" program. Filipinos and people in Hong Kong can report crimes and police misbehavior with SMS messages. In India, the IT police program allows crimes to be reported via e-mail, and eCOPS allows reports of police misconduct. India's iVillages program informs villages about an impending tsunami, and Malaysia's agriculture department warns farmers via SMS of impending floods.

E-government has improved transportation systems in Asia, including online vehicle registration and driver's license applications; online parking inspections and payment of fees and fines; and online purchases of bus and train tickets. Japan's Vehicle Information and Communication System provides drivers with real-time information about traffic congestion, accidents, parking, and weather. Hong Kong allows drivers to calculate the most efficient path through its route advisory system. Malaysia's Road Transport Department offers e-insurance and payment of the e-road tax. Filipinos can complain about polluting buses by text message.

Another significant impact has been in the area of education, including distance-learning and online libraries. For residents, especially children, living in remote rural areas, such measures can lead to an expanding of social and geographic horizons and the opening of numerous opportunities. In some cases, this process may be as basic as delivering the news. Distance-learning programs exist in Laos, Thailand, Indonesia, the Philippines, Pakistan, India, Bangladesh, and Kazakhstan. Some online education experiments, such as in Bangladesh, failed due to underpaid teachers and shortages of computer hardware. Distance learning is not simply a service for the rural poor, however, even in urban areas such as Tianjin and Shanghai, educational programs are offered over the web.

Using the Internet to monitor and promote health is another significant impact. Japan's various programs for the elderly are exceptional in this regard. For people in remote rural areas, access to medical advice and care is difficult to obtain. Fortunately, many Asian countries have initiated telemedicine projects that offer information, tele-consultations, and links to specialists via the Internet. In China, e-health measures include the Golden Health project and telemedicine networks run by the People's Liberation Army. Many Chinese cities (notably Shanghai and Beijing), and a few in Vietnam, offer digital alerts about air quality. Telehealth programs also exist in Thailand, Malaysia, the Philippines, India, Pakistan, Bangladesh, the Maldives, Uzbekistan, and Mongolia. In Cambodia, this takes the form of telediagnoses from digital camera mounted on motorcycles. Some countries have dabbled in telepsychiatry, teledermatology, and telegynecology. Some of these allow users to access services via their smartphones, and several governments have sent SMS messages to alert the public about epidemics such as SARS.

Smart cards of various sorts are another e-government by-product. These serve various purposes: as identification, to access government services, as a means of storing personal information, as a credit card, as a driver's license, and as a security measure. Some, such as Japan's Juki-Net, were viewed with great trepidation. China's Golden Card system was multipurpose in intent and design, while Shanghai developed a unique system of different cards for different groups of people. Thailand's smart card system collapsed due to poor design and administration, whereas Malaysia's Government Multi-Purpose Card succeeded reasonably. Other countries that have made attempts at government-issued smart cards include Laos, Bangladesh, and Kazakhstan.

As the use of the Internet by tyrannical states such as China, Vietnam, and most of Central Asia illustrates, e-government is not synonymous with democratization. In some countries, e-government seems more designed to serve officials than the public. Citizen input has certainly been enabled, as noted, but this is not the same as political freedom. Internet voting is still a rarity worldwide. In Asia, one example includes the e-voting system called Sailau in Kazakhstan. Singaporeans can register to vote over the web, while Bangalore has a get-out-the-vote program called Citizens Initiative. Indonesia's experimental Sistanas e-vote system never quite got off the ground.

7.4   E-government and Asian digital divides

Digital divides of varying types are a significant problem for e-government, which simultaneously reflects these social and spatial differences and offers a route to diminish such inequalities. The severity of digital divides in part reflects Internet penetration rates; countries with high rates of Internet access invariably have smaller and less serious divides. Conversely, those in which few people use the Internet often have the largest discrepancies. To the extent that the relatively well-educated and well-off use the Internet more than their poorer country cousins, e-government both reflects and amplifies social and spatial inequalities. Typically, digital divides are manifested in sharp dichotomies between urban and rural areas, and frequently netizens—and thus e-government beneficiaries—are concentrated in metropolitan areas.

The digital divide assumes different forms in different Asian nations. Japan has a "low tech underbelly" of underserved rural communities and Hokkaido. In Korea, it is essentially a "smart divide" based on broadband access. In China, it differentiates a well-connected and well-off coastal region from the country's interior; migrants from rural areas to cities who lack *hokou* permits are particularly vulnerable and have little access to the Internet. In Malaysia, it is manifested in the difference between the Western, peninsular part and the two provinces of Borneo, Sabah, and Sarawak, and in Indonesia in the schism between Java and the outer islands.

The list of Asian initiatives to reduce the digital divide is lengthy. Japan has its "Program for the Complete Dissolution of Geographical Digital Divide Areas," China its Village Access Project, Hong Kong has the Community Cyber Point project. Other examples include Malaysia's National Strategic Framework of Digital Divide, Singapore's Citizens Connect, Thailand's National Strategic Framework of Digital Divide, the Philippines's 700 e-centers, and Sri Lanka's Global Knowledge Centres program. In India it has been confronted with hundreds of telekiosks and various telecenter projects (Bhoomi, Akshaya, SARI, Simputer). Kazakhstan, Kyrgyzstan, and Afghanistan rely on foreign donors to do the job. Obviously the effectiveness of these phenomena varies greatly. In countries with low rates of literacy and computer literacy, they may have little meaningful impact without guidance and assistance. Electricity supplies are often problematic. In some countries, such as India, gender makes a difference: many women are not comfortable using telecenters staffed by men.

Mobile or cell phones are obviously one answer to the digital divide and give rise to so-called m-government. Most Asian countries have more mobile phones than people, although the rate of smartphone usage, i.e., those capable of Internet access, varies considerably. In some countries phones are the most common form of Internet access (e.g., Vietnam, Mongolia). The ability or willingness of Asian states to adapt e-government programs to smartphones also fluctuates widely. China has numerous smartphones but few e-government services through which they can be accessed. Obviously in some cases phones are critical to SMS interactions between the state and its citizens, notably the Philippines, the world's texting capital. Cities and countries that send text messages about epidemics, floods, or tsunami are another case in point. In Japan, smartphones are the basis of what is called "ubiquitous Japan." In Singapore, lawyers can appear in court via videophones. In several countries the state disseminates health information over the phone network (e.g., Pakistan). In Bangladesh, solar-powered phones are empowering people in remote areas who lack electricity, putting them in touch with their state representatives. Afghan farmers with smartphones can check crop prices, and pilot programs allow some with personal computers to obtain Internet access by connecting them to cell phones. Smartphones clearly represent the next stage in e-government, and their widespread use and popularity presages well for reducing the digital divide.

7.5   Asian Internet censorship and e-government

Although the Internet has long been touted as an emancipatory technology sure to bring democracy in its wake, the fact remains that many unsavory governments have adapted to it quite well. Unfortunately, Internet censorship is widespread in Asia and is an important, if often overlooked, dimension of e-government. Many governments— used to controlling the channels of information—are fearful of the Internet and its capacity to expose corruption, change public opinion, support unrest, and garner sympathy for marginalized groups and regions. Thus, governments engage in different practices, such as blocking websites, forcing owners of cybercafes to register clients and install censorship software, content filtering, and harassment of bloggers and cyberjournalists.

The type and severity of censorship obviously vary widely: in democratic states such as Japan, South Korea, and Taiwan censorship is nonexistent. Conversely, North Korea, where the Internet is confined to a tiny handful of elites, is Asia's—and the world's—worst offender in this regard. For sheer scale and scope of government limitation of people's access to information, China holds first place: its Great Firewall includes restrictions on Google and Yahoo!; filtering software; jamming of Gmail and Hotmail; monitors of websites, chat rooms, and cybercafes; and dismantling of blogs and harassment and imprisonment of bloggers. But China is caught in a dilemma, as is Vietnam; both need the Internet, and want e-government, but are fearful of unrestrained usage. It is also worth emphasizing that in dictatorships like China and Vietnam, self-censorship is widespread for understandable reasons.

Even many nominally democratic governments in Asia practice some degree of censorship, such as Thailand, Malaysia, Singapore, and Bangladesh. Blocking pornography, inciting violence, and combatting terrorism and cybercrime are commonly cited reasons. In countries such as India and Pakistan, websites promoting separatism are routinely blocked. Insulting the king is strictly forbidden in Thailand and Nepal. Central Asian countries, with the exception of Mongolia, routinely engage in strict censorship, including arrests of journalists.

Asian Internet censorship points to the deeply political nature of e-government. Aside from the office politics of resentful bureaucrats, the introduction of the Internet offers many people access to sources of information that are not state-sanctioned. Some countries, such as China, try to have it both ways, enjoying the efficiency and convenience of digital networks but without the freedom and opportunity they afford. In remains to be seen whether such states are forced to acknowledge their residents' civil liberties, or if they can persist in tightening their grip over the Internet indefinitely.

7.6   Final notes

In sum, e-government in Asia has become widespread, with numerous, albeit uneven effects. Overall, it has improved efficiency and reduced corruption. More Asians are better informed about the affairs of state than ever before and in some cases can make their voices heard. Long, time-wasting trips to government offices are declining. Life for many Asian has become safer, healthier, cleaner, and more convenient as a result. Digital divides are diminishing everywhere, particularly through smartphones. Rural masses are gradually becoming empowered, as when farmers can register land ownership and learn about crop prices. Telehealth and distance education are improving lives. There is no one-size-fits-all model: e-government means different things in different countries and must be understood as simultaneously reflecting national and local economic, political, and cultural contexts.

References

Abdullah, H., Kaliannan, M., 2006. The development of e-government in Malaysia: the role of leadership and organisational efficiency. In: Mitra, R. (Ed.), e-Government: Macro Issues. GIFT Publishing, New Delhi, pp. 190–202.

Ahmad, M., Markkula, J., Oivo, M., 2013. Factors affecting e-government adoption in Pakistan: a citizen's perspective. Transforming Government People Process and Policy 7 (2), 225–239.

Ahmed, A., 2002. Pakistan's blasphemy laws: words fail me. Washington Post May 19.

Ahn, M., Bretschneider, S., 2011. Politics of e-government: e-government and the political control of bureaucracy. Public Administration Review 71 (3), 414–424.

Allison, O., 2006. Selective enforcement and irresponsibility: central Asia's shrinking space for independent media. Central Asian Survey 25 (1–2), 93–114.

Aman, A., Kasimin, H., 2011. e-Procurement implementation: a case of Malaysia government. Transforming Government: People, Process and Policy 5 (4), 330–344.

Amarsaikhan, D., Lkhagvasuren, T., Oyun, S., Batchuluun, B., 2007. Online medical diagnosis and training in rural Mongolia. Distance Education 28 (2), 195–211.

Amatya, S., 2009. Functioning of rural tele-centers in Nepal: a case study of Kavre tele-centre. In: Proceedings of the 3rd International Conference on Theory and Practice of Electronic Governance. ACM, New York, pp. 311–313.

Ambali, A., 2009. e-Government policy: ground issues in e-filing system. European Journal of Social Sciences 11 (2), 249–266.

AmCham Vietnam, n.d. Senior Officials Face Corruption Charges in Botched e-Government Project 112. http://www.amchamvietnam.com/3026/senior-officials-face-corruption-charges-in-botched-e-government-project-112/.

Andersen, T., 2009. e-Government as an anti-corruption strategy. Information Economics and Policy 21, 201–210.

Anwaruddin, A., 2012. e-Leadership for e-government in Indonesia. In: Singh, A., Gonzalez, E., Thomson, S. (Eds.), Millennium Development Goals and Community Initiatives in the Asia Pacific. Springer, Dordrecht, pp. 177–188.

Anwer, M., Esichaikul, V., Rehman, M., Anjum, M., 2016. e-Government services evaluation from citizen satisfaction perspective: a case of Afghanistan. Transforming Government: People, Process and Policy 10 (1), 139–167.

Arai, Y., 2007. Provision of information by local governments using the Internet: case studies in Japan. NETCOM 21 (1–2), 315–330.

Arai, Y., Naganuma, S., 2010. The geographical digital divide in broadband access and governmental policies in Japan: three case studies. Netcom: Network and Communication Studies. 24, 1–2. https://netcom.revues.org/453.

Arbes, R., Bethea, C., 2014. Songdo, South Korea: city of the future? The Atlantic. (September 27) http://www.theatlantic.com/international/archive/2014/09/songdo-south-korea-the-city-of-the-future/380849/.

Arminen, I., 2007. Review essay: mobile communication society. Acta Sociologica 50, 431–437.

Asano, K., 2010. Electronic government in Japan. In: Berman, E., Moon, M., Choi, H. (Eds.), Public Administration in East Asia: Mainland China, Japan, South Korea, Taiwan. CRC Press, London, New York, pp. 305–325.

Aziz, M., 2012. Implementing ICTs for governance in fragile states – a case study of Afghanistan. In: Finger, M., Sultana, F. (Eds.), e-Governance: A Global Journey. IOS Press, Amsterdam, pp. 93–106.

Azmi, A., Bee, N., 2010. The acceptance of the e-filing system by Malaysian taxpayers: a simplified model. Electronic Journal of e-Government 8 (1), 13–22.

Baatar, T., Suldsuren, N., Bayanbileg, S., Seded, K., 2012. Telemedicine support of maternal and newborn health to remote provinces of Mongolia. In: Smith, A., Armfield, N., Eikelboom, R. (Eds.), Global Telehealth 2012. IOS Press, Amsterdam, pp. 27–35.

Bae, S., 2001. North Korea's policy shift toward the IT industry and inter-Korean cooperation. East Asian Review 134, 59–78.

Baimyrzaeva, M., 2011. Analysis of Kyrgyzstan's administrative reforms in light of its recent governance challenges. International Public Management Review 12 (1), 22–46.

Banday, M., Mattoo, M., 2013. Social media in e-governance: a study with special reference to India. Social Networking 2 (2), 47–56.

Basu, S., 2004. e-Government and developing countries: an overview. International Review of Law Computers 18, 109–132.

Baum, S., Mahizhnan, A., 2014. Government-with-you: e-government in Singapore. In: Baum, S., Mahizhnan, A. (Eds.), e-Governance and Social Inclusion: Concepts and Cases. IGI Global, Hershey, PA, pp. 229–242.

Baum, S., Yigitcanlar, T., Mahizhnan, A., Andiappan, N., 2008. e-Government in the knowledge society. In: Yigitcanlar, T., Velibeyogluand, K., Baum, S. (Eds.), Creative Urban Regions: Harnessing Urban Technologies to Support Knowledge City Initiatives. IGI Global, Hershey, PA, pp. 132–147.

BBC, December 10, 2012. North Korea: on the Net in the World's Most Secretive Nation. http://www.bbc.co.uk/news/technology-20445632.

BBC, April 26, 2013. BBC News and Technology. http://www.bbc.co.uk/news/technology-22308353.

Becker, J., Niehaves, B., Bergener, P., Räckers, M., 2008. Digital divide in e-government: the e-inclusion gap model. Lecture Notes in Computer Science, 5184, pp. 231–242.

Beklemishev, A., 2008. Kazakhstan. In: Finlay, A. (Ed.), Global Information Society Watch 2008. APC, Hivos and ITeM, pp. 135–138.

Beklemishev, A., 2012. Public access ICT in Kazakhstan. In: Gomez, R. (Ed.), Libraries, Telecentres, Cybercafes and Public Access to ICT: International Comparisons. IGI Global, Hershey, PA, pp. 330–343.

Belanger, F., Carter, L., 2008. Trust and risk in e-government adoption. Journal of Strategic Information Systems 17, 165–176.

Bertot, J.C., Jaeger, P.T., Grimes, J.M., 2010. Using ICTs to create a culture of transparency: e-government and social media as openness and anti-corruption tools for societies. Government Information Quarterly 27, 264–271.

Best, M., Kumar, R., 2008. Sustainability failures of rural telecenters: challenges from the sustainable access in rural India (SARI) project. Information Technologies and International Development 4 (4), 31–45.

Best, M., Maier, S., 2007. Gender, culture and ICT use in rural south India. Gender Technology and Development 11 (2), 137–155.

Best, M., Thakur, D., Kolko, B., 2009. The contribution of user-based subsidies to the impact and sustainability of telecenters – the eCenter Project in Kyrgyzstan. Information Technologies & International Development 6, 75–89.

Bhatia, D., Bhatnagar, S., Tominaga, J., 2009. How do manual and e-government services compare? Experiences from India. In: Information and Communications for Development 2009: Extending Reach and Increasing Impact. World Bank, Washington, DC, pp. 67–82.

Bhatnagar, S., 2006. Electronic delivery of citizen services: Andhra Pradesh's e-Seva model. In: Chand, V. (Ed.), Reinventing Public Service Delivery in India. Sage Publications, New Delhi, pp. 95–124.

Bhatnagar, S., Chawla, R., 2007. Online delivery of land titles to rural farmers in Karnataka. In: Narayan, D., Glinskaya, E. (Eds.), Ending Poverty in South Asia: Ideas that Work. World Bank Publications, Washington, DC, pp. 219–243.

Bhatnagar, S., Singh, N., 2010. Assessing the impact of e-government: a study of projects in India. Information Technologies and International Development 6 (2), 109–127.

Bhattacharya, D., Gulla, U., Gupta, M., 2012. e-Service quality model for Indian government portals: citizens' perspective. Journal of Enterprise Information Management 25 (3), 246–271.

Bhuiyan, S., 2006. e-Government in Bangladesh: prospects and challenges. Journal of Politics & Administration 1, 105–118.

Bhuiyan, S., 2010. e-Government in Kazakhstan: challenges and its role to development. Public Organization Review 10 (1), 31–47.

Bhuiyan, S., 2011. Modernizing Bangladesh public administration through e-governance: benefits and challenges. Government Information Quarterly 28, 54–65.

Bhuiyan, S., Amagoh, F., 2011. Public sector reform in Kazakhstan: issues and perspectives. International Journal of Public Sector Management 24 (3), 227–249.

Bleha, T., 2005. Down to the wire. Foreign Affairs 84 (3), 111–124.

Blythe, S., 2010. Rangoon enters the digital age: Burma's Electronic Transactions Law as a sign of hope for a troubled nation. International Business Research 3 (1), 151–161.

Borzo, J., 2004. It takes an internet village. Wall Street Journal January 23.

Brimkulov, U., Baryktabasov, K., 2014. Public transactional e-services through government web sites in Kyrgyzstan. Electronic Journal of e-Government 12 (1), 39–53.

Bruce, S., 2012. A double-edged sword: Information technology in North Korea. AsiaPacific Issues, 105. East-West Center, Honolulu, HI.

Burn, J., Robins, G., 2003. Moving towards e-government: a case study of organizational change processes. Logistics Information Management 16 (1), 25–35.

Buyong, W., Shaoyu, W., 2014. Social media development and implication on egovernance in China. In: Sonntagbauer, P., Nazemi, K., Sonntagbauer, S., Prister, G., Burkhardt, D. (Eds.), Handbook of Research on Advanced ICT Integration for Governance and Policy Modeling. IGI Global, New York, pp. 367–388.

Cambodian National Information Communications Technology Development Authority and Japan International Cooperation Agency, 2009. The Follow-up Study Report on e-Government Service Deployment Plan for Royal Government of Cambodia. http://www. jica.go.jp/project/cambodia/0609376/04/pdf/05_egov_2009_e.pdf.

Campbell, S., Park, Y., 2008. Social implications of mobile telephony: the rise of personal communication society. Sociology Compass 2 (2), 371–387.

Carter, L., Belanger, F., 2005. The utilization of e-government services: citizen trust, innovation and acceptance factors. Information Systems Journal 15, 5–25.

Cartier, C., Castells, M., Qiu, J., 2005. The information have-less: inequality, mobility, and translocal networks in Chinese cities. Studies in Comparative International Development 40 (2), 9–34.

Castells, M., 1996. The Information Age, Volume I: The Rise of the Network Society. Blackwell, Oxford.

Castells, M., 1997. The Information Age, Volume II: The Power of Identity. Blackwell, Cambridge.

Cecchini, S., Raina, M., 2004. Electronic government and the rural poor: the case of Gyandoot. Information Technologies and International Development 2 (2), 65–75.

Chadwick, A., May, C., 2003. Interaction between states and citizens in the age of the internet: 'e-government' in the United States, Britain, and the European Union. Governance 16, 271–300.

Chakraborty, J., Bosman, M., 2005. Measuring the digital divide in the United States: race, income, and personal computer ownership. Professional Geographer 57 (3), 395–410.

Chan, B., Al-Hawamdeh, S., 2002. The development of e-commerce in Singapore: the impact of government initiatives. Business Process Management Journal 8 (3), 278–288.

Chan, C., Pan, S., 2008. User engagement in e-government systems implementation: a comparative case study of two Singaporean e-government initiatives. Journal of Strategic Information Systems 17 (2), 124–139.

Chatfield, A., 2009. Public service reform through e-government: a case study of 'e-tax' in Japan. Electronic Journal of e-Government 7 (2), 135–146.

Chatfield, A., Reddick, C., 2015. Understanding risk communication gaps through e-government website and Twitter hashtag content analyses: the case of Indonesia's Mt. Sinabung eruption. Journal of Homeland Security and Emergency Management 12 (2), 351–385.

Chaudhri, N., Dash, S., 2006. Community information centres (CIC's) – e-governance for development. In: Sahu, G. (Ed.), Delivering e-Government. GIFT Publishing, New Delhi, pp. 96–104.

Chen, A., Huang, W., 2015. China's e-government. In: Pan, S.L. (Ed.), Managing Organizational Complexities with Digital Enablement in China: A Casebook. World Scientific Publishing, Singapore, pp. 97–106.

Chen, L., Lai, F., 2010. Crossing the chasm – understanding China's rural digital divide. Journal of Global Information Technology Management 13, 4–36.

Chen, C.K., Tseng, S.F., Huang, H.I., 2006. A comprehensive study of the digital divide phenomenon in Taiwanese government agencies. International Journal of Internet and Enterprise Management 4 (3), 244–256.

Chen, D.Y., Huang, T.Y., Hsiao, N., 2006. Reinventing government through on-line citizen involvement in the developing world: a case study of Taipei city mayor's e-mail box in Taiwan. Public Administration Quarterly 26 (5), 409–423.

Chen, A., Pan, S., Zhang, J., Huang, W., Zhu, S., 2009. Managing e-government implementation in China: a process perspective. Information and Management 46, 203–212.

Chen, D., Li, Z., Lai, F., 2010. Crossing the chasm – understanding China's rural digital divide. Journal of Global Information Technology Management 13 (2), 4–36.

Cheng, A., Mehta, K., 2013. A review of telemedicine business models. Telemedicine and e-Health 19 (4), 287–297.

Cho, J., March 20, 2013. North Korea Eyed in Huge Cyber Attack on South Korea. ABC News. http://abcnews.go.com/International/north-korea-eyed-huge-cyber-attack-south-korea/story?id=18769664.

Cho, Y.H., Choi, B.-D., 2005. e-Government to combat corruption: the case of Seoul metropolitan government. International Journal of Public Administration 27, 719–735.

Choe, S.-H., March 20, 2013. Computer Networks in South Korea are Paralyzed in Cyberattacks. New York Times. Retrieved from: http://www.nytimes.com/2013/03/21/world/asia/south-korea-computer-networkcrashes.html?pagewanted=all&_r=0.

Choney, S., 2013. North Korea's Internet? What Internet? For Most, Online Access Doesn't Exist. NBCNews.comhttp://www.nbcnews.com/technology/technolog/north-koreas-internet-whatinternet-most-online-access-doesnt-exist-1C9143426.

Clarke, R., Knake, R., 2010. Cyber War: The Next Threat to National Security and What to Do about It. Ecco, New York.

Comer, J., Wikle, T., 2008. Worldwide diffusion of the cellular phone, 1995-2005. Professional Geographer 60 (2), 252–269.

Crampton, J., 2007. The biopolitical justification for geosurveillance. Geographical Review 97 (3), 389–493.

Crang, M., Crosbie, T., Graham, S., 2006. Variable geometries of connection: urban digital divides and the uses of information technology. Urban Studies 43 (13), 2551–2570.

Crovitz, G., 2010. China's web crackdown continues. Wall Street Journal. January 11 http://online.wsj.com/article/SB10001424052748703948504574649021577882240.html.

Dada, D., 2006. The failure of e-government in developing countries: a literature review. Electronic Journal of Information Systems in Developing Countries 2697, 1–10.

Damm, J., 2007. The internet and the fragmentation of Chinese society. Critical Asian Studies 39 (2), 273–294.

Dann, D., Haddow, N., 2008. Just doing business or doing just business? Google, Microsoft, Yahoo! and the business of censoring China's internet. Journal of Business Ethics 79 (3), 219–234.

Davidrajuh, R., 2004. Planning e-government start-up: a case study on e-Sri Lanka. Electronic Government 1 (1), 92–106.

Davidrajuh, R., 2007. Towards measuring true e-readiness of a third-world country: a case study on Sri Lanka. In: Al-Hakin, L. (Ed.), Global e-Government: Theory, Applications and Benchmarking. Idea Publishing, London, pp. 185–199.

Davis, F., 1989. Perceived usefulness, perceived ease of use and user acceptance of information technology. MIS Quarterly 13 (3), 319–340.

Davis, F., 1993. User acceptance of information technology: system characteristics, user perceptions and behavioral impacts. International Journal of Man-Machine Studies 38, 475–487.

Davison, R., Vogel, D., Harris, R., Gricar, J., Sorrentino, M., 2003. Electronic Commerce on the New Silk Road: A Cornucopia of Research Opportunities. http://is2.lse.ac.uk/asp/aspecis/20030040.pdf.

Davison, R., Wagner, C., Ma, L., 2005. From government to e-government: a transition model. Information Technology & People 18 (3), 280–299.

Deibert, R., 2009. The geopolitics of internet control: censorship, sovereignty, and cyberspace. In: Andrew, H., Chadwick, P. (Eds.), The Routledge Handbook of Internet Politics. Routledge, London, pp. 212–226.

Deibert, R., Palfrey, J., Rohozinksi, R., Zittrain, J., 2008. Access Denied: The Practice and Policy of Global Internet Filtering. MIT Press, Cambridge.

Desai, M., Magalhaes, N., 2001. Vietnam's Tale of Two Cities. http://go.worldbank.org/ANV1MDO1C0H.

Dissanayake, S., Dissanayake, L., 2013. Development of e-Governance in Sri Lanka. In: Halpin, E., Griffin, D., Rankin, C., Dissanayake, L., Mahtab, N. (Eds.), Digital Public Administration and e-Government in Developing Nations: Policy and Practice. IGI Global, Hershey, PA, pp. 307–316.

Doarn, C., Adilova, F., Lam, D., 2005. A review of telemedicine in Uzbekistan. Journal of Telemedicine and Telecare 11 (3), 135–139.

Dobson, J., Fisher, P., 2007. The panopticon's changing geography. Geographical Review 97 (3), 307–323.

Dorasamy, M., Marimuthu, M., Raman, M., Kaliannan, M., 2010. e-Government services online: an exploratory study on tax e-filing in Malaysia. International Journal of Electronic Government Research 6 (4), 312–324.

Dugdale, A., Daly, A., Papandrea, F., Maley, M., 2005. Accessing e-government: challenges for citizens and organizations. International Review of Administrative Sciences 71, 109–118.

Dzhusupova, Z., 2013. Enabling democratic local governance through rural e-municipalities in Kyrgyzstan. In: Mahmood, Z. (Ed.), e-Government Implementation and Practice in Developing Countries. IGI Global, Hershey, PA, pp. 34–58.

Eberstadt, N., 2007. The North Korean Economy: Between Crisis and Catastrophe. Transaction Publishers, New Brunswick, NJ.

Eriksson, J., Giacomello, G., 2009. Who controls what, and under what conditions? International Studies Review 11, 206–210.

Eurasianet.org, 2009. In Turkmenistan, Internet Access Comes with Soldiers. http://www.eurasianet.org/departments/insight/articles/eav030807.shtml.

Faisal, N., Rahman, Z., 2008. e-Government in India: modelling the barriers to its adoption and diffusion. Electronic Government 5 (2), 181–202.

Fan, B., Luo, J., 2013. Benchmarking scale of e-government stage in Chinese municipalities from government chief information officers' perspective. Information Systems and e-Business Management 12, 259–284.

Faroqi, M., Siddiquee, N., 2011. Limping into the information age: challenges of e-government in Bangladesh. Journal of Comparative Asian Development 10 (1), 33–61.

Fath-Allah, A., Cheikhi, L., Al-Qutaish, R., Idri, A., 2014. e-Government maturing models: a comparative study. International Journal of Software Engineering & Applications 5 (3), 71–91.

Fietkiewicz, K., Stock, W., 2015. How "smart" are Japanese cities? An empirical investigation of infrastructures and governmental programs in Tokyo, Yokohama, Osaka and Kyoto. In: 48th Hawaii International Conference on System Sciences.

Fitzpatrick, M., July 13, 2010. Japan's Low-Tech Belly. BBC News. http://www.bbc.com/news/10543126.

Fong, M., 2009. Digital divide between urban and rural regions in China. Electronic Journal of Information Systems in Developing Countries 36 (6), 1–12.

Fountain, J., 2001a. Building the Virtual State: Information Technology and Institutional Change. Brookings Institution Press, Washington, DC.

Fountain, J., 2001b. The virtual state: transforming American government? National Civic Review 90, 241–251.

Freedom House, 2011. Kazakhstan. http://www.freedomhouse.org/images/File/FotN/Kazakhstan2011.pdf.

Fu, J.R., Chao, W.P., Farn, C.K., 2004. Determinants of taxpayers' adoption of electronic filing methods in Taiwan: an exploratory study. Journal of Government Information 30 (5–6), 658–683.

Fujita, M., Izawa, T., Ishibashi, H., 2005. The e-public administrative process in Japan. In: Druke, H. (Ed.), Local Electronic Government: A Comparative Study. Routledge, London, pp. 171–197.

Funilkul, S., Chutimaskul, W., Chongsuphajaisiddhi, V., 2011. e-Government information quality: a case study of Thailand. Lecture Notes in Computer Science 6866, 227–234.

Gadekar, R., Thakur, K., Ang, P., 2011. Web sites for e-electioneering in Maharashtra and Gujarat, India. Internet Research 21 (4), 435–457.

Gamage, P., Halpin, E., 2007. e-Sri Lanka: bridging the digital divide. Electronic Library 25 (6), 693–710.

Gao, X., 2011. The anatomy of teleneurosurgery in China. International Journal of Telemedicine and Applications 2011, 1–12.

Gao, X., Song, Y., Zhu, X., 2013a. Integration and coordination: advancing China's fragmented e-government to holistic governance. Government Information Quarterly 30, 173–181.

Gao, X., Xu, J., Sorwar, G., Croll, P., 2013b. Implementation of e-health record systems and e-medical record systems in China. International Technology Management Review 3 (2), 127–139.

Genus, A., Nor, M., 2007. Bridging the digital divide in Malaysia: an empirical analysis of technological transformation and implications for e-development. Asia Pacific Business Review 13 (1), 95–112.

Ghani, E., Said, J., Nasir, N., 2012. e-Government in Malaysia: a decade after. In: Bwalya, K., Zulu, S. (Eds.), Handbook of Research on e-Government in Emerging Economies. IGI Global, New York, pp. 290–306.

Goldfarb, A., Prince, J., 2008. Internet adoption and usage patterns are different: implications for the digital divide. Information Economics and Policy 20 (1), 2–15.

Goldsmith, J., Wu, T., 2006. Who Controls the Internet? Illusion of a Borderless World. Oxford University Press, New York.

Gomez, J., 2002. Internet Politics: Surveillance and Intimidation in Singapore. Think Centre.

Goranson, C., Thihalolipavan, S., di Tada, N., 2013. VGI and public health: possibilities and pitfalls. In: Sui, D., Elwood, S., Goodchild, M. (Eds.), Crowdsourcing Geographic Information. Springer, Dordrecht, pp. 329–340.

Gowda, M., Narayan, C., Ollapally, J., 2006. e-Lectoral reforms in India. In: Mitra, R. (Ed.), e-Government: Macro Issues. GIFT Publishing, New Delhi, pp. 24–34.

Grant, G., Chau, D., 2005. Developing a generic framework for e-government. Journal of Global Information Management 13, 1–30.

Gregor, S., Imran, A., Turner, T., 2014. A 'sweet spot' change strategy for a least developed country: leveraging e-government in Bangladesh. European Journal of Information Systems 23, 655–671.

Grönlund, A., 2011. Connecting egovernment to real government – the failure of the UN eparticipation index. In: Electronic Government. Springer, Dordrecht, pp. 26–37.

Guha, J., Chakrabarti, B., 2014. Making e-government work: adopting the network approach. Government Information Quarterly 31, 327–336.

Gunasekaran, A., Ngai, E., 2008. Adoption of e-procurement in Hong Kong: an empirical research. International Journal of Production Economics 113 (1), 159–175.

Gunawong, P., Gao, P., 2010. Understanding egovernment failure: an actor-network analysis of Thailand's smart ID card project. Proceedings of the Pacific Asia Conference on Information Systems. 773–784. http://unpan1.un.org/intradoc/groups/public/documents/UN-DPADM/UNPAN042473.pdf.

Guo, Y., Chen, P., 2011. Digital divide and social cleavage: case studies of ICT usage among peasants in contemporary China. China Quarterly 207, 580–599.

Gupta, M., 2012. Tracking the evolution of e-governance in India. In: Weerakkody, V. (Ed.), Technology Enabled Transformation of the Public Sector: Advances in e-Government. IGI Global, Hershey, PA, pp. 46–58.

Ha, H., 2013. e-Government in Singapore: critical success factors. In: Gil-Garcia, J. (Ed.), e-Government Success Around the World: Cases, Empirical Studies, and Practical Recommendations. IGI Global, Hershey, PA, pp. 176–194.

Ha, H., Coghill, K., 2006. e-Government in Singapore: a SWOT and PEST analysis. Asia-Pacific Social Science Review. 103–130. http://workspace.unpan.org/sites/internet/Documents/UNPAN042752.pdf.

Hachigian, N., 2001. China's cyber-strategy. Foreign Affairs 80 (2), 118–133 March/April.

Hachigian, N., 2002. The internet and power in one-party East Asian states. Washington Quarterly 253, 41–58.

Haldenwang, C., 2004. Electronic government (e-government) and development. European Journal of Development Research 16 (2), 417–432.

Hanna, N., 2008. Transforming Government and Empowering Communities: The Sri Lankan Experience with e-Development. World Bank, Washington, DC.

Haque, M., 2002. e-Governance in India: its impacts on relations among citizens, politicians and public servants. International Review of Administrative Sciences 68, 231–250.

Harris, R., Rajora, R., 2006. Empowering the Poor: Information and Communications Technology for Governance and Poverty Reduction. A Study of Rural Development Projects in India. Elsevier, New Delhi.

Harwit, E., 2004. Spreading telecommunications to developing areas in China: telephones, the internet and the digital divide. China Quarterly 180, 1010–1030.

Harwit, E., Clark, D., 2001. Shaping the internet in China: evolution of political control over network infrastructure and political content. Asian Survey 41 (3), 377–408.

Hasan, S., 2003. Introducing e-government in Bangladesh: problems and prospects. International Social Science Review 78 (3/4), 111–125.

Hashemi, S., Monfaredi, K., Masdari, M., 2013. Using cloud computing for e-government: challenges and benefits. International Journal of Computer, Electrical, Automation, Control and Information Engineering. 7 (9). http://www.waset.org/publications/17212.

Heeks, H., Stanforth, C., 2011. Understanding e-government project trajectories from an actor-network perspective. European Journal of Information Systems 16, 165–177.

Helbig, N., Gil-Garcia, J., Ferro, E., 2009. Understanding the complexity of electronic government: implications from the digital divide literature. Government Information Quarterly 26, 89–97.

Hermana, B., Silfianti, W., 2011. Evaluating e-government implementation by local government: digital divide in internet based public services in Indonesia. International Journal of Business and Social Science 2, 156–163.

Hirwade, M., 2010. Responding to information needs of the citizens through e-government portals and online services in India. International Information and Library Review 42 (3), 154–163.

Ho, T., 2002. Reinventing local governments and the e-government initiative. Public Administration Review 62, 434–444.

Holliday, I., 2002. Building e-government in East and Southeast Asia: regional rhetoric and national (in)action. Public Administration and Development 22, 323–335.

Holliday, I., Kwok, R., 2004. Governance in the information age: building e-government in Hong Kong. New Media and Society 6 (4), 549–570.

Holliday, I., Yep, R., 2005. e-Government in China. Public Administration and Development 25, 239–249.

Hoque, S., 2006. e-Governance in Bangladesh: a scrutiny from the citizens' perspective. In: Ahmad, R. (Ed.), The Role of Public Administration in Building a Harmonious Society. China National School of Administration, Beijing, pp. 346–365.

Hoque, K., Samad, R., Siraj, S., Ziyadh, A., 2012. The role of ICT in school management of Maldives. New Education Review 27 (1), 270–282.

Hori, Y., 2011. Creating a vision of Japan: achieving e-government. Japan Today. November 28 http://www.japantoday.com/category/opinions/view/creating-a-vision-of-japan-achieving-e-government.

Horibe, M., 2012. Digital identity management and privacy in Japan. In: Bus, J., Crompton, M. (Eds.), Digital Enlightenment Yearbook 2012. IOS Press, Amsterdam, pp. 97–108.

Hosman, L., Fife, E., 2008. Improving the prospects for sustainable ICT projects in the developing world. International Journal of Media and Cultural Politics 4 (1), 51–70.

Hossain, F., 2005. e-Governance initiatives in developing countries: helping the rich? Or, creating opportunities for the poor? Asian Affairs 27, 5–23.

Hsieh, R., Hjelm, N., Lee, J., Aldis, J., 2001. Telemedicine in China. International Journal of Medical Informatics 61 (2–3), 139–146.

Hsieh, P.H., Huang, C.S., Yan, D., 2013. Assessing web services of emerging economies in an Eastern country — Taiwan's e-government. Government Information Quarterly 30 (3), 267–276.

Huang, C.C., Farn, K.J., 2016. A study on e-Taiwan promotion information security governance programs with e-government implementation of information security management standardization. International Journal of Network Security 18 (3), 565–578.

Huang, A., Ismiraldi, Y., Thornley, A., 2016. Digital Governance in Indonesia: An on and Offline Battle. The Asia Foundation. http://asiafoundation.org/2016/05/18/digital-governance-indonesia-offline-battle/.

Hughes, C., Wacker, G. (Eds.), 2003. China and the Internet: Politics of the Digital Leap Forward. Routledge, London, New York.

Hui, W., Othman, R., Omar, N., Rahman, R., Haron, N., 2011. Procurement issues in Malaysia. International Journal of Public Sector Management 24 (6), 567–593.

Human Rights Watch, 2002. Human Rights Watch: World Report 2001, Vietnam. www.hrw.org/wr2k/asia/Vietnam.html.

Hung, S.Y., Chang, C.M., Yu, T.J., 2006. Determinants of user acceptance of the e-government services: the case of online tax filing and payment system. Government Information Quarterly 23 (1), 97–122.

Hung, S.Y., Chang, C.M., Kuo, S.R., 2013. User acceptance of mobile e-government services: an empirical study. Government Information Quarterly 30 (1), 33–44.

Hussein, R., Mohamed, N., Ahlan, A., Mahmud, M., Aditiawarman, U., 2010. G2C Adoption of e-government in Malaysia: trust, perceived risk and political self-efficacy. International Journal of Electronic Government Research 6 (3), 57–72.

Hwang, J., 2004. Digital divide in internet use within the urban hierarchy: the case of South Korea. Urban Geography 25 (4), 372–389.

Ibodova, P., Atoev, A., 2008. Tajikistan. In: Finlay, A. (Ed.), Global Information Society Watch 2008. APC, Hivos and ITeM, pp. 184–186.

Ibrahim, Z., Ainin, S., 2009. The influence of Malaysian telecenters on community building. Electronic Journal of e-Government 7 (1), 77–86.

Im, J., Seo, J., 2005. e-Government in South Korea: planning and implementation. Electronic Government 2, 188–204.

Iqbal, M., Seo, J.W., 2008. e-Governance as an anti-corruption tool: korean cases. Journal of Korean Association for Regional Information Society 6, 51–78.

Isa, W., Suhami, M., Safie, N., Semsudin, S., 2011. Assessing the usability and accessibility of Malaysia e-government website. American Journal of Economics and Business Administration 3 (1), 40–46.

Islam, M., Grönlund, A., 2007. Agriculture market information e-service in Bangladesh: a stakeholder-oriented case analysis. In: Electronic Government. Springer Verlag, Dordrecht, pp. 167–178.

Islam, M., Grönlund, A., 2010. An agricultural market information service (AMIS) in Bangladesh: evaluating a mobile phone based e-service in a rural context. Information Development 26 (4), 289–302.

Islam, M., Khair, R., 2012. Preparation of e-government in Bangladesh: an exploratory analysis. Journal of Information Technology 1, 19–26.

Ismailova, R., 2015. Web site accessibility, usability and security: a survey of government web sites in Kyrgyz Republic. Universal Access in the Information Society 1–8.

Jain, P., 2002. The catch-up state: e-government in Japan. Japanese Studies 22 (3), 237–255.

James, 2009. A Brief History of Chinese Internet Censorship. Time (March 18) http://www.time.com/time/world/article/0, 8599, 1885961,00.html.

Jamtsho, S., Bullen, M., 2007. Distance education in Bhutan: improving access and quality through ICT use. Distance Education 28 (2), 149–161.

Janenova, S., Kim, P., 2016. Innovating public service delivery in transitional countries: the case of one stop shops in Kazakhstan. International Journal of Public Administration 39 (4).

Jho, W., 2005. Challenges for e-governance. Protests from civil society on the protection of privacy in e-government in Korea. International Review of Administrative Sciences 71, 151–166.

Johnson, E., Kolko, B., 2010. e-Government and transparency in authoritarian regimes: comparison of national- and city-level e-government web sites in Central Asia. Digital Icons: Studies in Russian, Eurasian and Central European New Media 4 (3), 15–48.

Kalathil, S., Boas, T., 2003. Open Networks, Closed Regimes: The Impact of the Internet on Authoritarian Rule. Carnegie Endowment for International Peace, Washington, DC.

Kaliannan, M., Awang, H., Raman, M., 2007. Technology Adoption in the Public Sector: An Exploratory Study of e-Government in Malaysia. In: Proceedings of the 1st International Conference on Theory and Practice of Electronic Governance. ACM, New York, pp. 221–224.

Kaliannan, M., Awang, H., Raman, M., 2010. Public-private partnerships for e-government services: lessons from Malaysia. International Journal of Institutions and Economics 2 (2), 207–220.

Kalsi, N., Kiran, R., Vaidya, S., 2009. Effective e-governance for good governance in India. International Review of Business Research Papers 5 (1), 212–229.

Kamal, M., Hackney, R., Sarwar, K., 2013. Investigating factors inhibiting e-government adoption in developing countries: the context of Pakistan. Journal of Global Information Management 21 (4), 77–102.

Kapitsa, L., 2008. Towards a Knowledge-based Economy – Europe and Central Asia: Internet Development and Governance. United Nations Economic Commission for Europe Discussion Paper 2008. 1 UNECE Information Unit, Geneva. http://mgimo.ru/files/33016/ECE_DP_2008-1.pdf.

Karunasena, K., Deng, H., 2012. Critical factors for evaluating the public value of e-government in Sri Lanka. Government Information Quarterly 29, 76–84.

Karunasena, K., Deng, H., Singh, M., 2011. Measuring the public value of e-government: a case study from Sri Lanka. Transforming Government: People, Process and Policy 5 (1), 81–99.

Kaushik, P., Singh, N., 2004. Information technology and broad-based development: preliminary lessons from north India. World Development 32 (4), 591–607.

Kawtrakul, A., Mulasastra, I., Khampachua, T., Ruengittinun, S., 2011. The challenges of accelerating connected government and beyond: Thailand perspectives. Electronic Journal of e-Government 9, 183–202.

Kayani, M., ul Haq, M., Perwez, M., Humayun, H., 2011. Analyzing barriers in e-government implementation in Pakistan. International Journal for Infonomics 4 (3/4), 494–500.

Ke, W., Wei, K., 2004. Successful e-government in Singapore. Communications of the ACM 47, 95–99.

Ke, W., Wei, K., 2006. Understanding e-government project management: a positivist case study of Singapore. Journal of Global Information Technology Management 9 (2), 45–61.

Kellerman, A., 2002. The Internet on Earth: A Geography of Information. John Wiley, Hoboken, NJ.

Kellerman, A., 2010. Mobile broadband services and the availability of instant access to cyberspace. Environment and Planning A 42, 2990–3005.

Kendzior, S., 2010. A reporter without borders: internet politics and state violence in Uzbekistan. Problems of Post-Communism 57 (1), 40–50.

Keniston, K., Kumar, D. (Eds.), 2004. IT Experience in India: Bridging the Digital Divide. Sage, New Delhi.

Kevreaksmey, P., Bing, W., Virak, M., Sokim, T., Samkol, T., Sotheara, H., 2015. e-Governance: a key to good governance in Cambodia. Public Policy and Administration Research 5 (1), 1681–2176.

Khadaroo, I., Seng, W., Abdullah, A., 2013. Barriers in local e-government partnership: evidence from Malaysia. Electronic Government 10 (1), 19–33.

Khan, N., Bawden, D., 2005. Community informatics in libraries in Pakistan: current status, future prospects. New Library World 106, 532–540.

Khan, G., Moon, J., Swar, B., Zo, H., Rho, J., 2012. e-Government service use intentions in Afghanistan: technology adoption and the digital divide in a war-torn country. Information Development 28 (4), 281–299.

Khan, M., Hasan, M., Clement, C., 2012. Barriers to the introduction of ICT into education in developing countries: the example of Bangladesh. International Journal of Instruction 5 (2), 61–80.

Khanh, N., Danh, M., Gim, G., 2015. e-Government in Vietnam: situation, prospects, trends, and challenges. In: Sodhi, S. (Ed.), Trends, Prospects, and Challenges in Asian e-Governance. IGI Global, Hershey, PA.

Kifle, H., Cheng, P., 2009. e-government implementation and leadership – the Brunei case study. Electronic Journal of e-Government 7 (3), 271–282.

Kim, Y., 2004. North Korea's cyberpath. Asian Perspectives 283, 191–209.

Kim, J. Selling North Korea in new frontiers: profit and revolution in cyberspace. Joint U.S.-Korea Academic Studies Emerging Voices, 22. (Unpublished manuscript).

Kim, S., Kim, D., 2003. South Korean public officials' perceptions of values, failure, and consequences of failure in e-government leadership. Public Performance & Management Review 26 (4), 360–375.

Kim, H., Pan, G., Pan, S., 2007. Managing IT-enabled transformation in the public sector: a case study on e-government in South Korea. Government Information Quarterly 24, 338–352.

Kim, S., Kim, H.J., Lee, H., 2009. An institutional analysis of an e-government system for anti-corruption: the case of OPEN. Government Information Quarterly 26, 42–50.

Kim, G.H., Trimi, S., Chung, J.H., 2014. Big-data applications in the government sector. Communications of the ACM 57 (3).

Kita, T., 2006. Electronic government in Japan: towards harmony between technology solutions and administrative systems. In: Whittaker, D., Cole, R. (Eds.), Recovering from Success: Innovation and Technology Management in Japan. Oxford University Press, Oxford, pp. 286–297.

Kluver, R., 2005. The architecture of control: a Chinese strategy for e-governance. Journal of Public Policy 25 (1), 75–97.

Knox, C., 2008. Kazakhstan: modernizing government in the context of political inertia. International Review of Administrative Sciences 74, 477–496.

Knox, C., 2009. Dealing with sectoral corruption in Bangladesh: developing citizen involvement. Public Administration and Development 29, 117–132.

Ko, K., Jang, S., Lee, H., 2007/2008. kp North Korea. Digital review of Asia/Pacific, pp. 244–250. Retrieved from http://books.google.com/books?

Ko, K., Lee, H., Jang, S., 2009. The internet dilemma and control policy: political and economic implications of the internet in North Korea. Korean Journal of Defense Analysis 21 (3), 279–295.

Kodukula, S., Nazvia, M., 2011. Evaluation of critical success factors for telemedicine implementation. International Journal of Computer Applications 12 (10), 29–36.

Koga, T., 2003. Access to government information in Japan: a long way toward electronic government? Government Information Quarterly 20, 47–62.

Kolsaker, A., Lee-Kelley, L., Mitra, R., Gupta, M., 2007. Analysis of issues of e-government in Indian police. Electronic Government, An International Journal 4 (1), 97–125.

Korupp, S., Szydlik, M., 2005. Causes and trends of the digital divide. European Sociological Review 21, 409–422.

Kozhamberdiyeva, Z., 2008. Freedom of expression on the internet: a case study of Uzbekistan. Review of Central and East European Law 33 (1), 95–134.

Krairit, D., Choomongkol, W., Krairit, P., 2004. Strategic and technology policy implications for e-government: lessons from an empirical case study on information security in Thailand. Information and Security 15 (1), 21–35.

Kretchun, N., Kim, J., 2012. A Quiet Opening: North Koreans in a Changing Media Environment. http://www.audiencescapes.org/sites/default/files/A_Quiet_Opening_FINAL_InterMedia.pdf.

Krishnan, C., 2010. Are rural e-governance programmes in India at crossroads? Information Technology in Developing Countries 20 (3), 2–7.

Kubo, S., Shimada, T., 2007. Local e-governments in Japan: IT utilization status and directions. In: Al-Hakin, L. (Ed.), Global e-Government: Theory, Applications and Benchmarking. Idea Publishing, London, pp. 300–318.

Kudo, H., 2010. e-Governance as strategy of public sector reform: peculiarity of Japanese IT policy and its institutional origin. Financial Accountability and Management 26 (1), 65–84.

Kumar, R., 2004. eChoupals: a study on the financial sustainability of village internet centers in rural Madhya Pradesh. Information Technologies and International Development 2 (1), 45–73.

Kumar, R., Best, M., 2006. Impact and sustainability of e-government services in developing countries: lessons learned from Tamil Nadu, India. The Information Society 22, 1–12.

Kuriyan, R., Ray, I., 2009. Outsourcing the state? Public-private partnerships and information technologies in India. World Development 37 (10), 1663–1673.

Lake, E., 2009. Hacking the Regime. The New Republic. September 3 http://www.tnr.com/article/politics/hacking-the-regime.

Lallana, E., Pascual, P., Soriano, E., 2002. e-Government in the Philippines: benchmarking against global best practices. Philippine Journal of Third World Studies 17 (2), 235–272.

Lambroschini, A., February 24, 2011. No Twitter Revolt for Central Asia's Closed Regimes. Physorg.comhttp://www.physorg.com/news/2011-02-twitter-revolt-central-asia-regimes.html.

Layne, K., Lee, J., 2001. Developing fully functional e-government: a four stage model. Government Information Quarterly 18, 122–136.

Lean, O., Zailani, S., Ramayah, T., Fernando, Y., 2009. Factors influencing intention to use e-government services among citizens in Malaysia. International Journal of Information Management 29, 458–475.

Lee, S., 2016. Smart divide: paradigm shift in digital divide in South Korea. Journal of Librarianship and Information Science 48 (3), 260–268.

Lee, K., Hong, J.H., 2002. Development of an e-government service model: a business model approach. International Review of Public Administration 7 (2), 109–118.

Lee, H., Hwang, J., 2004. ICT development in North Korea: changes and challenges. Information Technologies and International Development 21, 75–87.

Lee, K., Lee, K.S., 2009. The Korean government's electronic record management reform: the promise and perils of digital democratization. Government Information Quarterly 26, 525–535.

Lee, J., Sparks, P., 2014. Sustaining a Nepali telecenter: an ethnographic study using activity theory. International Journal of Education and Development Using Information and Communication Technology 10 (2), 41–62.

Lee, S., Tan, X., Trimi, S., 2005. Current practices of leading e-government countries. Communications of the ACM 48 (10), 99–104.

Lee, J., Hancock, M., Hu, M., 2014. Towards an effective framework for building smart cities: lessons from Seoul and San Francisco. Technological Forecasting and Social Change 89, 80–99.

Liao, S.H., Jeng, H.P., 2005. e-Government implementation: business contract legal support for Taiwanese businessmen in mainland China. Government Information Quarterly 22 (3), 505–524.

Lili Cui, L., Zhang, C., Zhang, C., Huang, L., 2006. Exploring e-government impact on Shanghai firms' information process. Electronic Markets 16, 312–318.

Lim, J., Tang, S.Y., 2008. Urban e-government initiatives and environmental decision performance in Korea. Journal of Public Administration Research and Theory 18, 109–138.

Lim, E., Tan, C.W., Cyr, D., Pan, S., Xiao, B., 2012. Advancing public trust relationships in electronic government: the Singapore e-filing journey. Information Systems Research 23, 1110–1130.

Linders, D., 2012. From e-government to we-government: defining a typology for citizen coproduction in the age of social media. Government Information Quarterly 29, 446–454.

Ling, R., Donner, J., 2009. Mobile Phones and Mobile Communication. Polity Press, Cambridge, UK.

Lintner, B., April 24, 2007. North Korea's IT revolution. Asia Times Online. http://www.atimes.com/atimes/Korea/ID24Dg01.html.

Liou, K., 2007. e-Government development and China's administrative reform. International Journal of Public Administration 31 (1), 76–95.

Liu, C., 2012. The myth of informatization in rural areas: the case of China's Sichuan province. Government Information Quarterly 29 (1), 85–97.

Liu, C., 2016. Sustainability of rural informatization programs in developing countries: a case study of China's Sichuan province. Telecommunications Policy 40 (7), 714–724.

Lollar, X.L., 2006. Assessing China's e-government: information, service, transparency and citizen outreach of government websites. Journal of Contemporary China 15 (46), 31–41.

Loo, B.P.Y., Ngan, Y., 2012. Developing mobile telecommunications to narrow digital divide in developing countries? Some lessons from China. Telecommunications Policy 36, 888–900.

Lu, Z., Zhang, J., Han, B., Deng, Z., Lu, J., 2007. The development of urban e-government in China. In: Al-Hakin, L. (Ed.), Global e-Government: Theory, Applications and Benchmarking. Idea Publishing, London, pp. 214–237.

Luckman, E., October 21, 2013. Indonesia's Anti-corruption Website Is Now Getting 1,000 Crowdsourced Reports Every Day. Tech in Asia. https://www.techinasia.com/lapor-indonesia-200000-users.

Luk, S., 2009. The impact of leadership and stakeholders on the success/failure of e-government service: using the case study of e-stamping service in Hong Kong. Government Information Quarterly 26 (4), 594–604.

Luk, S., 2013. e-Government in China: opportunities and challenges for the transformation of governance in the information age. In: Wu, B., Yao, S., Chen, J. (Eds.), China's Development and Harmonization: Towards a Balance with Nature, Society, and the International Community. Routledge, London, pp. 192–206.

Luo, G., 2009. e-Government, people and social change: a case study in China. Electronic Journal of Information Systems 38 (3), 1–23.

Ma, L., 2013. The diffusion of government microblogging: evidence from Chinese municipal police bureaus. Public Management Review 15, 288–309.

Ma, L., Chung, J., Thorson, S., 2005. e-Government in China: bringing economic development through administrative reform. Government Information Quarterly 22, 20–37.

MacKinnon, R., 2008. Flatter world and thicker walls? Blogs, censorship and civic discourse in China. Public Choice 134, 31–46.

Madden, G., Bohlin, E., Oniki, H., Tran, T., 2013. Potential demand for m-government services in Japan. Applied Economics Letters 20 (8), 732–736.

Madon, S., Sahay, S., Sudan, R., 2007. e-Government policy and health information systems implementation in Andhra Pradesh, India: need for articulation of linkages between the macro and the micro. The Information Society 23, 327–344.

Mahmood, K., 2005. Multipurpose community telecenters for rural development in Pakistan. Electronic Library 23 (2), 204–220.

Mahmood, S., 2010. Public procurement and corruption in Bangladesh confronting the challenges and opportunities. Journal of Public Administration and Policy Research 2 (6), 103–111.

Mambetalieva, T., Shramko, Z., 2008. Kyrgyzstan. In: Finlay, A. (Ed.), Global Information Society Watch 2008. APC, Hivos and ITeM, pp. 146–149.

Mansourov, A., 2011. North Korea on the Cusp of Digital Transformation. The Nautilus Institute. http://www.nautilus.org/wp-content/uploads/2011/12/DPRK_Digital_Transformation.pdf.

Mao, Y., Zhang, Y., Zhai, S., 2008. Mobile phone text messaging for pharmaceutical care in a hospital in China. Journal of Telemedicine and Telecare 14, 410–414.

Mar, N., 2004. Utilizing information and communication technologies to achieve lifelong education for all: a case study of Myanmar. Educational Research for Policy and Practice 3 (2), 141–166.

Marcelo, A., 2009. Telemedicine in developing countries: perspectives from the Philippines. In: Wootton, R., Patil, N., Scott, R., Hopp, K. (Eds.), Telehealth in the Developing World. Royal Society of Medicine Press, London, pp. 27–33.

McGlinchey, E., Johnson, E., 2007. Aiding the internet in central Asia. Democratization 14 (2), 277–288.

McWilliams, B., June 2 2003. North Korea's school for hackers. Wired. http://www.wired.com/politics/law/news/2003/06/59043.

Mauro, R., July 13 2009. North Korea's cyber war. Front Page Magazine. Retrieved from http://www.freerepublic.com/focus/f-news/2291454/posts.

Mensah, I., Jianing, M., 2016. e-Government, China internet plus, and the one belt one road initiative: the Africa connection. International Journal of Social, Behavioral, Educational, Economic, Business and Industrial Engineering 10 (8), 2425–2429.

Mills, B., Whitacre, B., 2003. Understanding the non-metropolitan-metropolitan digital divide. Growth and Change 34 (2), 219–243.

Misra, H., Das, U., 2014. Role of connectivity in citizen centered e-governance in Myanmar: learning from Indian experience. In: Proceedings of the 2014 Conference on Electronic Governance and Open Society: Challenges in Eurasia. Association for Computing Machinery, New York, pp. 121–126.

Miyata, M., 2011. Measuring impacts of egovernment support in least developed countries: a case study of the vehicle registration service in Bhutan. Information Technology for Development 17 (2), 133–152.

Mo, D., Swinnen, J., Zhang, L., Yi, H., Qu, Q., Boswell, M., Rozelle, S., 2013. Can one-to-one computing narrow the digital divide and the educational gap in China? The case of Beijing migrant schools. World Development 46 (1), 14–29.

Mohamed, N., Hussin, H., Hussein, R., 2009. Measuring users' satisfaction with Malaysia's electronic government systems. Electronic Journal of e-Government 7 (3), 283–294.

Mol, A., 2009. Environmental governance through information: China and Vietnam. Singapore Journal of Tropical Geography 30, 114–129.

Monga, A., 2008. e-Government in India: opportunities and challenges. Journal of Administration and Governance 3 (2), 52–61.

Moon, J., Hossain, M., Kang, H., Shin, J., 2012. An analysis of agricultural informatization in Korea: the government's role in bridging the digital gap. Information Development 28, 102–116.

Murdoch, S., Anderson, R., 2008. Tools and technology of internet filtering. In: Deibert, R., Palfrey, J., Rohozinksi, R., Zittrain, J. (Eds.), Access Denied: The Practice and Policy of Global Internet Filtering. MIT Press, Cambridge, MA, pp. 57–72.

Nair, M., Han, G.S., Lee, H., Goon, P., Muda, R., 2010. Determinants of the digital divide in rural communities of a developing country: the case of Malaysia. Development and Society 39, 139–162.

Naughton, T., Ullman, O., 2012. Public access ICT in Mongolia. In: Gomez, R. (Ed.), Libraries, Telecentres, Cybercafes and Public Access to ICT: International Comparisons. IGI Global, Hershey, PA, pp. 356–369.

Ndou, V., 2004. e-Government for developing countries: opportunities and challenges. Electronic Journal on Information Systems in Developing Countries 18, 1–24.

Netchaeva, I., 2002. e-Government and e-democracy: a comparison of opportunities in the North and South. Gazette: International Journal for Communication Studies 64 (5), 467–477.

Neupane, A., Soar, J., Vaidya, K., 2014. An empirical evaluation of the potential for public e-procurement to reduce corruption. Australasian Journal of Information Systems 18 (2), 21–44.

Nguyen, T., Shauder, D., 2007. Grounding e-government in Vietnam: antecedents to responsive government services. Journal of Business Systems, Governance and Ethics. 2 (3), 35–52. http://workspace.unpan.org/sites/internet/Documents/UNPAN041927.pdf.

Nishida, T., Pick, J., Sarkar, A., 2014. Japan's prefectural digital divide: a multivariate and spatial analysis. Telecommunications Policy 38 (1), 992–1010.

Nurdin, N., Stockdale, R., Scheepers, H., 2015. Influence of organizational factors in the sustainability of e-government: a case study of local e-government in Indonesia. In: Sodhi, S. (Ed.), Trends, Prospects, and Challenges in Asian e-Governance. IGI Global, Hershey, PA, pp. 281–324.

Nurgaliyeva, G., Artykbayeva, E., 2011. Content provision for information and educational environment in the Republic of Kazakhstan. In: ICT in Teacher Education: Policy, Open Educational Resources and Partnership. UNESCO Institute for Information Technologies in Education, St. Petersburg, pp. 112–117.

Nurmandi, A., Kim, S., 2015. Making e-procurement work in a decentralized procurement system: a comparison of three Indonesian cities. International Journal of Public Sector Management 28 (3), 198–220.

Ó Beacháin, D., 2010. Turkmenistan. In: Ó Beacháin, D., Polese, A. (Eds.), The Colour Revolutions in the Former Soviet Republics. Routledge, London, pp. 217–236.

Obi, T., Hai, N., 2010. e-Government project implementation: insight from interviews in Vietnam. Journal of Asia-Pacific Studies. 14, 37–55. http://unpan1.un.org/intradoc/groups/public/documents/un-dpadm/unpan041923.pdf.

Obi, T., Ishmatova, D., Iwasaki, N., 2012. Promoting ICT innovations for the ageing population in Japan. International Journal of Medical Informatics 82 (4), 47–62.

Ojha, A., Sahu, G., Gupta, M., 2009. Antecedents of paperless income tax filing by young professionals in India: an exploratory study. Transforming Government: People, Process and Policy 3 (1), 65–90.

Oo, A., Than, M., 2008. mm Myanmar. Digital Review of Asia Pacific 2007–2208, pp. 223–228. http://www.digital-review.org/uploads/files/pdf/2007-2008/2007_C18_mm_Myanmar _223_229.pdf.

OpenNet Initiative, 2006. Internet filtering in Burma in 2005: a country study. http://www. opennetinitiative.net/studies/burma/.

OpenNet Initiative, 2007. Singapore. https://opennet.net/sites/opennet.net/files/singapore.pdf.

OpenNet Initiative, 2010a. Kyrgyzstan. http://opennet.net/sites/opennet.net/files/ONI_Kyrgyzstan _2010.pdf.

OpenNet Initiative, 2010b. Turkmenistan. http://opennet.net/research/profiles/turkmenistan.

OpenNet Initiative, 2010c. Uzbekistan. http://opennet.net/sites/opennet.net/files/ONI_Uzbekistan_ 2010.pdf.

OpenNetInitiative,2010d.Kyrgyzstan.http://opennet.net/sites/opennet.net/files/ONI_Kyrgyzstan_ 2010.pdf.

OpenNet Initiative, 2012. Pakistan. https://opennet.net/research/profiles/pakistan.

Intelligent Community Forum, 2016. List of Intelligent Communities. http://www.intelligent-community.org/intelligent_communities_list.

Orazbayev, S., 2012. The role of ICT in social and economic development of Turkmenistan. In: Sultana, F., Finger, M. (Eds.), e-Governance, a Global Journey: Volume 4 Global e-Governance. IOS Press, Amsterdam, pp. 23–38.

Oreglia, E., 2014. ICT and (personal) development in rural China. Information Technologies & International Development 10 (3), 19–30.

Orihuela, L., Obi, T., 2008. e-Governance in Japan: analysis of the current status of e-government and local e-services. Proceedings of the Eighth International Conference on Electronic Business. 72–79. http://iceb.nccu.edu.tw/proceedings/2008/#page=80.

Otani, S., 2003. Social, cultural and economic issues in the digital divide – literature review and case study of Japan. Online Journal of Space Communication. (5) http://spacejournal. ohio.edu/issue5/social.html.

Paltemaa, V., Vuori, J., 2009. Regime transition and the Chinese politics of technology: from mass science to the controlled internet. Asian Journal of Political Science 17 (1), 1–23.

Pan, S.L., Pan, G., Devadoss, P., 2005. e-Government capabilities and crisis management: lessons from combating SARS in Singapore. MIS Quarterly Executive 4 (4), 385–397.

Pan, S.L., Tan, C.W., Lim, E., 2006. Customer relationship management (CRM) in e-government: a relational perspective. Decision Support Systems 42, 237–250.

Park, S.L., Choi, Y.T., Bok, H.S., 2013. Does better e-readiness induce more use of e-government? Evidence from the Korean central e-government. International Review of Administrative Sciences 79 (4), 767–789.

Patak, R., Prasad, R., 2005. Role of e-governance in tackling corruption: the Indian experience. In: Ahmad, R. (Ed.), The Role of Public Administration in Building a Harmonious Society. China National School of Administration, Beijing, pp. 434–463.

Phong, K., Sola, 2015. Mobile Phones and Internet in Cambodia 2015. https://asiafoundation. org/resources/pdfs/MobilePhonesinCB2015.pdf.

Pick, J., Sarkar, A., 2015. The Global Digital Divides: Explaining Change. Springer, Dordrecht.

Pick, J., Gollakota, K., Singh, M., 2014. Technology for development: understanding influences on use of rural telecenters in India. Information Technology for Development 20 (4), 296–323.

Pierre, A., 2000. Vietnam's contradictions. Foreign Affairs 79 (6), 69–86.

Poon, S., 2002. ESDlife of Hong Kong egovernment application with an ebusiness spirit. In: Americas Conference on Information Systems (AMCIS) Proceedings Paper 86.

Prahono, A., 2015. Evaluating the role of e-government in public administration reform: case of official city government websites in Indonesia. Procedia Computer Science 59, 27–33.

Prasad, K., 2012. e-Governance policy for modernizing government through digital democracy in India. Journal of Information Policy 2, 183–203.

Qaiser, N., Khan, H., 2010. e-Government challenges in public sector. International Journal of Computer Science 7 (5), 310–317.

Qiang, C., Bhavnani, A., Hanna, N., Kimura, K., Sudan, R., 2009. Rural Informatization in China. World Bank, Washington, DC.

Qiu, J., 2009. Working-Class Network Society: Communication Technology and the Information Have-Less in Urban China. MIT Press, Cambridge, MA.

Radhakumari, C., 2006. Akshaya – a grass root level IT project in Kerala – a unique experiment with broadband. In: Sahu, G. (Ed.), Delivering e-Government. GIFT Publishing, New Delhi, pp. 105–122.

Rahardjo, E., Mirchandan, D., Joshi, K., 2007. e-Government functionality and website features: a case study of Indonesia. Journal of Global Information Technology Management 10, 31–50.

Rahman, M., Low, P., Almunawar, M., Mohiddin, F., Ang, S.-L., 2012. e-Government policy implementation in Brunei: lessons learnt from Singapore. In: Manoharan, A., Holzer, M. (Eds.), Active Citizen Participation in e-Government: A Global Perspective. IGI Global, New York, pp. 359–377.

Rajapaksha, T., Fernando, L., 2016. An analysis of the standards of the government websites of Sri Lanka: a comparative study on selected Asian countries. Transforming Government: People, Process and Policy 10 (1), 47–71.

Rajon, S.A., Zaman, SkA., 2008. Implementation of e-governance: only way to build a corruption-free Bangladesh. In: Proceedings of the 11th Computer and Information Technology, 2008. IEEE, pp. 430–435.

Rakhmanov, E., 2009. The barriers affecting e-government development in Uzbekistan. In: Proceedings of the Fourth International Conference on Computer Sciences and Convergence Information Technology. Seoul National University, Seoul, pp. 1474–1480.

Raman, V., 2008. Examining the 'e' in government and governance: a case study in alternatives from Bangalore City, India. Journal of Community Informatics 4 (2).

Ramos, A., Nangit, G., Ranga, A., Triñona, J., 2007. ICT-enabled community education in the Philippines. Distance Education 28 (2), 213–229.

Rao, S., 2005. Bridging digital divide: efforts in India. Telematics and Informatics 22, 361–375.

Rao, N., 2007. A framework for implementing information and communication technologies in agricultural development in India. Technological Forecasting & Social Change 74, 491–518.

Rattakul, R., Morse, A., 2005. An assessment of e-learning market opportunities in the government sector in Thailand. In: Proceedings of the Second International Conference on eLearning for Knowledge-Based Society. http://www.elearningap.com/eLAP2005/Proceeding/PP34.pdf.

Ray, D., Sirajee, S., Dash, S., 2006. A study on e-government readiness of Indian states. In: Mitra, R. (Ed.), e-Government: Macro Issues. GIFT Publishing, New Delhi, pp. 107–122.

Rehman, M., Esichaikul, V., 2012. Factors influencing e-government adoption in Pakistan. Transforming Government People Process and Policy 6 (3), 258–282.

Reporters Without Borders, n.d. Turkmenistan. http://en.rsf.org/Internet-enemie-turkmenistan, 39772.html.

Reporters Without Borders, 2004. Pakistan Annual Report 2004. http://www.rsf.org/article. php3?id_article=10794.

Rocheleau, B., 2007. Whither e-government? Public Administration Review 67, 584–588.

Rodan, G., 2000. Singapore information lockdown: business as usual. In: Williams, L., Rich, R. (Eds.), Losing Control: Freedom of the Press in Asia. Asia Pacific Press, Canberra.

Rose, M., 2004. Democratizing information and communication by implementing e-government in Indonesian regional government. International Information and Library Review 36, 219–226.

Rose, W., Grant, G., 2010. Critical issues pertaining to the planning and implementation of e-government initiatives. Government Information Quarterly 27, 26–33.

Rubenstein, C., November 29, 2012. China's government goes digital. The Atlantic. http://www. theatlantic.com/international/archive/2012/11/chinas-government-goes-digital/265493/.

Rye, S., 2008. Exploring the gap of the digital divide: conditions of connectivity and higher education participation. Geojournal 71 (2), 171–184.

Saeed, S., Wahab, F., Cheema, S., Ashraf, S., 2013. Role of usability in e-government and e-commerce portals: an empirical study of Pakistan. Life Science Journal 10 (1), 484–489.

Sahay, S., Walsham, G., 2006. Scaling of health information systems in India: challenges and approaches. Information Technology for Development 12 (3), 165–200.

Sahu, G., Gupta, M., 2007. Users' acceptance of e-government: a study of Indian central excise. International Journal of Electronic Government 3 (3), 1–21.

Saji, K., 2006. A case study approach to model the e-commerce adoption capability of Indian rural market co-operatives. In: Sahu, G. (Ed.), Delivering e-Government. GIFT Publishing, New Delhi, pp. 123–137.

Sambasivan, M., Wemyss, G., Rose, R., 2010. User acceptance of a G2B system: a case of electronic procurement system in Malaysia. Internet Research 2 (2), 169–187.

Samborsky, A., Popiv, I., 2015. Developing a concept of integrated information system for real property registration and cadastre for Uzbekistan. International Journal of Geoinformatics 11 (4), 9–13.

Sambuu, U., Tudevdagva, U., Erdene, G., 2008. e-Government initiatives in Mongolia. In: Proceedings of the 2nd International Conference on Theory and Practice of Electronic Governance. ACM, New York, pp. 474–477.

Sang, S., Lee, J.D., Lee, J., 2009. e-Government challenges in least developed countries (LDCs): a case of Cambodia. Advanced Communication Technology 3, 2169–2175.

Sang, S., Lee, J.-D., Lee, J., 2009. e-Government adoption in ASEAN: the case of Cambodia. Internet Research 19, 517–534.

Sang, S., Lee, J.D., Lee, J., 2010. e-Government adoption in Cambodia: a partial least squares approach. Transforming Government: People, Process and Policy 4 (2), 138–157.

Sang-Hun, C., March 23, 2013a. Computer Networks in South Korea are Paralyzed in Cyberattack. New York Times, p. A5.

Sang-Hun, C., March 16, 2013b. North Korea Sees South and U.S. Behind Hacks. New York Times, p. 7.

Santhanamery, T., Ramayah, T., 2014. Explaining the e-government usage using expectation confirmation model: the case of electronic tax filing in Malaysia. Public Administration and Information Technology 3, 287–304.

Sartor, V., 2010. Teaching English in Turkmenistan. English Today 26 (4), 29–36.

Schellong, A., 2008. Government 2.0: an exploratory study of social networking services in Japanese local government. Transforming Government: People, Process and Policy 2 (4), 225–242.

Schiesel, B., October 8, 2006. Land of the Video Geek. New York Times, p. 1. http://www.nytimes.com/2006/10/08/arts/.

Schlaeger, J., 2013. e-Government in China: Technology, Power and Local Government Reform. Routledge, London.

Schlaeger, J., Jiang, M., 2014. Official microblogging and social management by local governments in China. China Information 28 (2), 189–213.

Schware, R., 2000. Information technology and public sector management in developing countries: present status and future prospects. Indian Journal of Public Administration 46, 411–416.

Schwartz, S., April 11 2005. The Kyrgyz take their stan: A democratic revolution in Central Asia? The Weekly Standard, 10 (28), 12.

Schwartz, M., 2013. How South Korea traced hacker to Pyongyang. Information Week. http://www.informationweek.com/security/attacks/how-south-korea-traced-hacker-to-pyongya/240152702.

Seifert, J., Chung, J., 2009. Using e-government to reinforce government-citizen relationships: comparing government reform in the United States and China. Social Science Computer Review 27 (1), 3–23.

Sein, 2011. The "I" between G and C: e-government intermediaries in developing countries. Electronic Journal of Information Systems in Developing Countries 48 (2), 1–14.

Seng, W., Jackson, S., Philip, G., 2010. Cultural issues in developing e-government in Malaysia. Behaviour & Information Technology 29, 423–432.

Sethi, R., 2006. Issues and initiatives in ICT and e-governance: a study of transport sector in India. In: Mitra, R. (Ed.), e-Government: Macro Issues. GIFT Publishing, New Delhi, pp. 325–330.

Shafiev, A., Miles, M., 2015. Friends, foes, and Facebook: blocking the internet in Tajikistan. Demokratizatsiya: The Journal of Post-Soviet Democratization 23 (3), 297–319.

Shafique, F., Mahmood, K., 2008. Indicators of the emerging information society in Pakistan. Information Development 24 (1), 66–78.

Shah, S., Khan, A., Khalil, M., 2011. Project management practices in e-government projects: a case study of electronic government directorate (EGD) in Pakistan. International Journal of Business and Social Science 2 (7), 235–243.

Shao, B., Luo, X., Liao, Q., 2015. Factors influencing e-tax filing adoption intention by business users in China. Electronic Government 11 (4).

Shareef, M., Ojo, A., Janowski, T., 2008. A readiness assessment framework for e-government planning – design and application. In: Proceedings of the 2nd International Conference on Theory and Practice of Electronic Governance. ACM, New York, pp. 403–410.

Shareef, M., Ojo, A., Janowski, T., 2010. Exploring digital divide in the Maldives. In: Berleur, J., Hercheui, M., Hilty, L. (Eds.), What Kind of Information Society? Governance, Virtuality, Surveillance, Sustainability, Resilience. Springer, Dordrecht, pp. 51–63.

Sharma, G., Bao, X., Peng, L., 2014. Public participation and ethical issues on e-governance: a study perspective in Nepal. Electronic Journal of e-Government 12 (1), 82–96.

Sheryazdanova, G., Abdina, A., Abdildina, H., Kakimzhanova, M., Sadykova, T., Gappasova, A., 2016. Development of electronic government in Kazakhstan as a tool to combat corruption. Indian Journal of Science and Technology 9 (5).

Shi, Y., 2006. e-Government web site accessibility in Australia and China: a longitudinal study. Social Science Computer Review 24 (3), 378–385.

Shi, Y., 2007. The accessibility of Chinese local government web sites: an exploratory study. Government Information Quarterly 24, 377–403.

Shin, D.-H., 2007. A critique of Korean national information strategy: case of national information infrastructures. Government Information Quarterly 24, 624–645.

Siar, S., 2005. e-Governance at the local government level in the Philippines: an assessment of city government websites. Philippine Journal of Development 32 (2), 135–168.

Siddiquee, N., 2005. Innovations in governance and service delivery: e-government experiments in Malaysia. In: Ahmad, R. (Ed.), The Role of Public Administration in Building a Harmonious Society. China National School of Administration, Beijing, pp. 366–384.

Siddiquee, N., 2008. e-Government and innovations in service delivery: the Malaysian experience. International Journal of Public Administration 31, 797–815.

Siddiquee, N., Faroqi, M., 2013. A road far too long? e-Government and the state of service delivery in Bangladesh. In: Halpin, E., Griffin, D., Rankin, C., Dissanayake, L., Mahtab, N. (Eds.), Digital Public Administration and e-Government in Developing Nations: Policy and Practice. IGI Global, Hershey, PA, pp. 206–223.

Siew, L., Leng, L., 2003. e-Government in action: Singapore case study. Journal of Political Marketing 2 (3–4), 18–30.

Singer, D., Barboza, D., Perlroth, N., February 19 2013. China's army seen as tied to hacking against U.S. New York Times, p. A1, 9.

Singla, M., 2005. e-Governance potential for rural India. Journal of Management Research 5 (2), 102–109.

Sodhi, S. (Ed.), 2015. Trends, Prospects, and Challenges in Asian e-Governance. IGI Global, Hershey, PA.

Song, H., 2002. Prospects and limitation of the e-government initiative in Korea. International Review of Public Administration 7, 45–53.

Song, W., 2008. Development of the internet and digital divide in China: a spatial analysis. Intercultural Communication Studies 18 (3), 20–43.

Song, S.H., 2010. S. Korea exports e-government system to many countries. Pulse. http://pulsenews.co.kr/view.php?year=2010&no=687466.

Soon, C., Soh, Y., 2014. Engagement@web 2.0 between the government and citizens in Singapore: dialogic communication on Facebook? Asian Journal of Communication 24, 42–59.

Soriano, C., 2007. Exploring the ICT and rural poverty reduction link: community telecenters and rural livelihoods in Wu'an, China. Electronic Journal of Information Systems in Developing Countries 32, 1–15.

Srinivasan, R., Fish, A., 2009. Internet authorship: social and political implications within Kyrgyzstan. Journal of Computer-Mediated Communication 14 (3), 559–580.

Srinuan, C., Srinuan, P., Bohlin, E., 2012. An analysis of mobile internet access in Thailand: implications for bridging the digital divide. Telematics and Informatics 29 (3), 254–262.

Sriramesh, K., Rivera-Sanchez, M., 2006. e-Government in a corporatist, communitarian society: the case of Singapore. New Media and Society 8 (5), 707–730.

Srivastava, S., Teo, T., 2009. Citizen trust development for e-government adoption and usage: insights from young adults in Singapore. Communications of the Association for Information Systems 25. article 31 http://aisel.aisnet.org/cais/vol25/iss1/31.

Stevens, D., 2006. Inequality.com: Money, Power and the Digital Divide. Oneworld Publications, Oxford.

Stone, B., Barboza, D., January 16, 2010. Scaling the Digital Wall in China. New York Times, p. B1.

Subramanian, M., Saxena, A., 2006. e-Governance initiatives in an Indian state. Some observations from a gender perspective. In: Mitra, R. (Ed.), e-Government: Macro Issues. GIFT Publishing, New Delhi, pp. 130–140.

Suerte-Cortez, V., 2016. Does e-governance in the Philippines really mean 'e-inclusion'? http://www.makingallvoicescount.org/blog/e-governance-philippines-really-mean-e-inclusion/.

Surborg, B., 2008. On-line with the people in line: internet development and flexible control of the net in Vietnam. Geoforum 39 (1), 344–357.

Takao, Y., 2004. Democratic renewal by "digital" local government in Japan. Oirs 77 (2), 237–262.

Tan, C.W., Pan, S., Lim, E., 2005. Managing stakeholder interest in e-government implementation: lessons learned from a Singapore e-government project. Journal of Global Information Management 13, 31–53.

Tan, M., Xiaoai, D., Qiushi, Y., Chen, C., 2013. An investigation of e-government services in China. Electronic Journal of Information Systems in Developing Countries 57 (5), 1–20.

Tanaka, H., Matsuura, K., Sudoh, O., 2005. Vulnerability and information security investment: an empirical analysis of e-local government in Japan. Journal of Accounting and Public Policy 24, 37–59.

Tang, J., 2000. Recent internet developments in the People's Republic of China: an overview. Online Information Review 24 (4), 316–321.

Taubman Center of Brown University, 2007. South Korea Climbs to Top Rank in Global e-Government. http://www.brown.edu/Administration/News_Bureau/2006-07/06-007.html.

Teo, H.H., Tan, B.C.Y., Wei, K.K., 1997. Organizational transformation using electronic data interchange: the case of Tradenet in Singapore. Journal of Management Information Systems 13 (4), 139–165.

Thao, V., Trong, V., 2015. Examining the influence of society and technology in Vietnam e-government adoption. IPASJ International Journal of Management 3 (10), 8–12.

Thomas, P., 2009. Bhoomi, Gyan Ganga, e-governance and the right to information: ICTs and development in India. Telematics and Informatics 26 (1), 20–31.

Thompson, C., 2002. Enlisting on-line residents: expanding the boundaries of e-government in a Japanese rural township. Government Information Quarterly 19 (2), 173–188.

Thunibat, A., Zin, N., Sahari, N., 2011. Identifying user requirements of mobile government services in Malaysia using focus group method. Journal of e-Government Studies and Best Practices 2011, 1–14.

Tipton, F., 2002. Bridging the digital divide in Southeast Asia. ASEAN Economic Bulletin 19 (1), 83–99.

Tleuberdinova, A., Britskaya, Y., 2013. Problems of the e-government development in the Republic of Kazakhstan and their solutions. Education and Science Without Borders 4 (8), 44–47.

Trimi, S., Sheng, H., 2008. Emerging trends in m-government. Communications of the ACM 51 (5), 53–58.

Tsai, W.H., Purbokusumo, Y., Cheng, J., Tuan, N., 2009. e-Government evaluation: the case of Vietnam's provincial websites. Electronic Government 6 (1), 41–53.

Tung, L., Rieck, O., 2005. Adoption of electronic government services among business organizations in Singapore. Journal of Strategic Information Systems 14, 417–440.

Ulman, M., Ualiyev, N., Toregozhina, M., 2016. Do digital public services matter? A comparative study of the Czech Republic and the Republic of Kazakhstan. AGRIS On-line Papers in Economics and Informatics 8 (2), 121–133.

Ulziikhutag, O., 2011. e-Government Policy in Mongolia. Lambert Academic Publishing.

Unnikrishnan, P., 2006. Strengthening local self governments through IT: a case study of Kerala. In: Sahu, G. (Ed.), Delivering e-Government. GIFT Publishing, New Delhi, pp. 208–221.

Venkatesh, V., Sykes, T., Venkatraman, S., 2014. Understanding e-government portal use in rural India: role of demographic and personality characteristics. Information Systems Journal 24 (3), 249–269.

Verma, S., 2006. Law and regulation of e-government procurement (EGO) in India. In: Mitra, R. (Ed.), e-Government: Macro Issues. GIFT Publishing, New Delhi, pp. 177–188.

Verma, N., Mishra, A., Thangamuthu, P., 2006. One-stop source of government services through the national portal of India. In: Sahu, G. (Ed.), Delivering e-Government. GIFT Publishing, New Delhi, pp. 88–95.

VietNam News, August 29, 2013. e-Government Best Way to Go. http://vietnamnews.vn/society/244139/e-government-best-way-to-go.html#jEQL0TlTiA6CD3tL.97.

Villeneuve, N., 2006. The filtering matrix: integrated mechanisms of information control and the demarcation of borders in cyberspace. First Monday 11, 1–2.

Wahid, F., 2004. Lessons from e-government initiatives in Indonesia. Media Informatika 2 (2), 13–21.

Walsham, G., 2010. ICTs for the broader development of India: an analysis of the literature. Electronic Journal of Information Systems in Developing Countries 41 (4), 1–20.

Wanasundera, L., 2012. Public access ICT in Sri Lanka. In: Gomez, R. (Ed.), Libraries, Telecentres, Cybercafes and Public Access to ICT: International Comparisons. IGI Global, Hershey, PA, pp. 406–428.

Wang, F., Chen, Y., 2012. From potential users to actual users: use of e-government service by Chinese migrant farmer workers. Government Information Quarterly 29 (Suppl. 1), S98–S111.

Wang, Z., Gu, H., 2009. A review of telemedicine in China. Journal of Telemedince and Telecare 15 (1), 23–27.

Warf, B., 2010. Geographies of global internet censorship. GeoJournal 76, 1–23.

Warf, B., 2014. Asian geographies of e-government. Eurasian Geography and Economics 55 (1), 94–110.

Waseda University, 2009. 2009 Waseda University e-Government Rankings. http://www.obi.giti.waseda.ac.jp/e_gov/World_e-Gov_Ranking09_en.pdf.

Waththage, K., Deng, H., Karunasena, A., 2012. Developments of e-government in Sri Lanka: opportunities and challenges. In: Joseph, B., Zulu, S. (Eds.), Handbook of Research on e-Government in Emerging Economies: Adoption, e-Participation, and Legal Frameworks. IGI Global, Hershey, PA, pp. 1–19.

Weerakkody, V., Dwivedi, Y., Kurunananda, A., 2009. Implementing e-government in Sri Lanka: lessons from the UK. Information Technology for Development 15 (3), 171–192.

Wei, C., Kolko, B., 2005. Resistance to globalization: language and internet diffusion patterns in Uzbekistan. New Review of Hypermedia and Multimedia 11 (2), 205–220.

Wescott, C., 2011. e-Government in the Asia-Pacific region. Asian Journal of Political Science 9 (2), 1–24.

West, D., 2007. Global e-Government, 2007. http://195.130.87.21:8080/dspace/bitstream/123456789/1028/1/Global%20E-Government,%202007.pdf.

Wijers, G., 2010. Determinants of the digital divide: a study on IT development in Cambodia. Technology in Society 32 (4), 336–341.

Williams, M., June 10, 2010. North Korea Moves Quietly onto the Internet. Computerworld. http://www.computerworld.com/s/article/9177968/North_Korea_moves_quietly_onto_the_Internet?taxonomyId=18&pageNumber=2.

Williams, M., April 9, 2013. DPRK Reconfigures Its Internet Connection. North Korea Tech. http://www.northkoreatech.org/tag/star-jv/.

Windsor, S., Royal, C., 2014. Different telecentre models in ICT for development and their impact on organizational sustainability. International Journal of Technology Management & Sustainable Development 13 (2), 161–175.

Wong, P.K., 2003. Global and national factors affecting e-commerce diffusion in Singapore. The Information Society 19, 19–32.

Wong, E., June 3, 2016. China's Internet Speed Ranks 91st in the World. New York Times. http://www.nytimes.com/2016/06/04/world/asia/china-internet-speed.html?_r=0.

Wriston, W., 1997. Bits, bytes, and diplomacy. Foreign Affairs 76 (5), 172–182.

Xia, J., Lu, T.-J., 2008. Bridging the digital divide for rural communities: the case of China. Telecommunications Policy 32 (9–10), 686–696.

Xinhuanet, 2004. Myanmar to Launch e-Procurement System. http://news.xinhuanet.com/english/2004-04/01/content_1395904.htm.

Xiong, J., 2006. Current status and needs of Chinese e-government users. Electronic Library 24 (6), 47–762.

Xiue, Y., Liang, L., 2007. Analysis of telemedicine diffusion: the case of China. IEEE Transactions on Information Technology in Biomedicine 11 (2), 231–233.

Yadav, N., Singh, V., 2012. e-Governance: past, present and future in India. International Journal of Computer Applications 53 (7), 36–48.

Yan, T.M., Zheng, L., Pardo, T., 2012. The boundaries of information sharing and integration: a case study of Taiwan e-government. Government Information Quarterly 29 (Suppl. 1), S51–S60.

Yang, K., Zhang, C., Tang, J., 2012. Internet use and governance in China. In: Chen, Y.-C., Chu, P.-Y. (Eds.), Electronic Governance and Cross-Boundary Collaboration: Innovations and Advancing Tools. IGI Global, Hershey, PA, pp. 305–324.

Yapa, P., Guah, M., 2012. Public-sector accounting and e-governance in developing countries: case of Sri Lanka. Journal of Asia-Pacific Business 13 (1), 37–58.

Yeow, P., Loo, W., 2010. Acceptability of ATM and transit applications embedded in multipurpose smart identity card: an exploratory study in Malaysia. In: Weerakkody, V. (Ed.), Applied Technology Integration in Governmental Organizations: New e-Government Research. IGI Global, Hershey, PA, pp. 118–137.

Yigitcanlar, T., Baum, S., 2006. e-Government and the digital divide. In: Khosrow-Pour, M. (Ed.), Encyclopedia of e-Commerce, e-Government, and Mobile Commerce. IGI Global, Hershey, PA, pp. 353–358.

Yildiz, M., 2007. e-Government research: reviewing the literature, limitations and ways forward. Government Information Quarterly 24, 646–665.

Yonemaru, T., 2004. Electronic government in Japan. In: Eifert, M., Ole Püschel, J. (Eds.), National Electronic Government: Comparing Governance Structures in Multi-layer Administrations. Routledge, London, New York, pp. 136–181.

Yong, J.S., 2003. Enter the dragon: informatization in China. In: Yong, J.S. (Ed.), e-Government in Asia: Enabling Public Service Innovation in the 21st Century. Times Media, Hong Kong, pp. 85–96.

Yongnian, Z., Wu, G., 2005. Information technology, public space, and collective action in China. Comparative Political Studies 38, 507–536.

Yoon, C.H., Lau, L., 2001. Transformation of the telecommunications infrastructure in North Korea. In: Yoon, C.H., Lau, L. (Eds.), North Korea in Transition: Prospects for Economic and Social Reform. Edward Elgar, Cheltenham, pp. 199–213.

Yu, C.C., Wang, H.I., 2004. Digital divide in Taiwan: evidence, comparisons, and strategies. Electronic Government 1 (2), 179–197.

Zaynuddin, I., 2008. Uzbekistan. Tajikistan. In: Finlay, A. (Ed.), Global Information Society Watch 2008. APC, Hivos and ITeM, pp. 197–199.

Zeller, T., October 22, 2006. North Korea, the Internet is Only for a Few. New York Times. http://www.nytimes.com/2006/10/22/technology/22iht-won.3251122.html?_r=0.

Zhang, J., 2002. Will the government serve the people? The development of Chinese e-government. New Media and Society 4, 163–184.

Zhang, J., 2006. Good governance through e-governance? Assessing China's e-government strategy. Journal of e-Government 2 (4), 39–71.

Zhang, C., 2007. The institutional framework of the United nations development programme-ministry of science and technology (UNDP-MoST) telecenter project in rural China. Information Technologies & International Development 4 (3), 39–55.

Zhang, N., Meng, Q., Guo, X., Yin, C., Luo, H., 2015. Key e-government issues in China: an empirical study based on the orientation-maturity framework. Electronic Commerce Research 15 (3), 407–425.

Zhao, X., 2004. e-Government in China: a content analysis of national and provincial web sites. Journal of Computer-Mediated Communication 9 (4).

Zhao, Q., 2010. e-Government evaluation of delivering public services to citizens among cities in the Yangtze River delta. International Information and Library Review 42, 208–211.

Zhao, J., Zhang, Z., Guo, H., Ren, L., Chen, S., 2010a. Development and recent achievements of telemedicine in China. Telemedicine and e-Health 16 (5), 634–638.

Zhao, J., Zhang, Z., Guo, H., Li, Y., Xue, W., Ren, L., Chen, Y., Chen, S., Zhang, X., 2010b. e-Health in China: challenges, initial directions, and experience. Telemedicine and e-Health 16 (3), 344–349.

Zhao, J., Zhao, S., Alexander, M., Truell, A., 2015. The impact of Chinese e-government-to-citizens on government transparency and public participation. Issues in Information Systems 16 (1), 51–59.

Zheng, L., 2013. Social media in Chinese government: drivers, challenges and capabilities. Government Information Quarterly 30 (4), 369–376.

Zook, M., 2005. The geography of the internet. Annual Review of Information Science and Technology 40, 53–78.

Index

Printed in the United States
by Baker & Taylor